Ni

MW01487916

Nils Thor Granlund

Show Business Entrepreneur and America's First Radio Star

LARRY J. HOEFLING

McFarland & Company, Inc., Publishers
Jefferson, North Carolina, and London

LIBRARY OF CONGRESS CATALOGUING-IN-PUBLICATION DATA

Hoefling, Larry J.
    Nils Thor Granlund : show business entrepreneur and America's
first radio star / Larry J. Hoefling.
        p.   cm.
    Includes bibliographical references and index.

    ISBN 978-0-7864-4849-4
    softcover : 50# alkaline paper

    1. Granlund, N.T.   2. Theatrical producers and directors—
United States—Biography.   3. Broadway (New York, N.Y.)—
Biography.   4. Radio broadcasters—United States—Biography.
5. Actors—United States—Biography.   I. Title.
PN2287.G67H64   2010
792.02'32092—dc22
[B]   2010011995

British Library cataloguing data are available

Cover image: A 1946 CBS announcement for an audience
participation show featuring Granlund, "You're in the Act"
(courtesy McHuston Archives)

Manufactured in the United States of America

*McFarland & Company, Inc., Publishers
    Box 611, Jefferson, North Carolina 28640
        www.mcfarlandpub.com*

For my son,
Dustin Edward Hoefling
A beautiful boy — an ardent man

Acknowledgments

My sincere appreciation is extended to all who offered their support and encouragement during the process, not only those library and reference desk staffers who anonymously answered my many queries, but also my bookshop clients and acquaintances who regularly asked about the progress of the project.

A great deal of effort was expended early on in attempting to track down any surviving heirs of Nils Thor Granlund, and despite some early clues, leads struck dead ends until much later. Thanks are due to Rovena Baron, a staff member of the *Lincoln County News*, Newcastle, Maine, who went above and beyond in attempting to track down details of the latter life of Mabel Granlund and the Howard family, and to the staff at the Strong Funeral Home, Damariscotta, Maine, for providing pertinent information.

A tip of the researcher's hat and sincere thanks to Bronx historian Thomas X. Casey, who provided the postcard image of Zeltner's Hall, which was later called Niblo's Garden, a rare bit of Bronx history.

Deepest appreciation to Mr. B for the continued support of the project, and for introducing to me the enigmatic NTG.

My gratitude to Avery Amanda Howard for contacting me and sharing photographs and papers of her grandfather Nils Thor Granlund and her grandmother Mabel Avery Granlund, along with reminiscences and information — and additional thanks to her family members for their support and aid in providing materials.

As always, heartfelt thanks for the encouragement provided by my family, including my amazing daughter Kristen Pike, my talented son Dustin Hoefling, my energetic and supportive sisters Kathy Williams and Linda Collins — and all their respective families. *Doy reconocimiento a Fabiola, mi patrona y mi amor por muchos años.* Loving thanks to Martha Lee Huston Hoefling, a mother with enough patience to listen to unending stories about a forgotten Broadway showman.

A Note on Illustrations

While materials to document the life of Nils Thor Granlund are available from disparate sources, photographic images have been difficult to locate and vary in quality from studio portraits to grainy newsprint. After lengthy consultation with the editors at McFarland, it was determined to allow the inclusion of some of the lesser-quality images that — in my opinion — serve to provide a glimpse of NTG in settings not otherwise afforded. I am glad for the inclusion of these scarce items, despite their marginal quality.

Table of Contents

Unless a man enters upon the vocation intended for him by nature, and best-suited to his particular genius he cannot succeed.
— P.T. Barnum

Preface

The initials NTG came to light as part of a minor research project regarding a Jazz era entertainment venue called Niblo's Garden. The public hall, a former German beer garden in the Bronx, had borrowed the name from the original and well-known Niblo's Garden on Broadway at Prince Street that in 1835 hosted showman P.T. Barnum's first-ever exhibition, marking his debut in the world of public entertainment.

A small newspaper ad associated with the research featured only the three initials, a line of chorus girls, and the name Niblo's Garden. That venue, at Third Avenue and 170th Street, was originally part of a park-like tract known as Zeltner's Garden, built in 1870 by German immigrant Henry Zeltner across from his already successful brewery. His public hall, used for gatherings from dances to political rallies, later became known as the Bronx Lyceum and hosted similar functions until it burned to the ground in 1929.

Little evidence remains of the second venue to bear the name Niblo's Garden, and the man behind the initials NTG is nearly as obscure.

Nils Theodore Granlund, who adopted the middle name of Thor as a tribute to his Swedish birth, is perhaps one of the most famous Broadway personalities to be nearly forgotten. It was a testament to his fame at the time that Granlund was recognized with only his initials, in the same manner that later years saw the mention of the initials FDR referring to Franklin D. Roosevelt. On Broadway in New York City, during the time of the Great Depression and the birth of the Jazz Age, there was perhaps no name in America more closely associated with entertainment on all fronts than that of Nils Thor Granlund.

To be certain, there were stars in their particular fields who were famous then and remain as icons of that particular period — the time of emerging new forms of media such as film, radio, and television. The true vaudeville greats, the stars of the "serious" stage, the singers, the dancers, the producers, and early film stars would leave a solid legacy of performance history within their fields of endeavor. It was not the case for Granlund, a media innovator and promoter whose practices and techniques evolved with technology while his own brand of entertainment remained entrenched in the tried-and-true.

1

It is beyond the stretch of irony that NTG, a shameless self-promoter during his lifetime, a man as easily recognized on the street as on the stage, a radio voice simultaneously loved and hated on the greater New York air waves, a talent scout relied upon by Flo Ziegfeld and other showmen — could end his long career without a single tribute, with the credit for his many innovations completely lost to history.

Almost.

A few public acknowledgments do exist: The actress known as Joan Crawford disclosed that it was Granlund who wired the cash for her ticket to Hollywood after the screen test he arranged resulted in a contract, and Yvonne De Carlo, once famous for her harem-style movie roles but better known to later generations as Lily Munster on a campy television comedy, noted in her autobiography that she was first hired by NTG as a dancer in his Hollywood revue and that he remained an integral figure in her life. A biography of burlesque queen Lili St. Cyr includes an account of her discovery by Granlund at his Florentine Gardens nightclub in Hollywood.

There were many, many others who owed their fame to an opportunity provided by Granlund, and countless others who managed to survive tough times only by virtue of his benevolence. It is important that the story of one of the most creative of the New York entertainers be remembered not only for his talent discoveries but also for his collective social and technical innovations. Arriving in New York City at the time when so many forms of entertainment were in their infancy, and as the publicity agent for the largest American theater chain, Nils Thor Granlund was in a singular position to not only influence the entertainment being offered, but the manner in which the product was delivered.

In his later years, when he had been long-forgotten by all but his closest associates, he landed a contract for his memoirs. A car crash claimed Granlund's life within weeks of the book's publication and his story, without the requisite promotional appearances, died along with him.

Granlund traveled during the course of his life from New England to Hollywood and back to New York. Gifted with a quick mind and an eye for promotion, he managed to obtain coverage in newspapers, radio, and television. In his early years, making the news was his job as a press agent, and later he used the media contacts he maintained over the years to promote his causes. In researching his life, it was necessary to travel that same New York to Hollywood route, sifting through accounts of his passage that ranged from boxing commentaries in the Oshkosh, Wisconsin, *Daily Northwestern*, to pleas for financial aid that were delivered on his behalf in the nationally syndicated columns of Walter Winchell.

Granlund related his own life story as a series of adventures that are almost incredibly over-the-top. Amazingly enough, nearly every outlandish claim can be substantiated by independent sources. His memoirs centered on the stories he had told and retold in his later years, the accounts of the early stars, his now-famous finds, the shows and the venues, and his encounters with New York crime figures during Prohibition.

The life of Nils Thor Granlund — even tempered somewhat from his own account — is a remarkable tale of show business evolution. He omitted much in the telling of his own story, making no mention of an earlier family, his troubles with the law, and his desperation in later years.

Discovering the truth about the man became a process of understanding the sort of man Granlund was, a perception that falls somewhere between the glowing self-written biographies contained in the printed programs distributed in his nightclubs and the sometimes savage reviews of his acts by entertainment industry writers. He appeared in several now-obscure movies which provide a rare opportunity to hear his stage patter and view his mannerisms. His radio and television programs are likely lost to history, with the exception of a network television game show that remains in existence due only to the appearance of the well-known actor Errol Flynn in the same episode.

The discovery and examination of such rare ephemera as period postcards of his restaurants, his nightclubs, and the chorus lines of his musical revues aided in filling in aspects of his creative reach. Letters and postcards to his family members came to light much later.

Only the *New York Times* obituary contained the fact that Granlund had been previously married, although no additional information was revealed. The study of genealogical records in New York, Rhode Island, Connecticut, and Maine provided clues to the family and its earliest days as Swedish immigrants, but held no facts as to the whereabouts of his first wife and family. Some extraordinary measures finally provided contact with the descendants of Nils Thor Granlund, and their assistance added to the understanding of his story.

From his birth in Sweden to his 1957 death in a Las Vegas car accident, his life crosses through such notable territory as Prohibition bootlegging, mob hits, beautiful chorus girls, and American entertainment. He discovered show business stars, was the first to provide live coverage of sporting events, and — with a microphone in hand — he introduced the Jazz Age to the world through his New York City radio shows broadcast live from the nightclub stages. He socialized regularly with F. Scott Fitzgerald and was among the first to ever appear on a television screen. On the West Coast, he partied with film stars at his Hollywood mansion. He neither smoked nor drank. He died nearly penniless.

There is no other account of the man and his complete life, and as a career radio reporter and broadcaster, I could not help but think of Nils Thor Granlund as a man deserving of a place in the entertainment industry's collective memory.

Prologue

The truth is, the more kind and liberal a man is, the more generous will be the patronage bestowed upon him.
— P.T. Barnum

The young man, a Hollywood High School senior, had an appointment to meet the radio announcer at the man's home in Hollywood. The year was 1946, and the eighteen year old named Richard had just landed a part in the film *Tomorrow Is Forever*. A couple of Richard's friends had caught a ride in the car of a casting director, Jack Murton, who asked the students if they were in the school play.[1]

The two riders weren't, but they enthusiastically heaped praise on their buddy Richard, in fact, so much so that Murton felt compelled to audition the young man for a movie part.

The tale of how the high school senior wound up in the movies by way of two hitchhiking buddies was exactly the sort of story the Los Angeles radio announcer loved to talk about on his show.

The veteran broadcaster, known almost exclusively by his initials, NTG, was a fixture from New York to Los Angeles. Over the course of his career he had given plenty of opportunities to amateurs looking for a shot on the stage or radio. As part of his regular show, NTG was particularly fond of serving up the "lucky break" stories that everybody loved to hear — the waitresses discovered over lunch, the talent show winners who got a contract. They were accounts that made every listener believe they too had a shot at fame and fortune.

In the case of the young actor, he was to relate the story of his discovery by answering questions on NTG's live radio program on KHJ.

The meeting at the broadcaster's home was to be an ice-breaker — a chance for the young man to become comfortable in advance of the live interview, but Richard, coming from a modest home-life, might have instead been intimidated by the awe-inspiring mansion above Franklin Avenue, east of Vine near the Greek Theatre.[2]

The war had just ended, but there remained a bustling military presence throughout Southern California, with civilians and servicemen from all parts of the United States preparing to return home. It was a time of last chances in the place where dreams came true. Gone were the grave concerns about the troops and the war, and radio listeners were anxious to hear the hot movie items, reports about what stars might be spotted later in the restaurants and nightclubs of Hollywood.

The young actor was slightly early, but he mustered his courage and knocked at the entrance. What he saw when the door opened surprised him. He was expecting the radio-man, or perhaps a maid or butler, but he wasn't particularly disappointed at his reception. The woman standing before him was striking — not casually attractive or cheerleader-pretty — but breathtaking, stunningly beautiful.

Richard explained to the woman that he had an appointment. She stepped back and let him in, introducing herself as the secretary, and promising that his wait would be brief.

It amounted to half-an-hour, and during that time, at almost regular intervals, one beautiful woman after another passed through the foyer, each introducing herself as the secretary, each exchanging genuine pleasantries with the young actor before exiting with the promise that he would be met with shortly. Each of the women was as beautiful as her predecessor.

His host finally appeared, a tall, lanky man with an easy smile and a firm handshake that exuded confidence. It was almost a disappointment to the young actor that his wait was over, that the introductions and pleasantries with the beautiful women in the foyer had come to an end. The two adjourned to the heart of the spacious house, into a room rich with ornamentation and well-stuffed furnishings.

They completed the run-through of the intended interview and NTG was leading the young actor back through the hallways to the front door when he suddenly turned and proposed to show the young man through the home. It was a house of many doorways and curiosities, and one that invited tours.

The young actor accepted the offer and followed his host through the party room, with its long, fully stocked bar and walls lined with expensive paintings of hunting scenes.[3] The two moved from room to room until, at last, they reached one of most expansive spaces in the house. Stepping through the doorway, Richard was taken aback by the sight.

Situated on the opposite wall was an immense bed, perhaps ten feet by twenty feet.[4] It was the grandest bed the actor had ever seen, and in his astonishment, without thinking, he blurted, "How come you've got this big bed?"

"Well," NTG began, in a softened voice that hinted of foreign places.[5] "We all live here."

The answer clarified nothing for the puzzled young actor, but only served to prompt a second question. "Who?" he asked, still staring at the massive bed.

The tall man smiled. "My secretaries," he said. "My secretaries and I. We all live here."

"What? Do you all sleep together?"

There was the slightest pause before the answer came, and the slightest look of bewilderment on the face of the tall man, as though considering whether the young actor lacked the ability to comprehend.

"Yes," NTG replied at last, before smiling and escorting the younger man to the door.

The actor was Richard Long, and the radio interview on KHJ gave him some much-needed publicity at the beginning of a nearly thirty-year career in films and television. The story of how he got into the movies, however, was never told with the same enthusiasm as the anecdote of his *true* lucky break, the one that came the day he was invited to the big Hollywood house, and his amazement at meeting the radio-man bachelor with the great appetite and the four, five, six beautiful secretaries.

"Sleeping in the one bed," he would say, his face betraying his continuing astonishment, mixed with the slightest trace of envy. "And every time they came through the room — I'm so-and-so, glad you're here. Period. It was quite the experience."[6]

The radio-man kept company in his life in much the same fashion as he solicited companionship in his home. He relished familiarity and camaraderie. He was rarely found without the company of others.

By the time of the radio interview with young Richard Long, the announcer named Nils Granlund was experiencing changes that would affect him greatly, placing him in situations he had never before encountered. Increasingly, his golden touch began to fail him and times were lean.[7] The many friends and acquaintances that kept his constant company began to drift away, and soon, the atmosphere at the big house on Franklin Avenue was not the center of attraction it had once been.

There was time to think about his earliest days, time spent truly alone in the bitter north of Sweden, the land of the Nordic gods.

His name was Nils Theodore Granlund, but he had long ago dropped the middle name that was his bookkeeper father's, and when he penned an autograph he drew from the Viking god of thunder and proclaimed himself...

Nils Thor Granlund.

• ONE •

Sweden to America

We are all, no doubt, born for a wise purpose.
— P.T. Barnum

The Land of the Midnight Sun is also the land where darkness reigns in the middle of the day, where the villagers hunker down against an icy wind and temperatures approaching twenty below zero. In the north of Sweden, the village called Korpilombolo was tamped into the hard ground, fastened to the earth with ropes and reindeer hides to ward off the wind and cold. The Saami villagers know the cold as their heritage. They escaped the ancient Vikings by moving to the north, into the Lapland territories above the Arctic Circle, an expanse that extended from Norway through the northernmost areas of Sweden, Finland, and Russia.[1]

In that forbidden country, the Saami people, numbering in total less than the population of a mid-sized nineteenth-century American town, spoke the language of an ancestry spanning thousands of years and lived in tent-like dwellings laid together with long poles and sewn animal hides. Little could be grown in that northern climate, and little remained stationary. Even the origin of the name they were given seems to have blown away on the crisp gusts that swirled the Nordic snowfall.

The Portuguese philosopher Damião de Góis in 1540 tried to explain Lapland as meaning "the dumb and lazy land," since any piece of earth that refused to grow a healthy crop of vegetables was lazy, and does not speak, where other lands show their voice with growth and harvests. The men of Sweden, Norway, and Finland called the Saami people Lapps, although none could remember why. To the Saami, it has never been a term of endearment.[2]

When their Saami ancestors began settling near the coastal fjords in the time of de Góis, there were a small number who retained the nomadic lifestyle, trapping, fishing, and following the herds of reindeer until the time of their winter month encampments.

Nils Thor Granlund loved to relate the tale of how he was born "just north

9

of the Arctic Circle, near the tiny village of Korpilombolo,"[3] a story repeated countless times throughout his life and career, although the location was generally identified only as "Lappland" or "Swedish Lapland." His descendents express skepticism regarding the accuracy of the story, attributing the narrative to creative license on the part of Granlund's enterprising writers intending to punch up the copy of his 1957 memoir *Blondes, Brunettes, and Bullets.*[4] Without question, there are gaps and inaccuracies throughout Granlund's own telling of his adventures, related previous to the existence of the Internet and easily facilitated fact-checking, but most of his errors are likely the result of simple memory lapses regarding exact dates and precise names of peripheral characters. However, his claims to have been born in Lappland date to the earliest newspaper biographical sketches, and predate by decades the account edited by Sid Feder and Ralph Hancock.

Comparatively speaking, any non–Saami residents of the Swedish north would be considered latecomers to the region, in the Västerbotten province where trees are scarcely found amidst the hard and beautiful Scandinavian geography.

For non-nomadic Swedes, to live in that frontier in suitable structures would require the dragging of logs across the snow-covered hills and the clear, frigid rivers to build the sort of cabin that Granlund remembered at Korpilombolo, a solid structure that dwarfed the homes of the villagers.[5] His recalled his uncles as "big, red-faced men, weathered by the harsh northland," who made their living trapping and trading with the Saami.

Unlike his brothers, Theodore Granlund was of small frame and short stature, but he married tall. Amanda, born in 1860,[6] was a year younger than her bookish husband but was a sturdy and physically imposing woman who— at nearly six feet in height — towered over Theodore. As a result, she managed the heavy work associated with the maintenance of their trading post home, while Theodore Granlund kept the ledgers and the accounts associated with the family business.[7] Nils Granlund presumably inherited traits from both parents. Written accounts of his adult activities almost always included a reference to his height, and the regular use of such phrases as "lanky Swede" indicate that his physicality was something of note. With the exception of his sailing exploits, however, Granlund made his living using a creative thought process that might have had its origins in the mental acumen of a bookkeeping father.

Nils Granlund was born into a world in which success was completely dependent on personal enterprise, and the ability of anyone to survive in the Arctic circle at that time is a testament to their hardiness and ability to interact with the native villagers.

Leaving their crudely constructed dwellings during the summer months, the Saami people followed the herds of reindeer that supplied families with meat, hides, and materials for trading. At the trading posts throughout the Arctic Circle, furs, hides, and dried fish collected by the Saami could be exchanged for flour, hemp, axes, needles, and cloth that the Swedish traders brought from the markets to the south. Granlund's claims to have been in the company of the Saami on their expeditions herding reindeer are among those items that test credulity, given his age previous to emigration.

Regardless, hard times were to be found across Sweden following the industrialization of the late nineteenth century, and by 1879 the resulting manufacturing demands threw the timber and iron industries into an increasing state of crisis. Already, propagandizing pamphlets that offered cheap land in the American heartland circulated widely throughout Sweden, and over three-quarters of a million Swedes had taken up the offer by 1890.[8]

Amanda Granlund gave birth to the couple's first child, Frederick Eugene, in October of 1887,[9] and two years later Nils Theodore was born, in September of 1889.[10]

Nils claimed to have spent parts of those early summer months in the company of what he called the "Lappland herders," and could easily recall "the awful smell" of the tallow and reindeer hides that piled up in storage rooms of the trading post. He expounded on his travels as a child with the herders as they moved with the reindeer herds during the relatively mild summer weather.[11]

Granlund would have been too young to understand the sinking economy and the failing agricultural market, but its effect would feature in the decisions of Swedish families who opted to leave their homeland. Cheap American and Russian grain drove down prices, and the general rise in American prosperity presented a constant allure. A series of crop disasters befell the country over a period of consecutive plantings, resulting in widespread crop failures. The shortages that followed bordered on famine.

Even in the decade before Granlund's birth, times were so hard in Sweden that more and more families were giving up, choosing to try a new life in an unknown country rather than struggle through the problems. As early as 1867, Swedes began emigrating to the United States, gambling everything in hopes of finding a better life. When family members wrote letters back to Sweden, describing the success and general prosperity, it sparked a mass exodus.[12]

Several crossings were made previous to their final emigration, but Theodore Granlund and his family were among those who decided to leave their home in Sweden for good, settling in Rhode Island in 1893.[13] Amazingly, within thirty years, one out of every five persons born on Swedish soil moved away to live in the United States. The emigrants were primarily young unmarried men who stayed in the urban areas.[14]

It was typically a trip of nearly a month, after packing as many belongings as could be managed for the trip across the ocean to the United States. Many of the departing families booked passage on the steamships leaving from Oslo, Norway. From that port — then called Kristiana — the liners typically crossed the North Sea to Hull, England, where trains provided passage across the English countryside to the Atlantic port at Liverpool.

The Granlund family, according to accounts of the ship's passage, made the journey by way of Bremen and Hamburg, Germany, to Southampton, England, where they booked passage on the two-funnel steamship *Lahn*, operated by North German Lloyd.[15]

The *Lahn* carried a maximum of 1030 passengers, and — at the time of its 1887 maiden voyage — was the third-fastest steamship sailing the Atlantic.[16] Still, the oceanic crossing might take more than two weeks, with much of that time spent at the mercy of the seas and the operators providing the thin daily fare (primarily rice and bread).

Under gray skies and intermittent rain, the *Lahn* reached the American coast on March 15, 1894,[17] and steamed into the harbor at New York City, where the family of young Nils Granlund met with an exotic welcoming committee. A representative of the world-famous Barnum and Bailey Circus waited dockside with a gang of workers — strong circus wranglers who were ready to hustle portmanteaus and trunks down the gangplank. It would be Granlund's first brush with entertainment celebrities, although the circus official and his aides were certainly not searching the crowd for the arriving young Nils.

Disembarking into the care of the Barnum and Bailey representatives were the famed Sansoni sisters, a finely dressed pair of young women described as "the strongest human beings alive," and who — if the advance publicity was to be believed — were capable of "lifting heavier weights with apparatus than any other persons of either sex."[18]

The sisters were passengers on the *Lahn* for its Atlantic crossing, having already bested all comers on the vaudeville stages in Europe, and were looking forward to an American engagement with the Barnum and Bailey Circus for challenges by American strongmen.[19]

Rosa Meers, the renowned bareback equestrienne, arrived almost simultaneously on the steamer *Mobile* for a similar engagement under the circus big top, and the three women received a VIP welcome on the crowded boardwalks that marked the entry point into the United States. Meanwhile, amidst the many shouts and calls to the new arrivals by various vendors and hawkers who preyed on emigrant naiveté, the Granlund family shuffled along with a long line of newcomers, making their way to the Ellis Island officials for questioning and paperwork. Once that was completed, they could at last step onto the soil of New York City and their new home.

When Theodore Granlund and his family finally situated themselves in their new country, it was in Providence, Rhode Island, a world almost completely alien to the Lapland natives. The coastal state was a manufacturing stronghold,[20] employing much of its population in the production of goods for the wealthy. These items were unknown to the rustic Swedes.

When the Granlund family settled into their first Rhode Island abode, they were just a part of a population of nearly seven thousand Swedes to have relocated there; forty percent of them passed each other daily on the streets of Providence.[21] It was there that the textile and woolen industries hired immigrants into the thousands. Possessing the skills required of silversmiths, hundreds more could find steady employment in the many arms of the precious metals industry.[22]

The Gorham Manufacturing Company in Providence was the largest silverware manufacturer in the U.S. More than 200 smaller firms employed jewelers and silver workers of every sort, making Providence the nation's leader in jewelry production. Members of the Granlund family and many of their neighbors were quick to find their way into those better-paying jobs.

Theodore Granlund took the family's life savings, the amount left after paying their passage from Sweden, and spent it buying goods and merchandise for resale. It was the work he knew best. Granlund and his wife set up an urban version of their old trading post, opening a small grocery at 665 Eddy Street under the name Granlund and Company.[23] Later, Theodore landed a bookkeeping job at one of the many precious metal firms. His combined income from the steady fifteen-dollar-a-week paycheck and the proceeds from Granlund and Company allowed the family to move from their initial location into housing they considered more appropriate. Theodore would move four times over the next fifteen years.

It was spring of 1894, a warm one, but whether or not the temperatures reached record levels meant little to young Nils Granlund, who only knew that compared to the Arctic Circle, Rhode Island might well have been situated on the equator. The relative heat was only one of the trials facing the family as they acclimated themselves to a new environment. Learning the English language was vital to their success in their adopted homeland as was obtaining proper clothing that would reduce the conspicuousness of the dress that initially set them apart. Nils later recalled having arrived wearing "the first leather shoes I'd ever owned," a pair of crudely fashioned handmade shoes that made him the subject of childish criticism, but were, in actuality, much more similar to the footwear of his young neighbors than the wooden shoes and fur-lined Lapland boots he had previously worn.[24]

Although an industrious self-starter by nature, as a student Granlund lingered among the youngest elementary school classes because of his language deficiencies. Over the course of the next several years he worked his way back into the classes of his peer group by improving his English skills under the tutelage of James M. Sawin, the principal of Providence's Point Street Grammar School. Granlund's proficiency improved to the point that he eventually earned spending money by teaching English to a group of immigrants who met Sunday afternoons at the downtown Greek restaurant.[25] A portion of his earnings went to the family living expenses while they struggled to make ends meet.

Not far from the Granlund home on Narragansett Bay was the well-known Herreshoff Works at Bristol, the boatyards of John Brown Herreshoff and his brother Nathaniel. Despite losing his sight at age 14, J.B. Herreshoff was a well-respected shipbuilder who went into partnership with his brother Nat in 1878.[26] Captain Nat, as he was called, was an 1870 Massachusetts Institute of Technology graduate, and his designs revolutionized the sailing industry. The brothers produced a series of undefeated sailboats for the America's Cup race, and dominated the sport so dramatically that the 1893 to 1920 years are called the "Herreshoff Period."[27] By the time the Granlund family arrived in Rhode Island, the Herreshoff Manufacturing Company was already a force to be reckoned with on Narragansett Bay.

Nils loved the water and the sleek boats, and in his early teen years found part time work at Herreshoff, where he learned the basics of sailing and racing sloops.[28] When an acquaintance bought a racing boat from an owner north of Boston, Granlund was able to talk his way aboard as a member of the four-man crew sailing the boat from Marblehead to its new mooring at Providence. The salty old captain hired to lead them brought provisions for a two-day excursion, a trip that wound up being an arduous nine-day sail through the rough Atlantic around Cape Cod. At a point nearly halfway into the journey, the crew was greatly relieved to reach the waters of Provincetown Harbor, where they could regroup before tackling the rolling waters off the cape. Granlund, ever the talker, introduced himself to the captain of a fishing boat sailing out of Edgartown, Massachusetts, who offered a meal to the spent and hungry sailors.

Granlund's tale of the remainder of the excursion likely differs greatly from the version that would have been offered by the experienced fishing boat captain. Although he later boasted of his own efforts in bring the yacht to its destination, Granlund owed a debt of gratitude to the captain of the fishing boat. To his credit, Granlund admitted that, if not for "the big Portuguese fishing boat and her captain, Joe Silva," he might not have been able to tell the story at all.[29] It is a fact that Granlund, the racing sloop, the crew, and the aged acting-captain all managed to arrive safely at Providence.

The fishing boat was the *Louisa Silva*, and Joe Silva was a Portuguese immigrant, born in the Azores. The Silva family arrived in 1860 and settled at Edgartown when Joe was still a toddler.[30] Years later, he and his brothers bought a boat, named it for their mother, and began fishing the waters off Cape Cod, where they eventually crossed paths with Nils. As a courtesy, Silva told the departing sloop's crew they were welcome on his boat any time. Granlund took the invitation to heart.

Confident of his abilities and staunchly independent even at his young age, Granlund contacted Silva some months later inquiring about work, and the captain agreed to consider such a proposal if Granlund could meet the boat at Boston, while the crew unloaded their catch. Nils managed to find Silva and his boat, and soon after found himself employed as a crewman aboard the *Louisa Silva*.

Nils was sixteen when he hired on as captain's mate. He learned enough from his three-week adventure to crew on the racing boats in Narragansett Bay, and later sailed a number of yachts through the many local clubs. In 1913, he made the list of the Rhode Island Yacht Club, the same group in which the America's Cup Herreshoff family held membership. Granlund's brother Frederick took up sailing as well, and by 1919 he had his own vessel and a membership in the same club.[31]

To earn spending money, Granlund carried the printed news of the day to subscribers, and from delivering copies of the *Providence Evening Bulletin* and the morning daily *Providence Journal*, he eventually graduated to the copy desk, a move he attributed to John Revelstoke Rathom, then the managing editor of the papers.[32] Rathom was an Australian-born adventurer and journalist who came to the United States just three years before Granlund arrived, but settled instead on the West Coast and worked for a number of newspapers there, including the *San Francisco Chronicle*. Leaving for the Midwest and the *Chicago Times-Herald*, Rathom soon continued east, moving to Rhode Island in 1905 as an editor with the Providence papers. During his nearly twenty-year career in Rhode Island, he served as a director for the Associated Press and was elected to serve as president of the New England Press Association, in addition to running "one of the most money-making magazine combinations in the U.S."[33]

Granlund admitted that he never knew what it was that prompted the newspaper's managing editor to take an interest in him, but it may have been that Rathom recognized a fellow adventurer and the brand of fearlessness often required for a reporter to excel. It may also have been due in part to a recognition of a kindred spirit of sorts, given their shared penchant for exaggeration and their ability to massage the truth to achieve a desired effect. During World War I, Rathom toured as an after-dinner speaker, spinning wondrous fabrications as to how the *Journal* was involved in breaking up a ring of German spies, tales that were regularly picked up by wire service reporters to be related in other newspapers. Granlund was later able to use his quick-thinking and public speaking abilities as a promoter to rally his causes amid the cutthroat New York nightlife competition.

Granlund was quick to relate stories of his early days in the newspaper business, and although he later exaggerated or inaccurately recalled the dates, he was, in truth, working as a newspaper reporter by age seventeen, writing for the *Providence Tribune*, a newspaper that had no qualms about printing the works of young writers.[34] In addition to adding Granlund as a cub reporter in 1906, the *Tribune* also began printing a column on astronomy by a sixteen-year-old Providence native named Howard Phillips Lovecraft, who was penning a similar column for the *Pawtuxet Valley Gleaner*, and later achieved fame as the science fiction author H.P. Lovecraft.[35]

A young and inexperienced reporter, Granlund nonetheless imagined himself as a journalistic force.[36] When he spotted a description in a New York newspaper column that used similar wording to one of his own articles, Granlund assumed the metropolitan writer was pilfering his work. He fired off a letter to the writer, one Damon Runyon, who at the time covered sports for the *American*, demanding that Runyon give credit to the "little frog in Providence" for the work being printed in the big pond of New York City. Runyon wrote back that he had never heard of Granlund or his sports "lingo." In later years, after Granlund established himself in New York, he and Runyon became fast friends.

Granlund's editor at the Providence newspaper was a man named Eastman, who believed that his big-headed young reporter would benefit from being knocked down a peg or two, and envisioned an upcoming royal visit as a golden opportunity for Granlund to learn humility. The event was the arrival of Swedish Crown Prince Wilhelm in Newport, Rhode Island, for the Jamestown Exposition,[37] and subsequent appearances.

Granlund recalled the editor pointing out to him that "you're a Swede and this prince is about your age. Go down to Newport and get an interview with him,"[38] knowing full well that Granlund would be unable to gain entry to the event. Eastman did provide Granlund with expense money for transportation on the electric tram to Newport and back, and he set out immediately.

Nils Thor Granlund, circa 1907, during the period he worked as a sports editor for the *Providence Tribune* (courtesy Amanda Howard).

The arrival of King Oscar's grandson in August was seen as the primary social occasion of the 1907 season for the royalty of New England society, and a significant visit in the eyes of the many resident Swedes.

The royal visit set off a society matron's war among the Newport wealthy, including the widow of the younger Cornelius Vanderbilt, who had earlier emerged victorious as the primary hostess for the visiting Prince Henry of Prussia.[39] The honors fell to "Mrs. Stuyvesant Fish, to Mrs. E.J. Berwind, Mrs. Ogden Mills, and Mrs. Richard Gambrill."

A number of young Swedes had been selected to serve on the wait staff in attendance at the series of local events arranged in honor of the "Sailor Prince," including an exclusive, invitation-only dinner held at the mansion of Ogden Mills of Newport. Granlund recalled the hostess as Mrs. Ogden Goelet [*sic*]; although several accounts of the fete specifically noted the guest list exclusion of some members of Rhode Island's highest society, and particularly that of Mrs. Goulet, who had pushed her own candidacy as the prince's hostess.

Three thousand of Prince Wilhelm's former countrymen gathered at Battery Park on the morning of August 27, 1907, lining the seawall anticipating the arrival of the armored cruiser *Fylgia* in New York. The ship "passed in Sandy Hook a few minutes before eight o'clock, and an hour later the Swedes in Battery Park sighted her three funnels as she neared the Statue of Liberty."[40] Moments later, the *Fylgia*'s guns "thundered a salute to the American colors," which was met with a pounding reply from the American cannons atop the walls of Fort Wadsworth and on Governors Island. Thousands of handkerchiefs and Swedish flags danced in the air along the Battery in salute to the Swedish crew, which stood at attention at the sides of the *Fylgia* as it steamed past, heading up the North River to its anchorage off 86th Street.

Unknown to the energetic crowd, the prince was not aboard. He had departed the ship the previous afternoon to attend to the social "programmes" in his honor at Newport and Providence.[41]

At the same time, and undaunted at the prospect of interviewing Swedish royalty, a naïve seventeen-year-old Nils T. Granlund, cub reporter, made his way from Providence to Newport, where he found the lavish estate and attempted to talk his way onto the grounds. Security personal kept him outside the iron gates, and no amount of blustery Swedish claims or declarations of newspaper reporter's rights could get him inside for an interview. When it became apparent that his efforts were futile, Granlund reluctantly admitted defeat.

He made his way back from the rural estate to Newport proper, where he wandered for a time, before discovering an open-invitation Swedish ball being held in Wilhelm's honor. Granlund surmised the public event might hold some semblance of a news story that would keep him from returning to Providence empty-handed. He had been in the hall for only a short time, when — to his great surprise — the young prince made an unannounced appearance, mixing with the locals and even managing to accommodate several dance requests from the many young Swedish women in attendance.

At one point, when Wilhelm drew near, Granlund called out to him in their common language, trying to explain to the dancing prince that he had attempted an interview at the Mills Estate, but was turned away.[42] Prince Wilhelm did not end his dance for an interview with Granlund, but the young reporter mentally composed a story as he watched the Swedish royal being swept through the crowd. The story became that of the handsome prince turning up his royal nose at the high society gathering in order to dance with the local serving girls.

Eastman, the editor, was "flabbergasted and pleased" at the resulting story and challenged Granlund to try his luck the following day at Warwick Neck, where Wilhelm was to be the guest of Nelson Wilmarth Aldrich.

At the time, Aldrich, a U.S. Senator representing Rhode Island, was considered to be among the most powerful politicians in Congress.[43] Armed with a notebook and enough cash for the tram and dinner, Granlund made his way to Warwick and managed to locate the grounds of the Senator's large estate.

Moving surreptitiously along the perimeter of the grounds, Granlund eventually spotted an opening in the wall just large enough to allow him to slip through. Once inside, he trotted toward the house, but before he could reach the structure he was spotted by three security officers, who chased him down and physically detained him. Despite his many objections and explanations, Granlund was marched in the direction of the rear kitchen door.

When one of the men spoke, Granlund recognized his accent and pleaded his case anew in Swedish, drawing enough sympathy to be seated at a table in the large kitchen while someone in authority could be notified regarding a trespasser. Several Swedish members of the kitchen staff saw to it that Granlund received a quick meal while awaiting his fate.[44]

The senator's son Winthrop, who later served as head of Chase National Bank, strolled into the bustling kitchen some time later, and almost simultaneously, Granlund spotted Prince Wilhelm crossing in an adjacent hallway. It may have been his journalistic dedication or mere brashness that prompted his next move, but Granlund called out to the prince in Swedish. The largely Swedish serving staff was astonished when a member of their royal family entered the kitchen to speak to the young reporter. As the conversation continued, any thoughts Aldrich may have entertained about having the young trespasser prosecuted for his actions vanished altogether.

After speaking for a time with Prince Wilhelm, Granlund realized that the last tram bound for Providence had departed, leaving him stranded and on his own in Newport. As evidence of his persuasive gift of gab, the cub reporter managed to wrangle an automobile ride back to Providence. His transportation was no mere taxi: The car was that of the powerful state senator, and the ride was in the royal company of the crown prince, who had the driver drop Granlund off in front of the *Tribune* office, where a number of staff members were still working the typewriters.

Granlund remembered striding into the newspaper office and fielding questions about the interview he was not expected to manage, and then boasting that the prince "brought me back to town." He later boasted that the newspaper story netted him several hundred dollars when his article was sold by wire service to other papers around the country.

Years later, in New York, Granlund was formally introduced to Winthrop Aldrich, and the two men shared a laugh as they recalled the Swedish Prince and the Newspaper Pauper and the meeting in the kitchen of the Aldrich estate. Incredibly, it was not the last time Granlund would run into Prince Wilhelm of Sweden. In 1933, the son of King Gustaf undertook an expedition to N'Ahag-gar, located deep in the heart of the Sahara Desert, intending to write a book and perhaps release a film based on his experiences.[45] The royal expedition also included a visit to Ghat, in Libya, where Prince Wilhelm studied the nomadic Tuaregs, camel traders who descended from ancient North African tribes and ruled the Saharan trade routes. At the time of Wilhelm's expedition, Granlund was in the employ of Marcus Loew, one of the leading film promoters in the United States, and remembered when a "cadaverous-looking" fellow stroke into the office.

"I am Prince Wilhelm of Sweden," the man said to a surprised Granlund. "Do you remember me?"[46]

Granlund straightaway led the crown prince to the office of his boss and introduced him with a grand flourish. Marcus Loew naturally assumed his joke-loving publicity agent with the penchant for exaggeration, was kidding.

Two

Touring with Hanky Panky

Engage in one kind of business only, and stick to it faithfully
until you succeed, or until your experience shows you should
abandon it.

— P.T. Barnum

The Big Time — the venue all performers wanted to play — was The Palace
in New York City, but any American town that wanted to present itself to the
world as a place deserving designation on the artistic and social map had its
own music hall. Theaters at the end of the nineteenth century ranged from the
cavernous brick structures with velvet curtains and plush seating, to wooden
shacks that scarcely offered a room in which performers could change costumes.[1] As a general rule, they all offered raised stages, and most were equipped
with footlights, music, and seating to accommodate audiences willing to pay
the price of admission. In that time, which predated television, radio, and films,
there was little else besides summertime baseball and neighborly visits to serve
as entertainment, and nearly every community of any size had a theater to
showcase local talent or the troupes of traveling performers.

In Providence, one of the theaters was operated by B.F. Keith,[2] and for Nils
Granlund, it was the Big Time.

Benjamin Franklin Keith and Edward Franklin Albee were theater owners in Boston who in July 1885 developed a continuous daily variety show that
ran from ten in the morning until nearly midnight.[3] The acts ran in sequence
and repeated throughout the day, allowing a patron to buy a ticket and watch
until the program returned to the point at which the customer sat down. Vaudeville, notoriously risqué, underwent a family-oriented scrubbing[4] at the hands
of Keith and Albee, who began buying and remodeling East Coast theaters with
the intention of providing their own brand of "high class" entertainment.

In its earliest forms, vaudeville offered entertainment, crude bordering on
rude, with an audience restricted to men. Keith and Albee, recognizing the
income potential if an entire family bought tickets, began cleaning up the acts

as they cleaned up the buildings housing them. Crude remarks were out, along with the overtly suggestive performances and routines. The theater impresarios went so far as to police their audiences in an attempt to make the atmosphere appeal to mothers and children. As more theaters came under the Keith-Albee management, a circuit developed in which performers could tour from town to town.

From their base of operations in Boston, Keith and Albee developed a number of New England theaters, including several in Rhode Island, at Providence, Pawtucket, and Woonsocket. The holdings also included Keith's New Theater in Boston, run by A. Paul Keith; the Bijou in Philadelphia, managed by P.F. Nash; and the Union Square Theater in New York, run by J. Austin Fynes. In Providence, the Keith Theater listed B.F. Keith as proprietor, Albee as general manager, and J.T. Fynes as the resident manager,[5] and the playbill repeated the management's determination to provide a venue for family entertainment.

In his in-house program, Keith offered his compliments to the theatergoers of Providence, and his promise to "offer the best entertainments it is possible to provide for the ensuing season of 1895–96." Keith's determination to present family-oriented entertainment was reiterated with a pledge to "present the cleanest and most enjoyable type," and to "surpass the standard of excellence which has hitherto characterized the productions."[6]

There was a glamour to the Keith-Albee Theater that made it easy for Granlund to fall under its spell. With its towering, arched entryway and ornate columns, the building offered ornate stonework high above the street level, and a wide fixed awning that protected theatergoers from the rain. As with any "high class" theater, behind the curtain was a backstage area, and it was there than Granlund gravitated, rather than the cushioned seats beyond the ticket office.

Small-staff journalism requires much from its writers, and Granlund, now a seasoned seventeen year old, could flip over a page in his sports reporter's tablet and become drama editor of the *Providence Tribune*. He had drama experience: He played Shylock in *The Merchant of Venice*,[7] and that was enough to allow him to strut into the opera house and immediately head backstage. He felt himself an insider, someone who could make a difference in the success of the production. He was a writer, and he was unafraid to greet the headlining acts and write his reviews for print. Groomed at the sports desk, Granlund found himself increasingly drawn to the footlights and curtains, and a chance to talk with the stars.

"I got a tremendous kick every time I went backstage,"[8] he later recalled of his Providence interviews with notables such as Cecil Spooner, an actress and early feminist in a man's world, who left the trailing-e from her given name Cecile, hoping it would give her more power and respectability in a time when women had few rights.

At the tender age of twenty-two, Spooner opened a theater at 961 Southern Boulevard in the Bronx, which Loews bought years later and renamed the Loews Spooner Theater.[9] Spooner had achieved a degree of notoriety in New York, particularly after her performance in *House of Bondage*, a play that New York police determined to be beyond the limits of propriety. She and her manager were arrested just before the second night's opening curtain, and the resulting publicity brought lines of theater-goers for the subsequent night's performance — altered slightly in content as an appeasement.[10] Appearing in Providence earlier in her career, she made an immediate and lasting impression on Granlund, giving him his first taste of the audacity of New York and the type of women in whose company he could be found for the next forty years.

Wearing his drama editor hat, Granlund took his pad and pencil to the Keith Theater on an afternoon in 1909 for an interview with Pat Rooney, Jr.[11] The Rooney family was well-known to vaudeville audiences, who first met the Irish clan in 1867 when nineteen-year-old Pat Rooney, Sr., arrived from Ireland to begin a career of singing and dancing on New York stages. When he died at age 44, he left behind four children who would follow him into the business. Pat Jr. was a frequent performer in Providence, generally appearing with his wife Marion Bent, with whom he had a well-rehearsed dance-and-patter routine. It was Pat Jr. who danced with his hands jammed deep into his pockets to hike up his trousers legs, showing off his clogging footwork.[12] The style was widely imitated by other showmen of the time.

When the two married on April 11, 1904, a "large and jolly group" of performers saw the newlyweds off to Pittsburgh, where Pat was to perform without Marion, who claimed to have left the stage "for good."[13] It was an empty promise, and she played the Keith stage in Providence enough times that Granlund easily recognized the name.

Sitting across from the comedian in the dressing room, Granlund watched as Pat Rooney, Jr., leaned into the mirror to apply the finishing touches to his makeup before the afternoon matinee. Rooney was handed a telegram, which he quickly opened and read.[14] Granlund recalled that Rooney shouted, "I'm the father of a son!" and tossed him a telegram announcing the birth of Pat Rooney III — the latest in what would become a line of showmen bearing the Irish name.[15] Pat Jr. later divorced Marion; Granlund was in wartime Hollywood when a July 27, 1942, report announced the marriage of actress Janet Reade to Pat Rooney, Jr. The blonde-haired Reade was once a member of Eddie Cantor's production of *Whoopee*, and was the ex-wife of Pat Rooney III. In announcing her marriage intentions, Reade quipped that she had not seen her former husband in years, and "anyway, I like his father better."[16]

At the time of the Keith Theater interview, Granlund was already discovering an ability to be in the right place at the right time, a knack that — combined with his quick-thinking ability — allowed him to take advantage of a great many situations. Holding the telegram from Rooney's wife, Granlund may have been thinking of the woman he would shortly marry, a woman who would later require telegrams to communicate with her publicity-minded, on-the-road husband. For Granlund, the interviews at the Providence theater began his lifelong collection of anecdotes that would become the stock-in-trade of his later radio years.

The elegant and well-staffed vaudeville houses of the Keith-Albee chain, along with the nature of the entertainment they provided, earned them the nickname "the Sunday School Circuit" among the performers.[17] The B.F. Keith Theater would have been a respectable enough place for young Providence residents to be seen, particularly convenient for a member of the working press.

Granlund was taking courses at Brown University, the Ivy League school located in Providence, and was calling on an attractive young woman named Mabel Avery, a schoolmate from Classical High School[18] who lived with her parents about a mile from his own home.[19] Her parents were English-born, her father Frederick having come to the U.S. to work as a silversmith at Providence, and her mother, the former Emma Quinton, who had married Frederick in 1869.[20] Mabel, a surprise child born late in life, was nineteen years younger than her older brother Fred, and ten years the junior of her sister Florence.

Frederick Jr. followed in the trade of his father, and both men worked in the booming Providence silver industry, which had benefited from an 1842 tariff on silverware importation. Gorham Silver became an influential firm, with sales to Mary Todd Lincoln, who used her tea service in the White House, and commissioned trophies for the America's Cup, tennis' Davis Cup, and the Borg-Warner trophy for the Indianapolis 500 auto race.

With such large-scale industry, it was of little surprise to find several members of a family working in the silver trade, and in addition to the father-son employment in the Avery household, Theodore Granlund and his son Frederick were employed as silversmiths. There would have been plenty of common topics for conversation among the two families.

Nils Granlund and Mabel C. Avery were married on June 5, 1910,[21] but their home life would be interrupted from the beginning.

The young man who had struggled to catch up with his classmates continued to push himself, driven by a competitive nature and a love for sports. Granlund spent enormous amounts of time on the water, and the racing yachts of the Rhode Island Yacht Club at Newport became familiar and comfortable. It was more than racing competition, though. Before he married he had spent time in the local gyms, keeping up with the local boxing scene.

In addition to his day job reporting for the *Providence Tribune,* Granlund found himself in the favor of Felix Wendelschaefer, the former orchestra leader at the Providence Opera House, who was serving as manager.[22] Wendelschaefer hired Granlund at a rate of ten dollars per week as the theater's press agent, and despite the obvious conflict of interest, it allowed the reporter a boost to his income and an inside track to the show business backstage.

The Providence Opera House was constructed in 90 days in 1871,[23] and remained standing for sixty years at the northwest corner of Dorrance and Pine Streets. Next door sat the well-known Narragansett Hotel, and the two structures exemplified the capital-city dignity that adorned postcards and offered first-rate entertainment and accommodations. Granlund found himself almost nightly mingling with the top-billing acts of the day, while continuing his regular daytime employment as a reporter.

Covering sports for the *Providence Tribune*, Granlund traveled in November 1910 with the Brown University football team to New Haven, Connecticut, for a game against Yale. Football was a brutal sport at the time; just three years previous, eleven U.S. players were killed in a single season and nearly one hundred suffered serious bodily injury, including paralysis. In his 1912 book on football, Carlisle coach Glenn "Pop" Warner wrote that he could not encourage the use of helmets, but didn't hold it against those players who did, an attitude widely shared among players who disregarded the practicality of safety equipment. The 1909–1910 season marked a turning point in rules to reduce the game's high mortality rate.

Yale was a proponent of the forward pass, a play only recently added as legal, and was the dominant team in what would become the Ivy League. The year 1910 marked the beginning of modern football, and the end of the Yale dynasty. It was that year that Brown University, visitors on the Yale football field of play, recorded their first victory over their rivals, a stunning 21–0 upset, with young sports reporter Granlund on the sideline.

"The game made a big impression on me," Granlund later recalled, although it was not the highlight of his visit to Connecticut. "I saw a show at the Taft Theater the night before and I could describe every act, every number in the show."[24]

Increasingly, it was the sidelights rather than the sidelines that held his interest. When he saw an early performance of the vaudeville show *Hanky Panky*, featuring Florence Moore and her husband Billy Montgomery in the principal roles, it was enough to take Granlund out of reporting—and Rhode Island—for good.

Wendelschaefer booked *Hanky Panky* into the Providence Opera House and provided Granlund with publicity information for the year-end string of shows featuring Moore, who began touring at a young age with her brother's troupe, and managed a brief Broadway and silent film career before her death at age 49. In *Hanky Panky*, she found the start of a twenty-year stage career that took her to Broadway and across the country, as an actress on the newly emerging vaudeville circuit.

Opposite: Granlund's first wife, Mabel C. Avery of Providence, Rhode Island, circa 1910 (courtesy Amanda Howard).

Granlund was star-struck and outdid himself in providing publicity for the Providence performances. His suggestion for a theater-hotel package added business for the Narragansett, and the Providence run proved profitable for the company. It also brought Granlund to the attention of theater owner Marcus Loew.

Born into a poor New York Jewish family, Marcus Loew had no formal education, but possessed a head for business and an aptitude for entertainment.[25] From a series of menial jobs, he saved enough money to buy into a penny arcade business, and by 1900 was earning a living as a furrier, living in Manhattan with his wife Carrie and twin sons Arthur and David. Though Loew was dabbling in the theater by the time Granlund managed an introduction, he continued to consider his occupation as real estate rather than real entertainment. That would quickly change.

Another New York City furrier was Adolph Zukor, about Loew's age, who was a native of the Austro-Hungarian empire and emigrated to New York as a teenager in 1888.[26] He learned the fur trade and within ten years had twenty-five employees working at his Zukor's Novelty Fur Company and lived in the posh district of New York's West 149th Street. In 1903, Marcus Loew was among his employees when Zukor's cousin Max Goldstein asked for a loan to expand an arcade to accommodate Thomas Edison's new moving pictures.

As a penny arcade owner himself, Loew had an interest in pursuing such ventures, and convinced Zukor to form a partnership to open another theater. The New York City partnership marked the beginning of the Hollywood film industry, and Zukor founded the company that became Paramount Pictures. In the course of running his own small string of arcades, Loew eventually acquired a near monopoly on the vaudeville bookings, and purchased the production company backing *Hanky Panky*.[27]

Loew was as small as Granlund was tall, and where Granlund's style bordered on loud and overbearing, Loew was quiet and apologetic.[28] Although still a young man, Granlund already considered himself a significant contributor to the Providence scene, as the *Tribune*'s sports and drama editor, the press agent for the local opera house, and a proven sailor who was comfortable in the company of the wealthy local yachtsmen. In the back offices of the Providence Opera House, Loew offered Granlund a job, one that would take him on the road with the *Hanky Panky* production as its publicity agent. Granlund was hesitant to make the change, but when Loew promised to keep Granlund on after the end of the show's run, he accepted the offer.

The travel was not much different than what he had been doing covering sports for the *Tribune*, following the various Providence teams when they played on the road. Granlund was already familiar with most of the theater company's

Opposite: Nils Thor Granlund offers a sportsman's pose in Providence, circa 1910 (courtesy Amanda Howard).

scheduled stops, and had acquaintances from Boston to Buffalo. Still, he was reluctant to sever his Providence ties, so when he approached the *Tribune*'s managing editor Bill Dwyer, Granlund requested a leave of absence.

Granlund recalled that Dwyer admonished that the leave of absence would certainly become permanent, but offered reassurance that the *Tribune* would clear a desk for him should he ever decide to return. Over the course of his career, Granlund would land bylines on additional newspaper copies, but he never returned to the reporter's beat, and —for all practical purposes— spooled out distances between the job, his wife, and his family that could never again be reeled back in.

Plenty of change was in the air in 1912, not only for the Granlund family, but for Providence and the nation as well. Streets that not so long ago remained the exclusive domain of horse-drawn carriages began to find an increasingly shared usage with gasoline-powered automobiles. Arguments over the Grand Trunk railroad extension from New Haven to Providence forced an intervention by President Taft, who managed a restart to the construction. The Rhode Island Socialist Party nominated Helen Dougherty as their candidate for secretary of state; she was the first woman to run for state office, at a time when women were not allowed to vote for any candidate.

In the Granlund home, already partially vacated by the exit of Nils, the marriage in March of his brother Frederick emptied the nest of the now-grown children of Theodore and Amanda.[29] On March 12, Frederick married the daughter of Hugo and Elizabeth Schultz, who had emigrated to Rhode Island from Germany.[30] Twenty-four-year-old Pauline worked in the silver industry, along with her sisters, who packed the completed merchandise for shipping.

Alone for most of the day in her Providence home, Amanda Granlund continued to keep house for her husband, but late in the year she faltered, and after suffering through months of failing health, she died on September 2 at age 52.[31] Her burial in the Locust Grove Cemetery on Elmwood Avenue was the last occasion for the Granlund family to gather in Providence.

It was 1912 that marked Marcus Loew's construction of the Avenue B Theater in New York City. The theater officially opened on January 8, 1913, an opulent 1,750-seat showplace that cost Loew some $800,000 to build and which he described as his "most pretentious" house.[32] The site of the theater is still noted as the location of the humble apartment in which Loew was born. "I created the myth," Granlund later admitted. "It wasn't true but it made good publicity."[33]

During the Avenue B construction, Granlund was on the road, touring with the company of *Hanky Panky*. It was his on-the-job training for a position that he was eminently qualified, but had little experience or working knowledge. He also discovered that his Providence résumé amounted to "small pond" events that translated to naiveté in the bigger world.

It was a cross-country tour, showgirls high-kicking on stages from its start at the American Music Hall in Chicago, then onward to the Murat Theater in Indianapolis for a half-week engagement there before winding its way through the upper Midwest. On their way to the West Coast were company stars and two dozen chorus girls traveling with a 21 year old would-be publicity agent. Granlund was young and brash enough that he immediately began staging stunts that might have been nixed by any of his elder counterparts.

The show was booked into the Mason Opera House in Los Angeles, a lavish theater, looking as grand on the day Granlund and Company arrived as it had its opening in June 1903.[34] For Granlund, it was as spectacular a place as could be conceived, a wide, four-story art deco structure with a long, tiled lobby, a warm, red-carpeted foyer, and frosted incandescent bulbs casting a warm glow from their recesses in the ceiling. The Mason was a massive showplace; the orchestra pit alone could accommodate nearly 100 musicians. Standing on the stage, looking out over the empty house, Granlund could easily imagine the seats filled with patrons, and the applause ringing down from the sixteen box seats perched on the ivory and pale green walls like dainty bird's nests.[35] Below the box seats were three levels of seating and room for 1600 ticket holders. It was up to Granlund to sell those tickets.

He settled upon a scheme that he would later repeat in New York. It involved two dozen of the most daring chorus girls outfitted in a collection of rented and ill-fitting swimwear.

At the time, women's bathing suits consisted of two parts, a baggy and shapeless tunic top and long bathing knickers that — in their original design — came all the way down to the ankles. Annette Kellerman, an attractive Australian vaudevillian who made a name for herself as "the Queen of the Mermaids" and "Neptune's Daughter," was doing a water ballerina act in tanks of water on American stages.[36] She was arrested in 1907 on indecent exposure charges for her special bathing suit that revealed not only her arms and shoulders, but most of her legs as well. It was shortly after that event that the U.S. women's beach styles became slightly less stringent, at least in some areas of the country.

Still, the women's version covered considerably more than men's suits, which also sported a two-piece design, and featured a sleeveless shirt and a skirted pair of long shorts. Undeterred by the fact that the Venice, California, bathhouse only rented men's suits, Granlund paid the required fee, had his showgirls change, and then turned the ladies loose on the Venice beach sand and surf. Modesty was hardly an issue for the chorus girls, as their *Hanky Panky* costumes were cut from smaller cloth still, but for the Venice Beach public, it was an exciting and scandalous display.

Granlund slipped away to a telephone and called several newspapers, and shortly afterward the police, and within the hour twenty-four chorus girls were being herded into paddy wagons and transported to the local precinct house.[37]

He later recalled being forgiven by the cast when they saw the newspaper articles stemming from the publicity prank, and the resulting packed house.

The show was described as being "without a plot or anything to tax the mind, but is one long succession of laughs, catchy songs, pretty girls, shifting scenes, and a snap and a dash."[38] The Venice city trustees hastened to change the bathing suit regulations after Granlund's stunt, hurriedly passing an ordinance to make it "unlawful for any person to appear upon the beach, in the ocean, or in any public place in Venice in a bathing suit,"[39] unless the suit matched their specifications. That ideal and acceptable suit, which the mayor offered to parade down the boardwalk, was described as having "sleeves that come to the wrists, collar a half-inch high, bloomers, and a bona fide skirt at least thirty inches long hung from the waist. Women," it went on to say, "shall wear stockings of somber shade, and hair ribbons must be worn by girls under 14 years of age." Men's suits were allowed to be made in "mannish style," but of the same general fashion, and a $300 fine was enacted for any future violations.

Hanky Panky's run was extended to three weeks at the Mason and the cross-country tour had Granlund on the road for more than two years, rolling into New York City mid-tour for a Broadway performance. Show producer Lew Fields paid a surprise visit on his friend Marcus Loew on September 18, 1912, when ninety of the *Hanky Panky* chorus girls and the orchestra were "packed into automobiles after the show was over on Broadway and shot up into the Bronx, there to swell the regular Loew vaudeville bill of the evening."[40]

The show was the job, but as a PR agent, Granlund was not above a little self-promotion. When the touring company made Oshkosh, Wisconsin, for a series of performances at the Grand Opera House on High Avenue, Granlund discovered that middleweight boxer Eddie McGoorty was in town for a match. The sportswriter for the *Daily Northwestern* struck up a conversation with Granlund concerning the prospects of a local boxer, and later ran the comments as the opinion of an "Eastern Sporting Expert."[41] Granlund called McGoorty the greatest middleweight in the world, and the *Northwestern* gave the statement credibility by identifying N.T. Granlund as "formerly sporting editor of the *Providence Tribune*, manager of boxers for several years, and eastern fistic expert, who is in town today as press representative with *Hanky Panky*."

"McGoorty stands ace high in the east, especially around New York," Granlund was quoted as saying, "and I was surprised when I came here to find that he has never appeared to advantage here."

For all his self-importance, the young PR man gave a creditable account of the boxer's credentials, describing his victories and opponents by name, and went on to claim that the manager of another fighter wanted Granlund in the corner as a "second" in a match with McGoorty.

"Mike was scared to death that night," Granlund said of middleweight Mike Gibbons. "McGoorty got his goat with talk in the dressing room before

On a visit to Providence, circa 1913, following the time Nils Thor Granlund toured with *Hanky Panky* (courtesy Amanda Howard).

the fight, which Gibbons could hear over the top of the partition. I knew before the fight that Gibbons couldn't win. He was afraid to hit."[42]

For his own part, Granlund had no fear of verbal sparring. He was rough-cut, but gentle, and for all his blustering he could be surprisingly soft-spoken.[43] His genial style added to the camaraderie, and by the time the show reached Manitoba, Canada, in July 1913, the cast was being described as the "big, jolly, happy *Hanky Panky* company"[44] that had been touring for two years.

They had appeared at "every large city in the country" and the newspaper quoted from Granlund's advance publicity in describing the chorus girls as "the pick of America's garden of loveliness." In each city they visited, showgirls regularly joined the stars in parades, riding in cars at a time when the automobile was still a novelty and the presence of several in succession was reason enough for townsfolk to gather. The paper noted the "plethora of parades of late," but promised that the beauty parade would travel the downtown streets of the city with the theater orchestra and a band, seated on two big motor trucks, with the stars and chorus girls to "follow after in automobiles."[45]

During his travels, Granlund had kept in touch, not only with his wife Mabel, but his network of acquaintances and friends on the East Coast as well. His propensity for mixing in, reaching out, and signing up for the company of others allowed his name to be listed in some exotic circles.

By 1913, the Rhode Island Yacht Club already had a tradition of impressive and exclusive membership, and Granlund was pleased to be among the distinguished yachtsmen of Narragansett Bay, men like Nathaniel and John B. Herreshoff, the America's Cup yacht builders; Rhode Island Senator Nelson W. Aldrich, in whose home Granlund, as cub reporter, had been detained; Charles G. Bloomer, the Pawtucket jewelry manufacturer who was among the yacht club's early founders; William H. Cranston, of the major jewelry firm located in the Rhode Island city named after his ancestors; H. Earle Kimball, a sparkling beverage millionaire who began the still-active Kimball Foundation; Thomas Fleming Day, editor of *The Rudder*, described as the greatest American yachting and boating magazine ever published; Benjamin Franklin Keith, the theater magnate; United States Congressman Henry J. Spooner; and Charles F. Tillinghast, who won the first long distance amateur yacht race ever staged — a 1904, 330-mile event from New York City's Gravesend Bay to Marblehead, Massachusetts, by way of the tricky shoals off Nantucket and Cape Cod.

Granlund loved rubbing elbows with the rich and famous, perhaps as a testament as to how far he had already come as an immigrant to the United States, with humble beginnings. Name-dropping became a lifelong habit, and he took genuine pride in his association with those who went on to greater things, particularly when he believed he played a part in their success.

THREE

The Early Loew Years

If you hesitate, some bolder hand will stretch out before you and take the prize.

— P.T. Barnum

The Harland and Wolff Shipyards in Belfast, Northern Ireland, created the hull of what would be the most luxurious ocean liner of its time. The ship, when completed, was the RMS *Titanic*, and the May 1911 launch began the process of the final outfitting before its maiden voyage from Southampton to New York. Among the American notables who had a ticket was William Morris,[1] the founder of a theatrical agency that — by the time of its 100th anniversary in 1998 — had offices on both American coasts, both sides of the Atlantic, and claims to the title of "largest and most diversified talent and literary agency in the world."[2]

Morris cancelled his trip over a vaudeville booking problem[3] and thereby avoided the ill-fated voyage, marking the type of good fortune that seemed to follow his life and career. The luck may have begun with the sale of his independent theater chain to Marcus Loew on March 4, 1911.[4] It was Morris who was originally behind the production of *Hanky Panky* that Granlund promoted for two years, and Granlund's employment was prompted in part by Loew's purchase of the show and his immediate need for employees to oversee his new operations.[5]

At the time of his acquisition, Loew controlled 45 theaters and the agency known as the United Booking Offices,[6] which placed vaudeville acts and performers in theaters across the country. His purchase of the Morris theaters gave Loew an additional 100 theaters, including the American and Plaza in New York, the Fulton in Brooklyn, the American Music Hall in Chicago, the Princess in St. Louis, the Orpheum in Cincinnati, and numerous others in smaller cities through the South and the western states.[7]

The eye-popping, two-million-dollar deal gave Loew control of all of the Morris theatrical holdings except the talent booking agency. At the time of the purchase, Loew maintained his offices at the Columbia Theatre[8] building in New York. When Granlund was offered a position with Loew, at a salary of $75 a week, the Loew and Morris offices had already been consolidated in the recently purchased American Theatre.[9]

The American Music Hall was Morris' name for the American Theatre, built on the southeast corner of Eighth Avenue and 42nd Street by T. Henry French in 1893.[10] It was Loew's American when Granlund was given an office. He found he was in impressive company, not unlike the familiars of his Rhode Island Yacht Club. Nicholas and Joseph Schenck, two Russian-born brothers who built the Palisades Amusement Park in New Jersey[11]— with money advanced by Loew[12]— had offices down the hall. Nick, as he was called, was Loew's general manager, and by 1932 was running MGM and its 12,000 employees.[13] His brother Joe Schenck left Loew's in 1919 and went on to found 20th Century — later called 20th Century–Fox — and served as president of United Artists Corporation.

In the metropolis that was New York City, Granlund quickly discovered his self-opinion as the "big fish" from Providence carried little weight. His efforts for the theater chain were not making the newspapers, and — swallowing his Swedish pride — he entered Loew's office seeking advice.

"I'm not getting anywhere," he would later recall admitting to his boss. "I haven't gotten a break in any of the papers since I hit town."[14]

Just months previously, the *New York Herald*, in an extensive article by Garnet Warren, had profiled a woman described as "the best known press agent on Earth."[15] Loew shared Warren's opinion, and sent Granlund to introduce himself to Nellie Revell.

New York City has long been noted as the place where stars can shine most brilliantly — or crash to earth most spectacularly — and Granlund's success in his earliest Gotham ventures may have been singularly the credit of Nellie Revell. Granlund could recall others who lent assistance in his first uneasy year covering New York theaters, including William Barclay Masterson, who wrote a sports column for the *New York Morning Telegraph*. The writer was perhaps better known for his escapades as the Dodge City, Kansas, sheriff who was among the last of the Old West lawmen and better known as "Bat" Masterson. He had continued to make the most of his somewhat self-proclaimed reputation as a gunfighter, but relied on his previous newspaper background to make his daily deadlines.

It was Nellie Revell, though, who had the reputation and clout to give Granlund an inside track to the writers of the city's newspapers.

Living in the midst of an eclectic gathering of actors, actresses, agents, and managers at the Hotel Calvert at 41st and Broadway,[16] Revell — nearly twenty years older than Granlund — had the sort of background that was perfectly suited for promotion. She was a large woman, loud and opinionated, not afraid to step face to face with any man, and her brash and outspoken manner, quick-witted repartee, and love for humor made her one of the rare women operating in the men's world of newspapers and publicity.[17]

Years later, when she admitted once throwing a bottle of ink at her editor-boss, he clarified the account by specifying that she had not only thrown it at him, but had hit him in the head.

"P.T. Barnum was the best friend I ever had," she announced in her 1911 *Herald* interview, explaining how she had come to serve as press agent for Barnum and his circus. At the time of her interview, she was serving as a press agent for Percy Williams, who owned the Colonial Theater in Manhattan, the Alhambra in Harlem and nine others, all booked through William Morris. She claimed that her mother's family had been "circus people" and her father a newspaper publisher; her obituary in 1958 counted her as a "noted newspaper woman, radio commentator and publicist"[18] who left the newspaper business when they moved her column to the women's page, and went to work for singer Al Jolson as his publicity agent.[19]

At a time when most women stayed home, Revell was a rare character who earned the respect of her male counterparts. She was the first woman to enter the quarters of New York's Friar's Club,[20] which later made her an honorary member. For Granlund, she was exactly the sort of person who could ease his transition from on-the-road publicity to local press.

Revell gave Granlund access to her contacts, but she could not instill the confidence that was required to succeed in New York City. For the first time in his young life, Granlund began to doubt his abilities, and his continued failure to garner press clippings for the Loew's theaters took a toll on his self-esteem.[21] He was a man who took pride in earning his own way and producing for his pay; the first weeks back from the *Hanky Panky* tour left him feeling guilty and conspicuous. The enterprises surrounding Loew and his employees were clearly headed toward grander heights and a national focus. The comfort of his former Providence newspaper job began to have an allure, and his growing doubts at last prompted him to write a note to his one-time editor at the *Tribune*.[22]

The reply brought both a sense of relief and an amount of trepidation. A job was still there to be had, if he wanted it. He only had to admit to himself the humbling discomfort of defeat, resign his position with Loew, and return to Rhode Island.

Granlund believed that Loew had shown trust and honesty in making good on his promise of a New York job following the show tour, and considered Loew to be a quiet and unassuming man despite his position as head of one of the country's largest theater chains. As the chief officer for an expanding entertainment empire, however, Loew was a formidable presence. The man whose desk was found in a private office at the American Theatre was closer to the age of Granlund's father, and after being beckoned inside, Granlund recalled explaining his situation and apologizing for failing to meet Loew's expectations.[23]

According to Granlund, Loew countered the apology with a low-key response indicating he had not expected the new publicity agent to "set the world on fire." Granlund considered that moment to be a turning point in his relationship with Loew, viewing him more as a father figure than his own father had been, providing an unconditional support that would be expected only of family. Loew's sense of decency made a lasting impression on Granlund, and his later interactions with others were influenced by the tolerance and patience he recognized as traits that served Loew well.[24] Based on the show of confidence, Granlund agreed to stay in New York.

It took several months for his promotional efforts to make an impact, but when he finally connected, Granlund believed he had hit a home run for his boss. Loew, who is credited as being one of the most astute observers of trends in entertainment,[25] may have lobbed Granlund a grapefruit in his next at-bat.

The show was called *The Pleasure Seekers*, a musical comedy in two acts based on a book by Edgar Smith.[26] The cast included the familiar comedy team of Florence Moore and Billy Montgomery, along with numerous others recently attached to the run of *Hanky Panky*. From the nearly two years spent touring with that show, Granlund was markedly familiar with the cast members, and felt comfortable in promoting a musical, particularly one featuring a large collection of chorus girls.

The motion picture industry was in its infancy, with several moviemakers, including Sigmund Lubin of Philadelphia,[27] involved in turning out short films for the nickelodeons, the low-cost theaters that had given Marcus Loew his start. Films were sold to booking agents, who worked to get the one- and two-reelers scheduled in the theaters. Loew, who was not a filmmaker directly, recognized that controlling the product could greatly affect the profitability.[28] He was already dabbling with cameras and film — not as a director or cinematographer, but as an interested entertainment industry executive, and described his activities in that respect to an audience at Harvard Business School.[29]

Granlund had seen the cameras and was acquainted with Loew's chief camera operator, and perhaps Granlund's novice perspective and the popular novelty of the new "moving pictures" connected perfectly for the idea he was to hatch. Film presented Granlund with his perfect promotions opportunity, a stunt he believed would make its way into the newspapers and more importantly, create favorable publicity for his boss and the new production.[30] The stage for his stunt would be outside — cameras in that era requiring plenty of bright light — and would occur at the back door of the theater in which the new production would open on November 3, 1913.[31]

The Winter Garden was originally a trolley car barn between Fiftieth and Fifty-first, on Broadway, that was converted by the Shuberts into a theater in 1911,[32] and continued through the decades uninterrupted, still offering long-run productions through the twentieth century, like Andrew Lloyd Weber's

Cats, even as the house neared its one-hundredth anniversary. For his gimmicky stunt, Granlund enlisted one of the pretty chorus girls to star in the "movie" that he would shoot near the exterior stage door.

His premise was simple; a pretty girl intended to run away to work in the chorus line of a Broadway show, over the strong objections of her husband, who—in his melodramatic fit of passion—pulls out a gun and shoots her dead. A wild and boisterous commotion was to immediately ensue, arranged by Granlund and involving some of the trolley motormen and conductors lounging nearby who jumped at the chance to appear in a movie, along with a half-dozen Winter Garden stagehands.[33]

Unfortunately for the young promoter, he failed to adequately notify the passersby and neighboring tenants, who converged on the area at once after hearing the sound of a gunshot. Acting in good faith, rather than good skill, the unsuspecting crowd rallied valiantly in holding down the "murderous" husband, while calling for the police. The man portraying the husband managed to stay in character long enough to fool all who happened upon the scene. In the uproar that followed, the cameraman managed to collect his equipment intact, and spirit himself away. Granlund disappeared as well, recalling later how he slipped away from the pandemonium well ahead of the official investigation that followed.

When the finger-pointing began, the name of Nils Granlund surfaced at once.

After leaving the immediate area, Granlund encountered Loew's general manager Nick Schenck, who—having seen the aftermath of the stunt—warned Granlund that the police were searching for the man responsible. For several days Granlund laid low, reluctant to admit his involvement to either the police or his employer. At last, he confessed to Loew, who required that he make an appearance at the precinct house to settle the matter, but immediately recognized the value of the event.[34] The newspaper account called the publicity activity "an entirely new and unique 'stunt,'" and credited Loew with using innovative techniques in marketing his big musical shows such as *The Pleasure Seekers*.

Granlund was given a slap on the wrist by the police, who warned him that any future publicity involving the local precinct in an official capacity would be taken more seriously. Loew forgave the activity, and was pleased with Granlund[35] for concocting the idea of incorporating film into the promotion of live theater, creating—in effect—the first filmed Broadway ad, a commercial for an upcoming entertainment event.[36]

As Granlund remembered it, Loew asked, "Didn't I tell you you'd make good?" and he recalled Loew's calm reaction as a turning point in measuring up to his employer's expectations.

The effects of the staged publicity event were printed in a New York theater article promptly carried in newspapers across the country through syndication. It pointed out that Loew intended to film "moving pictures of the rehearsals and other incidents" which would be sent to theaters in advance [and] take the place of much of the bill board advertising."[37]

As for the production, the review was less solid for the acting than for Granlund's stunt. The *Times* reported in its November 4, 1913, edition that *The Pleasure Seekers* was a "Spectacle Only," lacking comedy, but having "a Big, Dazzling Chorus."

It was a review that members of Loew's inner circle would have worried over as much as the starring cast members. The Winter Garden show marked the first salvo of Loew's assault on the "high-brow" theater of Broadway, and although the official program at the theater identified the backers only as the "Winter Gardens Company," the *Times* named the production as "in reality the offering of Lew Fields and Marcus Loew [which] marked the entry of the latter, who is the moving pictures and vaudeville magnate, into the producing business on a large scale."

The comedy team of Montgomery and Moore "furnished most of the bright spots," according to the review, but it was obvious to the young Granlund that the real success of the show was in the staging, the props and, above all, the chorus girls.[38] Reading the newspaper's mixed appraisal, Granlund could wince at the depiction of the show's comedians as "sadly lacking," while noting with gratification the descriptions of the "glamour gals" in whose company he found a great amount of pleasure.[39] From the point in the article that mentioned the "girls and girls and girls" to the portrayal of the show's highlight, "where the chorus girls indulge in a snowball fight with the audience," it was clear enough to Granlund that the presence of pretty women interacting with the audience could sway even the toughest critic.[40]

The entertainment empire of Marcus Loew, the man who had given 24-year-old Granlund his first big break, continued to swell, and there would be no mistaking the high-powered company Granlund was keeping. Almost daily came news of acquisitions and transfers[41] — not all of which came without a struggle.

As the size of his theatrical holdings increased, Loew was able to offer better and longer bookings for acts and entertainers, a fact not overlooked by the competing theaters. Fred G. Nixon-Nirdlinger, who managed a vaudeville agency with his brother in Philadelphia, filed a formal complaint with the U.S. Department of Justice[42] alleging that Loew and others, including the chain owned by Sullivan and Considine, had virtually monopolized the vaudeville industry to the detriment of smaller owners. The complaint was taken seriously enough that a warrant was issued for Loew's employee Joseph Schenck, who was later arrested while stepping off a commuter train and taken into custody over the alleged federal violation.[43]

The Philadelphia Vaudeville War finally ended on December 13, 1913,[44] when Loew came to terms with Harry T. Jordan, representing Keith's Theatre in Philadelphia, along with Samuel F. Nixon, Fred Nixon-Nirdlinger, E.F. Albee, and J. Fred Zimmerman. In exchange for his stock in the Metropolitan Opera House and the Chestnut Street Opera House in Philadelphia, Loew received holdings in a new firm being created by B.F. Keith.[45]

Whether the deal lessened the virtual monopoly in theater bookings became a moot point, since all parties signed the agreement, including Nixon-Nirdlinger, who filed the initial complaint.

For Loew, it blasted the way open for new theater construction and renovations that in 1913 kept his attention focused on brick and mortar aspects of the entertainment world. It was not all good news.[46] Armies of construction employees working under the Loew's contractual umbrella were simultaneously starting and finishing projects.

On January 22, 1913, workers at the job site at 87th Street[47] near Third Avenue (the theater was later identified more closely with 86th Street[48]) finished for the day, and were gathering tools and equipment to head for home.

When Loew acquired the Yorkville Theatre on 86th in 1910,[49] it was a successful enterprise featuring two separate balconies and box seat tiers in a typical arrangement on each side of the stage. The Yorkville was one of Loew's earliest in New York City proper, in addition to the Lincoln Square, the Royal in Brooklyn, and the West End Theatre. Patron traffic was so impressive that Loew opted to construct a second vaudeville house in the same block. The proximity of the new theater to his original prompted references to the construction as the "new" Yorkville.

It would later be called Loew's Orpheum,[50] situated at 168 East 86th Street, and it was there that the workmen narrowly escaped disaster. Shortly after quitting time, with a roar that echoed through the neighborhood, the roof of the new theater collapsed to the ground, bringing with it the fronts of the completed balconies. The collapse triggered a fire that was quickly extinguished, but the construction faced setbacks lengthened by the extensiveness of the damage and the ensuing investigation instigated by the New York Building Department.

Loew was undaunted. Construction resumed and his opulent and modern theatre, which would "seat more than 3,000 persons and be used for vaudeville and pictures,"[51] opened on the night of October 18. It quickly became *the* place for Loew to showcase his better acts and productions, and was successful enough within a matter of months to attract the attention of thieves.

Early on the morning of December 26, 1913, three men broke into the darkened Orpheum and overpowered Joseph Lind, the night watchman.[52] Lind was bound and gagged while the three men attached explosives to the standing safe and blew it open. They escaped with $150, a paltry sum in the finances of Marcus Loew's enterprises.

Meanwhile, the 1,750-seat Avenue B Theater, which had opened earlier in

the year, was not drawing the crowds as Loew had envisioned.[53] The venue —
which had been built for vaudeville — was only showing films by late 1913, and
its name was no longer mentioned in the various newspaper entertainment listings. Loew turned to his publicity agent, asking Granlund if he could come up
with a scheme that would improve attendance.

Granlund recalled the theater as being in the heart of the East Side ghetto,
an area riddled with crime and violence. Much of the violence was related to
union workers in the trade industries, and a garment trade extortion gang
headed by Benjamin Fein.[54] "Dopey Benny," as he was affectionately known,
later outlined for police investigators the details of the elaborate crime syndicate, which held its own trials and meted out punishments to offenders,[55]
including broken bones and slashed ears.[56] His testimony resulted in more than
200 indictments[57] on charges including assault, extortion, and murder.[58]

It was in this atmosphere that Granlund first took center stage in front of
an audience.

Moving pictures had replaced live entertainment in the neighborhood,
and Granlund believed that the traditional stage fare still had viability among
the residents.[59] Lacking a budget, he put together a bill featuring amateur musicians and "pluggers"[60] who were employees of the various music houses hired
to perform and promote songs for the purpose of increasing sheet music sales.

"I had picked up a lot of Yiddish and a little Italian," Granlund recalled,
"and I sprinkled my M.C. monologue liberally with it. The audience ate it up."[61]

He was comfortable on the stage and, from the start, demonstrated an
ability to entertain the audience in between the various acts.[62] He scarcely realized it at the time, introducing the amateur performers at Loew's Avenue B,
but it was the calling he would follow for the rest of his life. There were numerous employers and avenues of employment, but after his theater premier,
Granlund never strayed far from the limelight of front and center stage.

He brought in singers and dancers. He found local comedians. There were
contests that had neighborhood locals on the stage competing for prizes. When
the house began to fill, Granlund brought in some professional acts, the sort
that could be had on the East Side stages, like "Lottie Mayer and Her Dancing
and Diving Nymphs,"[63] a group of one-piece-swimsuit–clad women who dove
into an onstage tank of water. It was high entertainment for the East Side, in
more ways than one, and it was an act that carried with it an inherent degree
of danger. Earlier in the year, previous to their performance at the 86th Street
Theatre, diver Gladys Kelly — one of the "Six Diving Belles"— died from a
fall backstage during practice, hitting her head on the edge of the pool while
the audience roared at the onstage antics of the comedian performing at the
time.[64]

Granlund, as Loew's primary publicity agent, had his hands full keeping
up with the astounding number of deals and purchases. A March 1914 transaction astonished media circles by its sheer magnitude. Loew purchased the

Sullivan and Considine Theatrical Syndicate of Kansas City.[65] The *New York Times* headline reported the sale as being closed at four million dollars, but the exact price was not released.

The transaction made Loew the largest figure in American vaudeville, holding nearly eighty theaters outright, and controlling some thirty theaters in the Midwest and on the West Coast.[66] The purchase included the so-called Empress chain, venues later identified as Loew's Empress theaters. In May he took possession of the Broadway Theatre and the Fulton, bringing to seven the number of Brooklyn houses under his control.

"Small-time" vaudeville, the entertainment product with which Loew had made his fortune, continued to decline as motion pictures increased in number and continued to draw patrons. In October 1915, Loew announced a deal with a German vaudeville promoter that would book European variety acts into the Loew chain, eliminating additional "small-time" acts in an attempt to compete with what was generally termed "first class" vaudeville.[67]

As more theaters became movie houses, local acts featuring all-but-amateur comedians, singers, and dancers increasingly found their performance venues eliminated. Granlund was sent to work under Joseph R. Vogel, who booked films into Loew's Seventh Avenue Theatre in Harlem.

When Granlund arrived, Vogel was working as assistant manager of the Seventh Avenue, in charge of booking movies. He stayed on the job with Loew for years, and after a career working for the corporation, in 1956 he was named president of the entertainment giant,[68] heading Metro-Goldwyn-Mayer studios, MGM Records, and nearly 170 theaters in the U.S. and abroad, taking charge of the multitude of employees and a $33 million debt; he became chairman of the board of MGM in 1963.[69] In 1915, however, Vogel was simply trying to fill the seats of a Harlem film house.

The film industry, having been developed on the East Coast, was centered in New York, but was just beginning to make its move to California, where the weather allowed a greater freedom in the photography.[70] In the early films, actors were uncredited, many seeing the medium as a step down from live theater, much in the way that later screen actors disdained television work.[71] Granlund was given the task of locating the name of an actor who had recently made his debut, and whose appearances proved popular enough to regularly fill a theater.

The actor was Charles Spencer Chaplin, Jr., better known as Charlie Chaplin. He was born to a theatrical family in England and, after playing the American vaudeville circuit, was offered a contract with the Keystone Film Company operated by Mack Sennett. His first movie, a one-reel comedy called *Making a Living*, hit the theater circuits on February 2.

Granlund knew the films had come from the Sennett studio in California, so he wrote a letter describing the little actor who wore an "old derby, floppy shoes, and sports a cane and a small mustache."[72] The description was that of the Little Tramp, the iconic character who debuted in Chaplin's second film. When the reply arrived identifying the actor, it also included a studio photograph.

Vogel immediately booked a series of Chaplin films, and Granlund set out to publicize the showings. The Loew's chain employed a staff of sign painters and printers to produce the numerous lobby cards and theater posters, and Granlund contacted them to produce prints to be scattered about Harlem.

The circus shows and traveling entertainers of the 1800s had already established a print style to publicize their appearances, and the silent films simply continued the fashion. The American Printer's Congress adopted a standard in 1911 for feature film posters, the 27 × 41 inch "one-sheet" being the most commonly used size. Granlund ordered a variety of one-sheet and the larger three-sheet posters as publicity for the run of Chaplin films at the Seventh Avenue.

Even in the pioneering days, theater owners recognized that theirs was a captive audience, and the practice of showing still "slides" allowed neighborhood merchants to deliver a brief advertisement. In the belief that he could instill in theater patrons the idea of regularly returning to view more of their favorite actor, Granlund ordered a set of promotional slides. Each of the already booked Chaplin movies were featured on slide projections offering the image of the Little Tramp and the name of the upcoming film, and were shown after the movie's completion.

In the same fashion that his film "stunt" prompted Loew to use film to promote upcoming live theater events, the showing of slides previewing future Chaplin films constituted the first film "trailer."[73] The term came later, and referred to material that "trailed after" or followed the feature film — like a "trailer" — but when it was noted that audiences began to leave immediately after the conclusion of the feature, the trailers were moved to a preview position. Despite the change in the order of presentation, the name stuck.[74]

Granlund, as publicity agent for the largest theater chain in the world, headquartered in New York at the time when it was the primary location of the American film industry, recognized that he was the first to employ what became an industry standard.

"This was the first," he recalled, in reference to the slides for the Chaplin films. "At least, Vogel and I got the credit for 'finding' Chaplin, advertising him, and being the first to see money potential in him." By the end of that first year, Chaplin's initial stint as a motion picture actor, he had appeared in nearly thirty films.

In truth, Granlund *was* in a position that would allow him to incorporate publicity, advertising signage, and projected images, to be the first to use a new form of publicity in a time when film entertainment growth was in its earliest stages. His claim to have shared credit with Vogel for "finding" Chaplin may be best described as a Granlund-ism, one of those one-degree-of-separation

THE SQUAW MAN

=== WITH ===

DUSTIN FARNUM

THE EMINENT ACTOR

FRIDAY MARCH **13th** *and* **Saturday** MARCH **14th**

Continuous Performance 2 to 10:30 p. m. No stop for supper hour.

Children's Tickets will be sold from 2 to 6 p. m. only.

6 Reels—264 Scenes—127 People in Cast.

AT THE BIJOU

Advertisement for *The Squaw Man* as it appeared in the LaCrosse Wisconsin *Tribune,* March 12, 1914 (courtesy McHuston Archives).

name-dropping claims that he continually incorporated into his conversations, radio work, and writings.

Despite the number of theaters, the grand openings, the remodelings, the new constructions, the promotions, and large-scale contracts, the Marcus Loew chain was still considered to be low-brow entertainment in comparison to the Keith-Albee Broadway "Big Time" vaudeville offerings.[75] Even Granlund, whose job was to generate publicity, believed the company needed something extra to move into the next league.

A year earlier, a filmmaker named Cecil B. DeMille rented a barn on the fringes of Los Angeles from Burns and Reiver Studio; it had been vacated by that company. It had a stage and some of the rudimentary requirements of a film studio.

DeMille was among the first to come west for filming, one of several who objected to the oversight and interference — not to mention the licensing fees— imposed by Thomas Edison, whose process patents gave him a stranglehold on the young industry.[76] The sunshine and dependable weather of Southern California had already caught the attention of D.W. Griffith and others, who had filmed projects as early as 1910 in the village called Hollywood.

None of those projects had the scale of DeMille's motion picture *The Squaw Man,* which was being backed by Samuel Goldwyn and Jesse Lasky. For American theatergoers the film was unprecedented,[77] a melodrama about an exiled Englishman who comes to America to buy a ranch in Wyoming and later marries a local, portrayed by an actual Native American woman named Red Wing. What the story may have lacked in plot development was more than eclipsed by the rip-roaring action, thrills and inter-racial love story. Beyond that was the matter of its sheer length: *The Squaw Man* encompassed a full five reels of film.[78]

Granlund recalled being in Loew's New York City office when Jesse Lasky arrived, bearing the results of their West Coast project.

"'Look what I got' was all he said," Granlund remembered. "Despair was in his voice."[79]

There was immediate discussion about the number of vaudeville acts that would have to be cut from an evening's bill to accommodate the length of the picture. Joe Schenck figured the number at three, and measured it as a threat to the reigning vaudeville business. Granlund considered the film as an evening's entertainment in itself and a different sort of business altogether. The men arranged a screening of the film, and afterward, Granlund excitedly encouraged Loew to give it a chance.

Loew agreed to book the five-reel film into his theaters and turned over promotion of *The Squaw Man* to his young agent.

Broadway audiences had a taste of a condensed version beginning in March, when William Faversham began a long tour through the B.F. Keith theaters in a one-act presentation which premiered at the Colonial Theatre. In promoting the film, Granlund played on the length of the picture, and the size of the production as among the chief assets, and including the number of cast members—which he pegged at 127.

"I figured that the title, the director, or the actors wouldn't mean anything to the public," Granlund noted. "The public, I thought, would react the same way I did. They'd go for the novelty of the five reels. I advertised it—*Five-Reel Motion Picture, First Time in Any Theater*." To play up the length he added, "Doors Open One Hour Earlier."

The publicity advance published in the La Crosse, Wisconsin, *Tribune* of March 12, 1914, had all the markings of a company press release, even to the point of sharing a descriptive term for the leading man with the adjective used in the paid advertisement for the showing.[80]

The Granlund release promoted Dustin Farnum, "the eminent actor," who opted to leave the stage to "continue his work to the productions marketed through the motion picture industry."

The preview piece carried in Montana's *Anaconda Standard* of March 19 included descriptions of the filming sets,[81] noting that shooting for the first two reels occurred at Shedham, England, the next two in "lower California at the Lasky studios," and the final two "with the entire company, numbering six score of artists, en route from Utah to Green River, Wyo, the company traveling hundreds of miles and traversing deep ravines, giant mountain ranges, and fording numerous streams."

The success of the film, which grossed over $200,000[82] (an amount, when adjusted for inflation, equal to more than two million dollars in 2007), at a time when films were considered secondary entertainment offerings. The glowing reviews, both by critics and audiences, made the extended reel production of films an industry standard.[83] It also had the effect of giving Granlund the supreme confidence that comes with success, an easy assurance he displayed in the many ventures he undertook over the next several decades.[84]

With his work on *The Squaw Man*, Granlund believed, he had finally hit the big time, making his own mark as a player in New York City.

• FOUR •

Radio and the Jazz Age

If I shoot at the sun, I may hit a star.
— P.T. Barnum

The matter of convenience weighed against the expense, and as a result Granlund took an apartment closer to the Bronx in what is now upper Manhattan, some thirty yards west of Broadway on 172nd Street,[1] a straight shot to his work at Loew's offices at 1493 Broadway. It was a demanding time for both Granlund and his employer.

The entertainment chain continued to expand, with Loew investing heavily in theater acquisitions. Before 1917 was out, he added houses in Quebec, Toronto, Hamilton, Ottawa, Montreal, and London to his holdings in Canada, purchased a long-established theater in Pittsburgh, and lengthened his reach westward with the purchase of theaters in Cleveland and St. Louis.[2]

With each acquisition, Loew tossed a new assignment to his publicity manager. Granlund scrambled to keep up with the press releases touting the latest buys, the entertainment schedules for the various houses, the advertising and signage needs, and the publicity demands for the touring companies.

For all the time spent in the company of his employer, Granlund might have been better served with a backstage cot in one of the theaters, or a pallet on the floor outside the office door of Marcus Loew. Granlund was twenty-seven years old, riding the front grill of a barreling locomotive of change, not only in the day-to-day structure of his employer's business, but in technology and entertainment as well. The demands on his time were great, and his priorities remained set in the fashion of young career men.

Early on, Mabel, his young wife, spent time traveling with Granlund and the crew of *Hanky Panky*. That practice came to an end when one of the chorus girls could not make the performance, and Granlund convinced his attractive wife to fill in. One experience on-stage was enough for Mabel, who returned the costume, packed her trunk, and returned to New York.[3] When his tour ended, Mabel had barely reacquainted herself with her traveling husband when

46

In 1915, Mabel Granlund returned to the home of her sister in Rhode Island, where Granlund's daughter June was born (courtesy Amanda Howard).

she became pregnant with their first child. During the course of her pregnancy, she shuttled back and forth between the Manhattan apartment and the home of her family in Providence.

The houses on Sackett Street in Rhode Island's capital city are perched close to the edge of the road, shoulder to shoulder like birds on a wire. They are two-story Victorian-style homes, built in a manner that easily allowed their partitioning to accommodate boarders, should the need arise. It was easy enough for Mabel to return.

Her career-minded sister, thirty-six-year-old Florence, worked as a book-keeper and could contribute toward the household expenses while remaining at the Avery family home on Sackett Street.[4] Her father Frederick brought home a decent wage as a silversmith, and her mother Emily could provide for her daughter's day-to-day needs in the home, keep her company, and prepare for an addition to the family. Brothers Frederick and Ernest were out of the family home, living as boarders in quarters closer to their jobs.

On June 2, 1914, the day their daughter June Emily Granlund was born,[5] Mabel was in Rhode Island.

Star-struck promoter Granlund would never again reside in Rhode Island, and the distance between his New York employment and his Rhode Island rel-

Doting Father Writes
of Daughter's Debut

SHE LOOKS LIKE 'LIL EVA

TEE HEE

FOND PAPA AND MAMMA

B'GOSH SHES A SLICKER

DOC RANKIN-

June Granlund, Aged Seven, Makes First Stage Appearance

Here's a letter we received one drab, cold morning this week, and as it handed us a laugh, we're passing it along to you, verbatim:

N. T. GRANLUND,
Director of Publicity,
Loew's Theatrical Enterprises,
1540 Broadway, New York.

Dear Friend Deitrich:

As a personal favor to me, will you please run some kind of line announcing the debut of my small daughter June, aged seven, as a stage star. The location of this noteworthy event was the village of Wickford, R. I. where I have a home.

Of course, it is needless for me to say that the kid was a knockout. She knocked 'em cuckoo with a gypsy dance which was more gypsish than anything else, and added to her dancing was her singing, in a voice that sounded like a bullfrog calling to its mate at 1 a. m. And she hit every seventh note right. However, she wore a tinseled dress and had her hair curled, so she was a riot.

I want to notify Meessrs. Ziegfeld, Dillingham and the Shuberts that in about ten years I'll have a new star for them. I'm considering all offers now.

She thinks she's good, so if you write anything on it, please don't razz her; she's liable to read it. The kid is a perfect Swede, with hair and blue eyes, and has a perfect an accent. This all suits my wife, who hates Swedes.

Hoping you are the same,

Sincerely,

atives, combined with the nature of his nighttime theatrical work, allowed only the most basic of relationships.

Within a few years of the ending of the *Hanky Panky* tour, there were fewer reasons for Granlund to visit Providence. His mother-in-law, Emily Quinton Avery, died in 1914 and was buried at the North Burial Ground in Providence. His own mother had died in 1912. His brother Frederick "removed to Cumberland" with his wife, and in 1917 registered for the Armed Forces in World War I, listing his occupation as a self-employed jeweler.[6] Frederick entered the Navy, serving as a naval cadet on the crew of the S.S. *Caracus* in the Dutch West Indies. He died in 1927 with the rank of ensign and was buried at Cypress Hills National Cemetery in Brooklyn.

Their father, Theodore Granlund, the Swede who brought his family from Lapland to America, was buried before the Great War.

As for Granlund, his own armed forces registration in 1917 is one of the few public acknowledgments of his first wife and child, whom he noted on the card as his dependents.[7] At the time, he listed his address as 636 West 172nd Street in New York, working as publicity manager for Loew's Theatrical Enterprise. He claimed exemption from the draft based on his dependent wife and child.

By the time June Granlund was ten years old, her father had remarried to an eighteen-year-old showgirl, and the former Mrs. Granlund lived as a working single mother in Providence. Mabel Granlund took a job working with her sister Florence, a career single woman who took over the reins of Edward J. McCabe, Inc., a real estate and insurance firm. Mabel kept the books and was minimally involved in real estate transactions, and was listed in the company paperwork of McCabe, Inc., as the corporate secretary.

She gave up the house she had taken up for an apartment, and then the apartment for a room in her sister's home on First Avenue in East Greenwich, Rhode Island. Mabel and her daughter continued to move, and were located in Cranston nearer her brother Ernest before 1938.[8] By World War II, she had relocated to Newcastle, Maine, where Mabel's older brother Fred Avery kept a house on River Road. Mabel moved in with daughter June and her husband Nathaniel Orson Howard, who had purchased an "1860s house" at 61 Mills Road, where Granlund's granddaughter Avery Amanda Howard was born in 1941.[9]

Granddaughters Natalie and Amanda spent the winter of 1946 with their grandmother Mabel at the Avery House on River Road.[10] The Howard family later moved to New London, Connecticut, where Nathaniel Howard had been assigned to the U.S. Navy submarine service. Mabel stayed behind, taking an

Opposite: Brooklyn Eagle editorial cartoonist Ainsworth H. "Doc" Rankin illustrated an article by N.T. Granlund on the occasion of seven-year-old June Granlund's stage debut (courtesy Amanda Howard).

apartment across the Damariscotta River and working at Nash's Clothing Store in Newcastle. When she retired in 1956, she joined her daughter June and her family, who were living in Merritt Island, Florida. A year later, when Granlund was in Florida for a personal appearance, he wrote to his ex-wife and asked if he could visit. She declined the meeting.

"I didn't want him to see that I had gotten old,"[11] was the reason she gave, although Amanda Howard recalls her grandmother as a "slim and elegant lady." It was a missed opportunity for the family to acquaint themselves with their famed family member, as Granlund died just months later. Mabel missed New England and returned to Maine, living a quiet life until her death and cremation in 1977, just shy of her 89th birthday. By then, she had been "widowed" for more than two decades, never having again cast a shadow into the spotlight in which her showman ex-husband thrived.[12]

By 1918's summer months, 10,000 American soldiers a day were donning the dark-cloth uniform of the "doughboy" to ship out for France, part of the army of four million young men drafted to help settle the Great War in Europe. Granlund deferred, electing to take a position "in charge of propaganda and publicity for the U.S. and the Allies in New York," a job description he provided some twenty-four years later for a Hollywood magazine. Although his title might have been somewhat self-inflated, Granlund did, in fact, supervise and provide the entertainment for a number of major Red Cross campaigns and bond rallies.[13]

Between 1917 and 1918, the United States raised money to offset the astonishing $30 billion cost of the war effort. Investment notes called Liberty Bonds were sold to the general public through public appeals and fundraising rallies. As publicity manager for the largest single theater owner in the country, Granlund was perfectly suited to fill the stages with entertainers

JUNE EMILY GRANLUND
IS MARRIED IN CRANSTON
Aug. 29 ——— 1935
Daughter of Radio Announcer Is
Bride of Chauffeur

Miss June Emily Granlund, daughter of Nils T. Granlund, former Providence sports editor and now a theatrical producer and radio announcer, was married yesterday at Cranston City Hall to Nathaniel O. Howard of 108 Gallatin street, Providence.

The ceremony was performed by Judge Louis W. Dunn of the Eighth District Court. The couple secured their marriage license shortly before 5 o'clock Tuesday. They gave their ages as 21 years and Mr. Howard said he is a chauffeur. The bride gave her address as 24 Crossway street, Cranston.

They had no attendants.

The 1935 announcement of the marriage of "radio announcer" Nils T. Granlund's daughter June to Nathaniel Howard (courtesy Amanda Howard).

and the seats with bond buyers. In addition to booking the theaters, entertainers, and publicity, he usually took to the stage to introduce the acts, calling out over the crowd in the days before public address systems.

On the night of September 15, 1918, over a thousand soldiers—part of the U.S. Tank Corps—arrived in New York by train from their camps at Gettysburg and Tobyhanna, Pennsylvania. The men marched as a group from the station to the Century Theater. A month earlier, composer Irving Berlin had been ceremoniously inducted into the National Army at the rank of sergeant and had presented a musical on the same stage at the Century, a 4,500-seat competitor of the Metropolitan Opera House. *Yip, Yip, Yaphank*, produced with military men filling the entire cast to raise money for war relief, marked the climax of Broadway's participation in the effort.

The Tank Corps Welfare League benefit of September 15 arranged by Granlund headlined Italian tenor Enrico Caruso and featured a star-studded lineup.[14] The audience overflowed into the aisles and raised an enthusiastic applause while a large group of soldiers took the stage. Emcee Ed Wynn introduced popular singers Anna Fitzin, George M. Cohan, and Al Jolson, who kicked off the rally with "The Star-Spangled Banner," followed by Caruso's presentation of Cohan's wartime hit "Over There."

Backstage, Granlund was trying to keep the acts in order for Wynn, the one-time assistant of W.C. Fields whose comic routine made him a star with the Ziegfeld Follies. Unlike regular performances in which the headlining act takes the stage as the finale, Granlund was dealing with a war rally lineup, in which the big-name acts hoped to appear early in the show, do their part, and then be free to leave the theater. Caruso, the top act of the night, appeared first. The large number of performers intending to make a stage appearance as part of the entertainment prompted Granlund to request of Caruso that he limit to only two the number of songs in his performance.[15]

When Caruso followed "Over There" with only two brief Italian war songs, it set a precedent followed by nearly all of the subsequent entertainers. Granlund had scheduled the performers to get there in two waves, and it was clear that the reduced-length bill of the first half of the program would not even fill the time until the second wave of artists was to arrive.

Backstage, a thin little fellow who had managed to find his way backstage had been respectfully nagging Granlund for a spot on the bill. It was a proposition that Granlund dismissed at the outset, explaining, "We got nothing but stars on this show. I can't put you on."[16]

As the entertainers continued their steady pace, though, giving a speech or singing a song or two, the likelihood of running out of acts midway through the rally became apparent. In addition to the thousand soldiers standing in the aisles, the seats of the Century Theater were filled with thousands of wealthy patrons who paid $25 a ticket,[17] a large sum at the time.

When the last of the performers on-hand walked off the stage, a nervous

A gift cartoon to June Granlund, from *Brooklyn Eagle* editorial cartoonist Ainsworth "Doc" Rankin, circa 1922 (courtesy Amanda Howard).

Granlund faced the choice of having to fill the gap himself, asking Ed Wynn to perform a routine, or finding another act that could manage the ten or fifteen minutes until the next group made its arrival.

"You say you can entertain?" Granlund asked the young man.

"I'm a very funny fellow."

By 1922, Granlund's wife Mabel and daughter June were living in this home in Wickford, Rhode Island, while Nils lived in New York City (courtesy Amanda Granlund).

"Then get out there," Granlund urged, getting Wynn's attention and giving the young hopeful an encouraging push in the back.[18]

George Jessel was only twenty years old when Wynn introduced him to the packed house, and where he proved that he was indeed a "very funny fellow" by keeping the audience entertained until Granlund signaled him off to a genuinely appreciative ovation. Before the year was out, the young comic had headlined his own show, "George Jessel's Troubles," appeared in a motion picture, and co-wrote the lyrics for a hit song. Ironically, toward the end of his long and successful career, Jessel was widely referenced by the nickname "Toastmaster General of the U.S.,"[19] in deference to his frequent appearances as master of ceremonies across the country.

The night of the fundraiser, standing with the entertainers gathered on the stage of the Century was a rising star of whom Granlund was completely unaware. When the 150-soldier unit of the Tank Corps took the stage, they were accompanied by Colonel I.C. Welborn, the director; Captain P.D. Poston, his assistant; Colonel W.H. Clopton, commander of the Tobyhanna Camp; and

Major Dwight David Eisenhower,[20] the camp commander at Gettysburg. Ike, as Eisenhower was later nicknamed, assumed the title of supreme commander of the Allied Forces in Europe during World War II, and was commander in chief of the U.S. military as a result of his election in 1952 as the thirty-fourth president of the United States.

Interstate highways have greatly reduced the travel time from Pittsburgh, Pennsylvania, to New York City — about a six-hour drive, most days — but there were no interstates during Granlund's time in New York. The nation was still trying to find a comfortable routine following the end of the Great War, when a new phenomenon atop the Westinghouse Building in East Pittsburgh allowed for an almost instantaneous traversing of the distance between the two cities. The transmitter in a makeshift studio that evening — November 2, 1920 — broadcast a signal that carried out over most of the eastern United States, though the electrical receivers to pick up the transmission were scarce.

It was what is considered to be the debut of radio broadcasting, when the switch was thrown at precisely 6:00 on that Tuesday evening, and a voice was cast through the atmosphere with news of the Harding and Cox presidential race.

The designation of official radio frequencies did not occur until May 1923. Previous to that date, broadcasts were experimental, irregular, and largely unheard. Westinghouse, expanding on its KDKA experience, moved into the New York market in 1921 with WJZ, although it was officially licensed to Newark, New Jersey. WJX was the call sign issued to the DeForest Radio Telegraph and Telephone Company in October, but the company lacked the financial wherewithal to provide programming on a regular basis.

Granlund remembered his first experience with radio as having occurred in the back of the DeKalb Theater in New York, a vaudeville house that was earlier called the Casino Theater, located on DeKalb Street in Brooklyn. His recollection was of a man named George Schubert, a backstage electrician, working a "queer-looking tangle of wires and black glass bulbs" while speaking into a "metal cup that hung by a wire in front of him."[21]

"He's sending his voice out over the air," the DeKalb manager whispered to Granlund as the two observed the engineer. It was a time when radio broadcasting was not far removed from the mystified reverence that an audience provides a magician at his tricks. Granlund recalled being amazed when told that "people all over town are listening to him."[22]

In his study of Jazz Age radio broadcasters, author Clifford J. Doerksen notes that George Schubert was most likely Granlund's mistaken recollection of the name George Schubel, who was publisher and editor of the weekly *Ridgewood Times*, a forward-thinking businessman who decided in late 1921 to experiment with the new medium.[23] The "electrician" was, in actuality, William Boettcher, a twenty-one year old who was running an experimental transmitter out of his parents' attic, and with Schubel's backing draped an antenna wire between the flagpoles of the Ridgewood Chamber of Commerce and the *Times* building.

Ironically, Granlund had no trouble recalling Boettcher later, working as his studio engineer. Doerksen asserts that Boettcher's own account of the Loew's Theater involvement in Schubel's radio operation began with an out-of-the-blue proposal put forward by Granlund in 1922.[24]

"I was flabbergasted,"[25] Granlund said, after being given an opportunity at the microphone. He recited the telephone number in the theater manager's office, and asked for calls from listeners if "anyone can hear me." Granlund recalled that more than twenty calls had been fielded by the time they finally made it back to the manager's office.

That chance encounter with the radio transmitter set the wheels turning, and Granlund began considering the opportunities the device might offer. At the end of World War I, he had taken on additional duties as a producer for Loew while maintaining his publicity work, and was running a revue at Murray's Gardens[26] as early as 1920. Sensing that the new technology might serve the theaters, he returned to the DeKalb the following evening for a real trial. In what amounted to the first true radio contest, at a time when radio listeners were being treated to irregular programs filled with cooking recipes and such discussions as "What Constitutes the Ideal Man?," Granlund dangled a ten dollar cash prize to the listener calling in from the most distant point.

"I was amazed," Granlund remembered. "One fellow had heard me from a little place over in Jersey nearly thirty miles away."[27]

It was enough to convince him of the potential of the electronic medium. Ever conscious of his primary duties, that of providing publicity for the Loew's chain of theaters, Granlund believed early on that the radio could provide an outlet that would distinguish his own offerings from the printed advertisements in general use. Still, before approaching Loew and his assistants, Granlund sought to ascertain the sort of demographic population that might be associated with the new technology. For his early-day poll, he again relied on a contest format.

His use of amateur acts in lieu of professional vaudeville performers at many of the Loew's outlets had met with success. (At the time, four of the Loew's venues carried amateur entertainment on a regular basis.) From those bills came a list of ten performers that Granlund believed would create enough interest among the listeners to generate the sort of response he wanted.

Promising prizes to the winning acts, Granlund asked his audience to take part in the judging, in the same manner that television's *American Idol* would select its winner more than eighty-five years later.

Granlund solicited an accordion player, a singer, a piano player, and a quartet, along with several others, whom he herded into the tiny studio to take up the microphone. His "amateur contest" would provide prizes to the performers selected by his listeners voting with mailed-in postcards.

The diversity and quantity of the responses convinced Granlund that the radio offered a genuine new outlet, one that could —from their position as ground-floor operators— be shaped into a tool that might best serve Loew's theater interests. He took the postcards and a proposal to Loew, but was met with resounding opposition, generally based on the same basic truths others had realized from the experimental technology. Although the earliest trials were intermittent, lately stations had begun to outline regular programming schedules. Since many, like WHN, were owned by businesses instead of electronics wizards, employees had to be hired to set up and maintain the equipment and studios, and still others were required to provide programming and a constant vocal presence.

Schubel, the newspaper publisher, apparently saw radio as an advertising outlet from the beginning, but was stymied by regulations and proprietary trademark claims of American Telephone and Telegraph, the manufacturer of many of the radio parts. Schubel's inability to charge advertisers legitimate fees for commercial announcements, along with the steady financial drain from station-related expenses, placed him squarely alongside others who had been issued licenses but soon felt strapped as a result of the acquisition.

Charles Moscowitz — who by 1951 would advance to a position as senior vice-president of MGM pictures— was the sole member of Loew's staff to side with Granlund. As for Loew himself, Granlund remembered his employer's reaction as "indignant."

"What do you want to do, put us out of business?" Loew asked during the meeting in his office. "You'd be encouraging something that could ruin the theater."[28]

Discussions continued for some time, but before the gathering broke up, Moscowitz and Granlund had convinced Loew and Nicholas Schenck to take a chance, and they struck an agreement with Schubel for a multi-year lease of the station and its equipment for the weekly sum of $100. By summer 1923, Loew's employees relocated the station to the top of the new Loew State Building on Times Square at Broadway and Forty-fifth, with the antenna on the roof and the transmission equipment in the corner of the business office.[29]

For his enthusiasm, Granlund was rewarded with the responsibility of running the station. No one within Loew's organization — Granlund included — knew anything about the new technology, and it was a learning curve from the start.

After sealing off a room with heavy curtains to create a studio, Granlund quickly discovered that the cramped quarters caused everyone to suffer, both those currently in the studio and those lining the halls waiting to perform. He set the program lengths at fifteen minutes to allow a change for sheer comfort's sake; that format became commonplace in the early radio days. While he began scheduling guests from among the acts on the Loew's circuit, other performers would drop by on the outside chance they might wrangle an appearance in front of the microphone.

On August 9, 1923 — less than two months after signing the lease with Schubel[30] — Granlund kicked off the new presentation on WHN. The gala broadcast included such notables as comedian Eddie Cantor, composer-entertainer Irving Berlin, Earl Carroll (whose later enterprise in Hollywood would directly compete with Granlund's Florentine Gardens), singer George M. Cohan, and two contemporary film stars. It was typical of the approach Granlund would take regarding the programming, favoring popular acts over the sorts of presentations considered more dignified.[31]

From the beginning of its move beyond the experimental stage, radio was considered to be an elite offering, with special expectations for those who took up the cause. Granlund employed an opposite tack from the start, and viewed radio as entertainment for the masses. He had no use for complaints lodged by the more genteel. Using the newcomers he had placed on the stages of the Loew's theaters, Granlund offered entertainment that he considered to be "of considerable higher quality than the average in competing stations."[32]

While WHN gave its listeners Al Jolson and Eddie Cantor (in their first radio appearances), other New York stations focused on educating the public with their programs. The *New York Times*, in a September 2, 1923, article, noted that "an organ recital will be radiated by WJZ tomorrow evening," while WEAF would feature at the same hour "the Story of the Pony Express by Professor Driggs of New York University." The following evening's highlights included a speech by Police Commissioner Enright, an hour-long performance by the Penn Trio from the University of Pennsylvania, and Civil War melodies sung by Arthur B. Hunt (baritone), with "talks and vocal solos" making up the remainder of the schedule.[33]

To call the time hectic for Granlund is to put it mildly, particularly since most within Loew's organization considered the radio station to be little more than Granlund's new toy. He remembered simultaneously holding down positions as general manager, announcer, booking department, program director — running "everything but the machinery."

Although Granlund cared nothing for the elitist attitude regarding the new technology, there remained a matter of personal respectability. "I decided at the beginning to conceal my real name," he noted years later, after his radio career had ended. "If I laid an egg, I wanted to lay it anonymously. I identified myself only by the initials NTG. It created a lot of curiosity. And one morning I opened the New York *Evening Journal*, and there was this headline *NTG Leads in Popularity Poll*. It was the first time the initials ever appeared in print."[34]

Although he kept his identity a secret on the air for only the first year, the initials became a part of his public persona for the rest of his life, and as often as not, references to the Broadway Swede in print included initials with more frequency than his given name. During his years at the Florentine Gardens in Hollywood, the initials were outfitted in neon lights on the front of the building, as they were in the wartime feature film *Goin' to Town*, featuring the Arkansas Ozarks comedy duo of Lum and Abner.

The "coming out" for NTG may have been in September 1924, when an exhibition at New York's Madison Square Garden featured 150 American and foreign radio manufacturers. Dubbed the "Radio World's Fair," the weeklong exhibition drew more than 100,000 visitors and hired some 250 employees to tout the benefits of the newest offerings in radio receiver technology. Granlund — with the technical expertise of station engineer William Boettcher — had already discovered a manner of broadcasting from remote locations through the use of leased Western Union telegraph wires, and took up his microphone at the Garden for the event, as did station WEAF.

RCA Corporation featured a sixteen-week newspaper poll with listeners sending in votes to determine the most popular radio announcers. Receiving the gold cup from the Radio World's Fair was George Hay of station WLS in Chicago, who received the most votes overall.[35] The top vote-getter in New York City was the announcer who identified himself only with the initials NTG.

"Well, I thought," Granlund recalled, "this thing looks like it might be a hit. In that case I'll tell 'em my name."[36]

The coming out also included a series of portrait-style publicity photos that showed the lean Swede in a thoughtful pose, immaculately attired in suit and tie. The earliest of the photographs that featured his real name and signature also included his middle initial, written in a firm hand as Nils T. Granlund. Later, and perhaps a result of his increasing confidence about his place among the city's entertainers, the initial no longer represented the middle name he had been given in honor of his father, Theodore.

Using his seemingly limitless talent for promotion, and playing on the increasing newspaper references to his Swedish Lapland ancestry, he dropped the middle initial in favor of a stronger Scandinavian reference, adopting the name of the hammer-wielding Norse god of thunder. Before the decade was out, the man the New York columnists called the "Broadway Swede" and the "Lanky Laplander" was always identified as Nils Thor Granlund. Even in the 1957 memoir of his life, *Blondes, Brunettes, and Bullets*, co-written by Sid Feder and Ralph Hancock, they called him Thor.[37]

In later incarnations of radio broadcasting, turntables (later compact discs and computers) allowed the direct broadcast of recorded music, giving staff members intervals in which they could step away from the microphone, to regroup, organize, and in many cases catch their breath. Granlund's early experiences required that he provide the entertainment through his own efforts, or introduce another performer or group to take up the cause. As a one-man show (allowing that Boettcher handled all the engineering), Granlund was required to manage the artists who would be featured on the day's broadcast, setting up their order, greeting them at their arrival and getting the performers in and out of the tiny studio. His singular attention to all facets was partly driven by the need to take the radio station from the loss column on Loew's books to a profitable enterprise like any of the other venues. Again, Granlund recognized opportunities for mutual benefit.

Making the rounds of the theaters and nightclubs, Granlund had come to know an entertainer by the name of Harry Richman, who at the time was serving as the accompanist for Mae West, already a star from the vaudeville circuit. For a brief period, Richman set out on his own, performing in the Keith circuit theaters, but after an article in *Variety* suggested that West's act had lost "the little touch of finesse" that it had previously enjoyed, she rehired Richman.[38]

After completing a Sunday matinee performance at the RKO-Colonial at Sixty-sixth and Broadway, Richman took a break and headed up Broadway, stopping at Granlund's apartment, where "the usual boisterous gang" was gathered. Over the course of the afternoon, the group began chiding Richman about his role as an accompanist.

In addition to the elaborately costumed Mae West, the Colonial's evening bill featured performances by tap dancer Bill "Bojangles" Robinson,[39] and Granlund and his crowd decided to attend. They took seats halfway up in the balcony and politely enjoyed the show until West completed her act, took her bows, and walked offstage. At that point, the Granlund crowd stood up and began calling in unison, "We want Richman, we want Richman,"[40] a chant taken up by the entire audience. Richman gave a smile and a slight bow, returned to the piano and banged out an extended version of "There's No Hot Water in the Bronx," finishing to a standing ovation.

Mae West was furious.[41]

"She fired him on the spot," Granlund remembered. "And that was the end of Harry Richman's career as an ordinary piano accompanist. But it was the beginning of Harry Richman café entertainer par excellence."[42]

Richman began working solo at the Ringside Café, run by the former lightweight boxing champion Benny Leonard, and was performing there regularly at the time Marcus Loew agreed to acquire WHN. Granlund invited Richman to visit the newly relocated radio station, and over the course of the next few months, Richman increasingly shared the small WHN studio with Granlund, who featured Richman's piano and vocals. Eventually, the two developed a regular stage patter that continued between acts by other in-studio performers.[43]

Although Richman received a decent wage playing at the Ringside, his work for Granlund was done gratis, a fact offset by the piano player's "on the side" compensation. At the time, music companies regularly paid "song pluggers" to perform their music, in hopes of increasing the popularity of a tune, resulting in greater sales of the sheet music. In his 1966 autobiography *A Hell of a Life*, Richman admitted receiving "five dollars per song per day," having already been reassured by Granlund that he was free to select his own material.

Granlund's WHN foil Harry Richman, circa 1938, with showgirl Hazel Forbes, whom he later married (courtesy McHuston Archives).

The result, according to Richman, was that he "would plug their songs incessantly," and since as a performer, he "was on the air seven days a week and for at least six hours a day," broadcasting from the Loew's Theater, "money was rolling in from those publishers."[44]

The steady supply of cash was directed at music performers, however, and did not benefit WHN or Loew. While radio broadcasters did manage to air a small amount of thinly disguised mentions for pay, regulations prohibited overt commercial advertising. The government might have been seen as the party responsible for the advertising limitations, but the real five-hundred-pound gorilla was AT&T, already established as an attorney-wielding, lawsuit-filing king of the electronic jungle.

Because it was behind the technology responsible for the medium, the communications company held an effective monopoly of the equipment and claimed rights to the types of usages allowed. Initially, the company anticipated that radio would be used as a point-to-point communications tool in direct competition to the telephone. To that end, they allowed RCA and GE to market radio wave "receivers," which had the end effect of a corporation shooting itself in the foot as transmissions quickly evolved into a one-to-many broadcast. As a further bit of irony, RCA, GE, and Westinghouse took up broadcasting in order to stimulate the sales of their receivers.

Station WEAF maintained its elitist approach to the medium, presenting such fare as the Metropolitan Opera and the Philharmonic Orchestra on an uninterrupted basis. Granlund and WHN, on the other hand, continued to offer programming solely for the entertainment benefit of those owning the radios.

In a 1925 interview with *The Wireless Age*, one of the first magazines devoted exclusively to the new medium, Granlund made clear his position: "The policy of the station is not to educate the masses. Let someone else elevate them. What I want to do is entertain people and to bring some frivolity into their homes."

From the number of complaints that Granlund incited, it is obvious that many preferred the "high road" approach taken by stations like WEAF. His affinity for bawdy humor and "programs of jazz" were singled out by critics as examples of "low uses" of the technology. Doerksen recounts in *American Babel* a piece of correspondence from the Department of Commerce file on WHN in which an example of the Granlund programming is noted by Joseph Callahan, a municipal court judge who indicated that the announcer continually described the beauty of the girls and their scanty attire.

"Then something of this sort occurred: The managers says, 'Isn't this girl marvelous? Did you hear what she said? She wanted me to kiss her where I just slapped her,' and then the voice of the announcer is heard saying, 'And did you see where he slapped her?'"[45]

Additionally, Granlund was contributing to the station's financial solvency through his advertising tactic, a sort of winking allusion to a company or vendor in the context of his broadcast. He might mention, for example, that the piano used by Richman came from a particular store, and could be had by anyone for a low weekly rental amount.

AT&T may have seen in WHN a vulnerable opponent for testing the legal waters regarding proprietary rights, filing a Federal District Court lawsuit against the station in March of 1924. The suit was viewed by many as the big-time operators against the independent stations, and its effect was little different than a neighborhood's reaction to an up-the-block bully kicking the scrawny stray dog that wandered the yards every day.

Granlund contributed to the battle through the airwaves. Already the first to establish a station slogan, the sort that would be later sung as *a cappella* jingles at the start of a record, he changed his portrayal of WHN as the "Birthplace of the Hits," to "The Station of Human Interest," with phrases like "Serving the Masses, Not the Classes." As a demonstration of his popular support, Granlund and others organized groups to pen letters of support, which came in a quantity greater than 10,000, and signed by various fire companies, community organizations, and radio clubs.

In the end, AT&T backed down, and the regulations and licensing rules were changed to accommodate financial support for broadcasters. Granlund was quick to take credit for the change, reflecting on the many "firsts" that occurred during his initial two years at the microphone.

"We put on the first newscast and, heaven forgive us, the first commercial. Ours was the first amateur show on the air, preceding the famous Major Bowes by several years," said Granlund,[46] citing radio's best-known talent show, which began on WHN in April 1934 and aired for nearly a decade. "We had the first audience participation show," Granlund recalled, "in a thing called *Country Store*. We inaugurated remote-control broadcasts from nightclubs and from a political forum."[47]

His leasing of a Western Union telegraph line from the New York Press Club allowed the broadcast of Senator James J. Walker's announcement of his plans to run for mayor, which Granlund claimed to be the first-ever "remote-control" broadcast of a political forum. His term for the event endured as well. Broadcasts—both by radio and television — that originate away from the studio are commonly called "remotes."

Those "remote-control" broadcasts were already well established by early 1925, when Granlund leased Western Union lines to link WHN to more than thirty New York City jazz nightclubs, including the Parody Club, the Silver Slipper, Club Moritz, and Harlem's Cotton Club. The *New York Times* early on began including a radio programming schedule for its readers, and among the listings were such luminaries and unknowns as Vail's String Trio; Theresa Lind, soprano; Bob Miller; Alfred Dulin, piano; the Club Alabam Orchestra; the White Way Entertainers; the Harry Richman Entertainers; Dantzig's Orchestra; Roseland Dance Orchestra; Boxing Celebrities; Tillie Linderman, soprano; and Estelle Grossman, piano.[48]

In its infancy, radio broadcasting had few steadfast rules, and little by way of precedent. Either to observe the nation's birthday in a "dignified" fashion, or to allow the performers to attend to other, more lucrative shows, WHN was "silent" on July 4, 1925, but most nights were given to less genteel offerings. The station offered half-hour shows from the Strand Roof, the Silver Slipper, the Roseland, and the Cotton Club almost nightly, placing Granlund as one of the foremost promoters of jazz music in New York City.[49]

The September 17, 1928, *New York Times* carried a listing for a 10:45 program, a fifteen-minute feature entitled *Poems by NTG*, which belied Granlund's assertion that the poetry was only used to fill time when acts failed to show. In his study of Jazz Age broadcasters, Doerksen offers skepticism about the validity of Granlund's assertions that the readings were prompted by mob-affiliated nightclub owners.

"I began to see more and more of them or their henchmen around," Granlund remembered.[50] "In fact, they even sauntered into our studio occasionally and requested me to read certain poetry. I often read poetry, Kipling or Service or Poe. I was a whiz with 'The Raven.' But it always puzzled me when these big tough guys asked me to read it."

Larry Fay, the owner of the then-infamous El Fey Club,[51] had hired Granlund to produce a chorus line revue, and one of the club employees pulled Granlund aside one night to tell him how much they enjoyed his poetry readings. Granlund recognized the man as one of Fay's liquor-running employees and asked why they were popular.

"We got to like it," came the nonchalant reply.[52] "That's how we listen for Fay's signals."

It was the recitation of certain poems, heard by boat crews waiting at sea, beyond the three-mile limit, that indicated that the "coast was clear," and the liquor could be brought to shore.

It was the age of Prohibition.

• FIVE •

Speakeasies and Prohibition

In this instance he is the man who pays while we receive, and you must therefore put up with his bad manners.

— P.T. Barnum

Two groups at opposite ends of the social and political spectrum — the African-American population and the Ku Klux Klan — found themselves in agreement on the subject of the new prohibition; as did the Methodists, Presbyterians, Quakers, and Scandinavian Lutherans, which might have been expected among American religious groups. There were religious groups that did not back the idea. Although not every member of the two major political groups agreed, there was a general concurrence among both the Republican and Democratic parties, and factions of both urban and rural society. When the Eighteenth Amendment to the United States Constitution went into effect on January 16, 1920, its backers hoped that the prohibition of the manufacture, sale, and transportation of alcohol would lift all Americans into that "army of the Lord to wipe away the curse of drink."[1]

People planning to give it up could treat the day as New Year's Day and the new law as an authoritative backbone to aid in keeping their New Year's resolution. Those choosing not to give up their drink had options. The wealthy could stock up (although the thirteen-year supply might prove cumbersome for most) and the others could visit their local saloon. Since enforcement was spotty at the outset, many retailers continued with business as usual until they found themselves padlocked. Others simply reopened, even after being shut down.

At the time of Prohibition, establishments selling alcoholic beverages fell under the heading of saloon, regardless of the social standing of the proprietor. In January 1920, it is estimated that there were some 16,000 saloons in New York City.[2] In the months that followed, to avoid raising suspicion about illegal liquor sales, an employee would ask the customer to keep his voice down and "speak easy." Those establishments called saloons in lawful times became known during Prohibition as speakeasies— illegal clubs that offered liquor sales, often in addition to legal fare such as food, music, and floor shows.

Granlund was working for Loew in 1920 when the law was changed, and additionally was producing a stage revue at Murray's Gardens, a Broadway nightspot that had been a favorite for more than a decade. Designed by architect Henri Erkins for Irishman John L. Murray, and originally called Murray's Roman Gardens, the establishment was New York's first theme restaurant at 42nd Street near Seventh Avenue.[3] Along with suspended mirrors, the building's exotic interior featured fountains, flowers, and wildlife, scattered through a six-floor building that was a combination of theatrical restaurant and luxury apartments. The establishment's trouble began at Murray's death in 1917; his high-end Roman Gardens Restaurant became one of the early casualties of Prohibition, to be replaced by the lowbrow Hubert Museum and Flea Circus.[4] Before the demise of the Gardens, Granlund was trying to resuscitate the ailing victim in the summer of 1920 with a flashy dance revue featuring that part of show business with which he had the longest single association — the chorus line.

From his travels through the theatrical district, he came into contact daily with show business hopefuls. Some were recent immigrants living in New York, many others had performances to their credit but sought the bigger and better venues that the Loew's theaters offered. Still others came east from Missouri, Ohio, Pennsylvania and other American states hoping to find a spot among the many performance companies in New York.

"Show business had hit a slump," Granlund recalled. "Chorus girls and other small-time talent were being laid off in droves. Things were becoming pretty rough."[5]

At Murray's Gardens, it was believed that Granlund could supply girls and a show that might revive the cabaret's fortunes. Toward that purpose he employed out-of-work showgirls with the stipulation that no chorines would be permitted to mingle with the clientele.

Granlund was no dancer, so he hired a director to provide the choreography for the revue, in which a woman named Patrice Gridier was a featured dancer.[6] Gridier became the focus of attention of newspaper writer Damon Runyon, whom Granlund had accused years earlier of copying his sports colloquialisms. Runyon became a regular at Murray's Gardens and later married Gridier.[7] The image of the hard-boiled and cynical reporter who was comfortable with gangsters and Broadway entertainers may have come from Runyon's own persona; *Guys and Dolls*, an immensely successful Broadway musical, is his best-known work, incorporating the slang that was adopted by writers such as Raymond Chandler for their own "hard-boiled" characters. Granlund's revues became habitual stops for Runyon, who regularly included the now-familiar NTG in his Broadway column "As I See It," written for the Hearst newspaper syndicate.

Granlund's status as a pilot led to this photograph of Mabel Granlund as a passenger on a demonstration flight, circa 1914. The pilot is unidentified (courtesy Amanda Howard).

It wasn't just the women who sought Granlund out, but it was generally the women who had a better opportunity of finding some form of entertainment work through him. He learned early on that his efforts as a publicist were greatly aided by his recruitment of a harem of pretty girls to accompany him at press events. In short order, his association with various venues drew some of New York's most notable. Helen Weller, who was later a partner in the Los Angeles nightclub Ciro's, recalled of Granlund's "Sunday salon" at New York's Hotel Des Artistes' swimming pool, "What a scene unfolded there! It was dreamlike. There was Dorothy Parker, F. Scott Fitzgerald, Clara Bow, George S. Kaufman, Lupe Velez, and Helen Morgan.... [C]ries of merriment approached fierceness, as luscious creatures in provocative dresses were being chased and gotten hold of with unexpected ease and no opposition."[8]

As early as 1921, Granlund started to feature the tall beauties as regular companions. That same year, he began to establish a reputation for himself, a talent he later used in describing himself as a "connoisseur of beauty." The women in his company also served the purpose of diverting attention from his own activities. Because of his frequent jaunts across the border to Canada, where Loew owned several theaters, Granlund had learned that a bottle or two of Scotch whiskey could go a long way in obtaining favors when it was "spirited" back to the United States. Although the activity was illegal, he was not exactly a bootlegger, in that Granlund's small-scale transports were never intended for monetary profit.[9]

He also had access to transportation in a variety of fashions. The aviation industry in the United States was still in its infancy, and air fields regularly featured shows that would demonstrate the latest technological advances. On July 21, 1921, Dutch aircraft designer Anthony G.H. Fokker exhibited a commercial passenger plane at what was then called Hazelhurst Field in Nassau County, Long Island.[10] (The air field near Mineola was renamed Curtiss Field until it merged with Roosevelt Field in 1929.)

The Fokker "Half Moon" had a track record in Europe as an alternative to train travel, and company officials hoped to establish a similar demand for air service in the United States. The New York Times noted that the plane was the last word in commercial airplanes, and that its passengers could "walk, talk and write" in the Half Moon's "comfortable cabin." The novelty of such a plane is apparent in the account of W.P. Connell, one of pilot Bert Acosta's passengers that afternoon.

"We had a wonderful view of the country," said Connell, "and it seemed hard to believe that we were in an airplane. We could talk, move about the cabin, and, as we experimented, even write. We noted that we were moving along at the rate of seventy miles an hour at one time, and one hundred at another time. We found it desirable to open one of the side windows and let in some of the breeze."[11]

Such demonstrations and newspaper accounts helped ease public fears concerning air travel. For his part, Granlund never felt uncomfortable. As he recalled, his friendship with Acosta and adventurers Richard E. Byrd, George Noville and Bernt Balchen would have had him crossing the Atlantic in a Fokker tri-motor plane called the *America*, in what would have been the first Atlantic crossing to Paris.

"There was some talk about taking me along as radio broadcaster," Granlund recalled. "Bird had been offered $10,000 by the *New York Times* if he would broadcast hourly bulletins as he flew toward Europe. But I turned down the invitation. I simply didn't know enough about the technical side of radio to qualify for such a job and I recommended instead that they take a Norwegian friend of mine named Bernt Balchen."[12]

Byrd, who had already flown over the North Pole, delayed the flight while the fate of two missing French fliers was determined, and in the interim, on May 20, 1927, American pilot Charles Lindbergh successfully made the Atlantic crossing in thirty-three hours. When Byrd, Acosta, and Balchen made their own flight a month later, they met with horrible weather; at one point, Acosta lost control of the plane, sending it spiraling toward the water. It was only through Balchen's last-second correction that a crash was averted, and he managed to bring the craft down in an emergency landing off the coast of Normandy.

Granlund acquired an adventurer label himself, likely due to his friendship with characters such as Acosta and Byrd. Long before the Atlantic flight, Acosta was giving demonstration flights on Long Island at Curtiss Field,[13] and Granlund brought his personal harem to a flying meet there on October 16, 1921, to "lend 'atmosphere' to the event."[14]

"I was out at the field attending a publicity part some press agent friends of mine were staging in connection with the launching of the new Fokker 12-passenger plane," recalled Granlund. "In the midst of the festivities I got a long-distance call from Enoch 'Nucky' Johnson, political boss of Atlantic City."[15] Johnson was staging a beauty contest and counted on Granlund to be a judge, even though the contest was scheduled for later in the day. Granlund not only agreed, but offered to provide some additional contestants.

Granlund immediately made flight arrangements with Charles S. Jones, better known as Casey Jones, a World War I pilot and operator of Curtiss Field. Jones loaned Granlund a plane and a pilot named Art Caperton. With the girls and Granlund aboard, the plane set out for Atlantic City and Johnson's beauty contest.

Nucky's father, Smith Enoch Johnson, had an auspicious start, and was elected sheriff of Atlantic County by the "South Jersey boss system"[16] that came under investigation for voter fraud in 1911, when Johnson was forced to call several grand jury probes. With the onset of prohibition, his son Nucky found himself on the other side of the law, and was the undisputed "lord" of Atlantic City during Prohibition.

The coastline and docks at Atlantic City became prime arrival real estate for the smuggling operations working off the East Coast, and Johnson quickly established the area as his personal domain for bootlegging, the numbers rackets, and other illicit activities. By 1929, Atlantic City was so firmly under his control that he brazenly held a national convention of bootleggers at the President Hotel, hosting racketeers from New York, Chicago, Kansas City, Cleveland, Philadelphia, and other cities, in an attempt to lay the groundwork for peaceful relationships in anticipation of a post–Prohibition era. His formation of the so-called "Seven Group" in 1927 is considered a forerunner to the Mafia Syndicate.[17] He was convicted in the 1940s on tax evasion charges and on the eve of being handed a ten-year prison sentence, he married a chorus girl named Florence Osbeck.

He also enjoyed a reputation as a world-class partier.[18] At the time, Johnson occupied most of the sixth floor at the Atlantic City Ritz; when Granlund pointed out the building, Caperton dropped the plane to sixth-floor altitude and flew in the tight airspace between the Ritz and the Ambassador Hotel. The group landed in a field at the edge of town, where Johnson later arrived to pick them up.

The festivities lasted well into the night. The only spare room for Caperton was the one that housed cases and cases of champagne and other illegal alcohol. When Granlund and the girls returned to New York the next morning, it was by train. Caperton stayed on as one of Nucky Johnson's guests.[19]

The success of the broadcasts from the cabarets brought arrangements with still other restaurants and nightclubs, and when Granlund arrived, it was usually with his group of women in tow. From his experience at Murray's Roman Gardens,[20] Granlund began to put together a regular revue, and worked with the house orchestras at the various clubs to provide music for his dancers. His vaudeville connections provided personnel for costuming, and within a short period of time, Granlund established his own cabaret entertainment circuit.

He and his revue found Gypsy Land through one of the regularly booked Loew's theater acts. The *New York Times*, in a 1914 article, mentions the "little folk" but referred to the relative age of the Hippodrome audience rather than the performers themselves. The act billed themselves at "Singer's Midgets,"[21] and had been "delighting Europe when political conditions cut short their activities and caused them to flee to America."[22]

"Baron" Leo Singer brought his troupe of twenty "little people" to the United States in 1914[23] and the group of Eastern European performers quickly discovered Gypsy Land, an authentic Hungarian restaurant, originally located in the East Seventies, but later relocated to 135 West 45th Street. It runs by Alexander Schwartz and his wife. In due course, Granlund also became a Gypsy Land regular.

"It was a typical little Hungarian place, with an elegant menu, but no matter what you ordered, you always got goulash," Granlund remembered. "It was patronized by neighborhood Hungarians, frequently in native costume."[24]

It was after a Loew's theater performance that Granlund arrived at Gypsy Land with a group that included actress Texas Guinan. It soon became a favorite among the entertainment crowd. Granlund proposed to Schwartz that he could increase the business for the restaurant, if Schwartz would agree to split the additional profits. According to Granlund, within a week's time, the relatively small location was packed to the walls, with chauffeur-driven limousines lined up for half a block. It is said that the oil millionaire Harry F. Sinclair spent $2,000 in an evening. According to Granlund, "the restaurant's entire stock of food and liquor and fixtures weren't worth that much when I first saw it."[25]

Once again, Granlund relied on his connections to the theaters and the list of chorus girls ready to take the stage. The results may have been a bit over the top, and Granlund blamed the downfall of the establishment on its own success.

In the early morning hours of December 17, 1922, Prohibition agents under Officer Gus J. Simons entered Gypsy Land, and cries of "Raid!" went up from the assembled crowd.[26] According to the *Times*, "Men and women diners abruptly left their tables" in the face of the federal crackdown. In a press conference announcement the previous afternoon, E.C. Yellowley, acting Prohibition director for the state of New York, outlined a plan of action that included the fact "that the names of patrons in raided places would be taken when such establishments were raided with bench warrants."

Arrests in the raid included "Alexander Schwartz, proprietor; Louis Zalud, manager, and Sam Bernard, a waiter." The three were charged with violations of the Volstead Act, the popular name given to Prohibition in reference to Andrew Volstead, chairman of the Senate Judiciary Committee, who oversaw the passage of the law.

The Gypsy Land raid wasn't the only one on the night of December 17. Fifteen others were arrested for Volstead Act violations in crackdowns on a Broadway delicatessen, where twelve bottles of gin were alleged to have been delivered, and a Moore Street warehouse, where sixty cases of rye whisky and ten of Scotch were discovered. At the warehouse of Oak Drug and Chemical Company at 964 First Avenue, agents found four hundred cases of grain alcohol and "3,000 gallons of wine in vats and bottles of the United Wine Company, 95 Forsyth Street."[27] The Wilton Club on East 188th Street in the Bronx lost 400 quarts of home brew and ten 10-gallon vats to the agents, who arrested Henry Seaboldt, the owner.

Granlund ended his association with Gypsy Land, but not with others known to deal in illegal spirits.

By 1923, Prohibition was in its third year, and the actress born as Mary Louise Guinan was 39 years old, past her on-camera prime, and had taken to working as an emcee of sorts for Emil Gervasini and John Levi, the owners of a cabaret on West 40th Street called Beaux Arts.[28]

Guinan was born in Texas and had a capacity as big as that state for the telling of tall tales, many of which were printed in the newspapers as gospel truth. Her accounts of riding bareback in rodeos, busting broncos, and herding cattle on a 50,000-acre ranch outside Waco were gobbled up by a naïve press corps that took years to learn that her stories were almost always just that — stories. They did earn her the nickname "Texas."

Texas Guinan left for France in 1917 as the U.S. entered the Great War, doing her part among the troops to the extent that she was awarded a medal from

Mary Louise Cecilia "Texas" Guinan came from Waco, Texas, to become the queen of the New York City Prohibition–era nightclubs (courtesy McHuston Archives).

General Joffre, the French commander. That was her claim. In truth, Guinan was in Hollywood making movies when the U.S. entered the war. She made 36 films before landing at the Beaux Arts Club, although "characteristically, she inflated the number to 300."[29] In court in 1928 on Prohibition-related charges and sworn to tell the truth, Guinan perhaps had come to believe some of her own stories when she claimed to have "made 312 motion pictures, played in vaudeville, and been five years with the Shuberts."[30]

The Beaux Arts, a Greek-themed speakeasy on the second floor, had been a reasonably popular spot previous to her arrival, but the popularity of Guinan's snappy on-stage patter began to attract the best crowds in town. Granlund caught her act one evening and suggested to Gervasini afterward that they put a revue together as a backing-act for Guinan, "to increase her prestige."[31]

As Granlund recalled, the deal was struck on the spot. He offered chorus line spots to a number of Ziegfeld's dancers and put together a show, complete

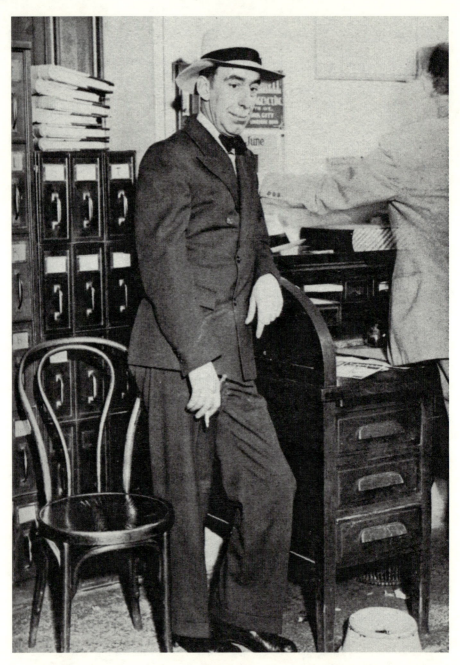

One-time taxi company owner and bootlegger Larry Fay made and lost a fortune before being gunned down by an irate employee in 1932 (courtesy McHuston Archives).

with costumes and rehearsals. A week later, Granlund arrived at the Beaux Arts to debut the act, and Gervasini declined to put them onstage.

Granlund was furious over the broken deal: "They had made a fool of Texas and embarrassed me before Ziegfeld."[32] He remembered the Beaux Arts fiasco when Larry Fay came looking for Granlund's assistance in putting in a new cabaret.[33]

It was sheer luck that launched Lawrence "Larry" Fay's career as a player in the Irish-American mob of Prohibition-era New York, that he hit a 100-to-one payout at Belmont Race Track[34] and bought his way into a taxi company. (Others say the money came as a loan from Arnold Rothstein, one of the early New York City gang leaders who brought "Legs Diamond" and other thugs into prominence. Still other accounts mention a cab drive to Canada and back that resulted in the discovery that a ten dollar case of Canadian whiskey could bring as much as ninety dollars in the United States.)

Regardless of the financial source, Larry Fay, described by T.J. English in *Paddy Whacked: The Untold Story of the Irish American Gangster* as a "scrawny, horse-faced Irish-American from Long Island," was so successful in his enterprises that he tried to legitimize his business by having it listed on the stock exchange. He was turned down. The idea of opening a nightclub appealed not only to Fay's search for legitimacy, but would also serve as an outlet for his supply of bootleg liquor. Fay was familiar with Granlund's experiences with Gypsy Land, and visited the Loew's offices to propose that the two work together in opening a new cabaret. Citing demands on his time that included Loew's publicity work, the WHN operations, and his increasing forays into chorus line revues, Granlund declined the offer.

"I had a brilliant idea," he recalled, believing he could not only take away the main draw for the Greeks' club, but do a favor for Texas Guinan while getting back in the good graces of Florence Ziegfeld. "I explained what a nice setup I had with Loew, how much I liked my work, and how in this capacity I could be more help to Fay's projects than I could working for him."[35]

He suggested that Fay hire Guinan as his emcee, a move he later joked was intended as a jab at Fay, believing that Guinan was set up to fail as an emcee. In 1957, though, his recollection was that the suggestion was a win-win situation for both Fay and Guinan, and it served as a settling of scores with Gervasini at the Beaux Arts.

"Besides, if you can get her," he remembered telling Fay, "she'll bring the business along with her."

Visiting the Beaux Arts to catch the performance, Granlund introduced Guinan to Fay and related to her the outline of a proposal for opening what he termed a "swank nightclub," that would place Texas Guinan in the top spot.

Fay, who had been uncommitted to that point, found himself described as intending to offer work to someone he had only moments before first seen as a performer, but he nonetheless jumped in with both feet, offering Guinan fifty percent of the profits with a $1000-a-week salary cap.[36]

Guinan agreed immediately, and Granlund offered his efforts as a show producer for $150 a week. While working for Fay, he began producing revues in earnest, setting up the rules and routines that would serve him for the remainder of his career. He accommodated the dancers with a dressing room, where they could visit with friends or family before or after a performance. His "no mingling with the trade" rule that began with the El Fey Club was strictly enforced, even when Granlund left Broadway for California.

The performances were strictly "late-night," with dancers arriving at eleven for a midnight performance, and shows that were repeated until four or five in the morning. Many of the dancers in Granlund's revues were also employees of Ziegfeld, trying to earn a little extra cash after the night's *Follies* performance. As a result of the acquired familiarity among the dancers, Ziegfeld began to call on Granlund when he needed to add to his own show's cast.

"The initials NTG were becoming synonymous with beautiful girls," recalled Granlund of his many ventures for cabarets, nightclubs, and benefits. "I was getting a reputation as the top talent scout in the country. Producers from all over came to me for girls."[37]

For her part, Guinan settled easily into the role of emcee at the El Fey. She was quick-witted and sharp — just to the edge of caustic. Her Texas-drawled line "Hello, sucker," first used to recognize big spenders who would quickly be parted from their money, became part of the popular culture of the time. Another was, "Give the li'l girl a great big hand," and came quickly after the end of a dance or singing routine. It was a line tossed back at her by a police captain to one of his officers when Guinan's club was raided and she was being assisted out the door. Her pet name for a big-spending dairy executive became the title of George S. Kaufman's classic play, *The Butter and Egg Man*.[38]

Photographs of Granlund and Guinan were featured on newspaper pages across the country as part of the Broadway Prohibition crackdowns that came later.

It was in 1923 that Granlund took a young dancer named Ruby Keeler, a veteran of his Loew's State talent show, to the El Fey.[39] His introduction led to a long-term series of appearances for the tap dancer, and she remember it fondly.

"You see," she said, "in those days word always got around town to the big producers about the good tap dancers. There was a gentleman by the name of NTG — Nils T. Granlund. All the girls called him Granny. He placed the girls in nightclubs. Someone had told him about me and Granny took me over to Texas Guinan's, the El Fey Club. I got a job in there, and you know, I had my fourteenth, fifteenth, and sixteenth birthdays there!"[40]

Already involved at the El Fey, and making appearances at nightclubs as part of his nightly WHN programming, Granlund expanded his interest in producing revues, within a year appearing every Sunday night on Long Island at the Pavilion Royal. Through the week, the revue would often move from one spot to the next, with the dancers all piling into a series of cars for the short trip to the next nightspot. Some of the clubs were refined, some had thinly disguised ties to the bootlegger mobs, and some — like Niblo's Garden at 170th and Third Avenue — were little more than public halls used for dance socials, where anything could happen.

In November 1920, the Bathgate Avenue police were called to Niblo's to quell a small riot involving dancers.[41] The namesake Niblo's Garden was a large legitimate stage near Prince Street built in 1928, when that area was part of the New York suburbs, torn down in 1895. The familiar name was borrowed by a hall at Third Avenue and 170th Street, the former Zeltner's Hall owned by a Bronx beer brewer. It took six patrolmen to bring about order, in a coat room filled with young men "struggling for the possession of various overcoats." When the crowd adjourned to the police station to sort out the matter, they found another twenty-five coatless young men, "waiting with complaints that their coats had been stolen."

In later years, newspaper ads for Niblo's simply carried the name of the club and the initials NTG; that, along with a tiny image of a chorus line, left no doubt as to the entertainment that would be found there that evening. In addition to Niblo's Garden, Granlund staged revues almost nightly at the Silver Slipper, the Parody Club, the Frivolity, and others.

Those were the stages that caught the attention of a Federal Grand Jury in the summer of 1928, when Granlund, Guinan, Helen Morgan, and 105 others were named in an indictment before Judge Frank T. Coleman. Morgan was a dancer with Ziegfeld's Follies and was a featured singer at Billy Rose's Backstage Club in 1925. While the *New York Times* article listed the names of all 108 charged in the indictment, the names of Guinan, Granlund, and Morgan were highlighted in the first paragraph, with Granlund further identified as "(NTG), radio announcer for Station WHN."[42]

Newspapers across the country created their own headlines for the wire-reported story, but they were all variations on the theme *Three Broadway Favorites Face Federal Prison Term*, as included with the Special United News Dispatch that ran in papers on July 28, 1928.

"A shocked and outraged Broadway was trying to apprehend the stunning news tonight that three of its most popular favorites faced a fight to escape two years in federal prison on bootlegging charges," the report began. "Texas Guinan, undisputed queen of local New York life: Helen Morgan, star of the Ziegfeld production *Show Boat*, and — Nils T. Granlund, announcer known to thousands of radio fans as 'N.T.G.' were all named by a federal grand jury in indictments charging them with violating the Prohibition law and maintaining nuisances."

It was the first occasion that charges came outside the circle of "rum rings, distillery operations, thefts from liquor store warehouses, and rum-running."

The charges included conspiracy, a newly utilized net being cast by Prohibition enforcers, and as a result scores of nightclubs began "wearing the shiny brass padlocks ordered clamped on by U.S. authorities."[43]

Guinan had her own club by the time of the raid, and Helen Morgan — reportedly with aid from a Chicago bootlegging syndicate — was operating Helen Morgan's Summer Home at 134 West 52nd Street.[44]

Guinan's Salon Royal made the list of clubs identified in the indictment, along with Granlund's Frivolity Club at 1674 Broadway, the Furnace Club at 26 West 53rd Street, the European Club at 26 West 53rd Street, and Club Mimic at 132 West 52nd Street.

Also raided were the Silver Slipper at 201 West 48th Street, the Don Royal at 136 West 50th Street, the Charm Club at 137 West 51st Street, the Knight Club at 115 West 51st Street, Pete's Blue Hour Restaurant at 157 West 49th Street, the Rose Room Club at 117 West 51st Street, the Greenwich Club at 125 West 51st Street, the Jungle Room at 201 West 52nd Street, Luigi's Restaurant at 134 West Houston, the La Frere Club at 692 Sixth Avenue, the Beaux Arts at 80 West 40th Street, and the Red Moon Supper Club at 114 West 52nd Street.[45]

The La Frere Club was co-owned with the Beaux Arts, and it might have been somewhat satisfying to Granlund that Emile Gervasani, Guinan's former employer who broke his word, faced a double indictment as a result of the probe, which included clubs identified as among the most "exclusive" and "elaborate in the night life of the city."[46] The *Times* noted that Guinan and Morgan had previously faced charges, although it failed to point out that the allegations were in connection with stage performances deemed inappropriate. The article identified Granlund as "producer of the revues staged in the Frivolity and the Silver Slipper Clubs. Frequently, radio hook-ups have been made with both clubs and station WHN and Granlund has announced the proceedings."

Bench warrants were issued for both Granlund and Morgan on Monday, August 7, 1928, when they failed to appear in Federal Court. Guinan made an appearance along with some forty others who were among the 138 named in the final indictment. She was released "in $1,000 bail," without the immediate setting of a trial date.[47]

The Broadway skirmish continued the next day when Morgan and thirty others who had failed to show for the hearing entered pleas of not guilty to the Volstead law violations. Granlund again failed to appear, and again his attorney promised to produce both Granlund and Texas Guinan's brother Tommy Guinan, who was also named in the indictment.

According to Gilbert Swan in his NEA syndicated column "In New York," Guinan was typically glib when she heard that Morgan was being carted off to jail. "Well," sighed Texas, "I hope they don't give her my room."[48] Months later, Clark Kinnaird mentioned in his column "The Diary of a New Yorker" that Guinan, on the eve of her trial, "is now doing a Henry Ford and teaching old-fashioned square dances to patrons of her club. And they're popular with the patrons. Jazz dances have become too strenuous for the tired businessmen."

As the week of August 7 wore on, the threats continued, but Granlund never entered the courthouse. Six months later, the Federal Court in New York issued a new set of warrants, and a list that again included the name of Nils Granlund among the thirteen who faced the new threat of arrest.

After issuing the warrants, Judge Edwin S. Thomas of Connecticut sentenced to prison five men associated with the Knight Club who had earlier entered guilty pleas. Henry A. Sundock, the club's proprietor, was sentenced to three months imprisonment and a $600 fine, while his partner Alvin Felshir and three employees received five-month sentences and fines of $200 each.

The activity was simply a warm-up for the main attraction, the heavyweight bout between Federal prosecutors and Texas Guinan, the only one charged to actually seek a date in court. That date was April 9, 1929, a Monday morning that the papers declared as "Broadway nightclub day in federal court." On the docket were Guinan and others who made initial appearances with her.[49]

Judge Thomas paused before beginning the case, to allow the parties a chance to enter guilty pleas to the nuisance charges related to Guinan's Salon Royale. Her ten co-defendants quickly took up the judge's offer. Guinan dismissed the manner in which her co-defendants quickly caved: "They are Greeks and don't know what guilty means. I will fight this out if it is the last thing I do in my life."

Another eleven of her fellow entertainment workers were less confident, and entered guilty pleas to charges stemming from their own nightclubs. As the judge wound down the plea agreements, the courtroom began to bristle with anticipation. The show was about to begin. Many had seen Texas Guinan only in the nickelodeon movie houses, but had seen enough of them to consider her a star of the film industry. Others were speakeasy patrons, come to cheer on their night-time hostess. The benches were crowded with reporters, too. Accounts of the pre-trial activities had been carried across the country by the wire services to be printed in newspapers from coast to coast. The steady buzz of muted voices might have just as easily be heard among the audience members at any of the highbrow Broadway theaters.

From the first bang of the gavel, Texas Guinan held court.[50] Readers nationwide followed the daily accounts carried like a soap opera in stories usually found on the front page. Guinan's brother Tommy anticipated the outcome nervously, as did Helen Morgan, Granlund, and the numerous others whose own cases might be affected by the results of Guinan's trial. As often as not, the newspaper accounts were situated near stories that outlined the federal crackdown on Prohibition violations, and how the use of nuisance and conspiracy charges was a powerful new tool in combating illegal liquor activities.

Throughout it all was a sense that more was at stake than simply the case of a nightclub hostess being charged as a nuisance.

For the government, the driving force was 38-year-old Assistant U.S. Attorney General Mabel Walker Willebrandt, a Kansas native who was known as the "First Lady of Law."[51] She had successfully prosecuted some of the biggest bootlegging rings in the country. Willebrandt, however, would not be handling the actual courtroom duties.

To tackle Texas Guinan, she sent a man.

Willebrandt's "most ferocious lawyer"[52] was Special Assistant Attorney General Norman J. Morrison, and from the opening moments he expressed no degree of intimidation at confronting the outspoken former actress. Guinan, however, held a decided advantage in playing for the jury.

She arrived in pearls and diamonds, smiling and waving to the gathered crowd that jostled along as she stepped up to the doors of the courthouse. Seating was at a premium, and the benches were filled to "double-capacity." The Associated Press reported that Guinan "did her best to show that she could be the life of the party even when she wasn't being paid for it."[53]

The bailiff had barely gotten Prohibition agent James L. White sworn in and situated, when the taffy-haired Guinan announced with a smile that she was going on a diet "in preparation for prison food." The off-the-cuff and out-of-order comment pretty well set the tone for the entire trial.

White was a member of the Washington investigative team dubbed by Broadway operators as the "Four Horsemen." He testified that he visited Guinan's Salon Royale several times the previous year and paid "$20 a quart for whiskey and $25 for champagne." The "long-nosed and sad-looking" White admitted to spending $400 obtaining evidence after being introduced to Guinan "as a rich oil man," and said that he saw waiters slip bottles wrapped in napkins into the laps of patrons, "some of whom had to be helped to the street."

Under cross-examination, it became clear that Guinan's attorneys intended to assert that the hostess was neither an "owner nor manager of the Salon Royale, but merely employed there as hostess and entertainer." It was the same arrangement that Granlund enjoyed in his association with the Silver Slipper and the Frivolity Club, and the outcome of Guinan's trial could have a direct bearing on his own case.

Tuesday morning brought S. David Beazell, another of the Washington quartet that assembled the majority of the evidence against the Broadway club operators and employees. Beazell was present when the Salon Royale was raided the previous June, and testified that when the raiders came charging in, he had "a quart of champagne and a pint of whiskey on his table that had been purchased in the place." Under cross-examination, though, Beazell admitted that he had not yet paid for his liquor when the raid got underway and that in all the "ensuing excitement he didn't get a chance to pay the check."

By afternoon, the courtroom had heard from John D. Mitchell, still another of the Washington enforcement group, who spent some time under questioning describing the duties of Texas Guinan, whom he said "seemed to act as master of ceremonies and to quiet patrons who kept 'raring up' every now and then."[54] It was also clear that Guinan had had her share of fun at the expense of Agent Mitchell.

"She was circulating around, quieting drunks," Mitchell told Morrison.

"Quieting drunks?"

"Yes. I asked her what she was famous for."

"What did she say?"

"Well," Mitchell began, "she said, 'I'm Mary Pickford.'"[55]

On the edge of being dulled by the line of questioning, an appreciative courtroom audience again erupted in laughter.

While the Academy Award–winning Pickford was a contemporary of Guinan, she represented the antithesis of Texas Guinan, and was known as "America's Sweetheart."

Mitchell went on to explain how he had seen Guinan reprimand a waiter for walking across the dance floor and threaten to fire him if he did it again. Drinking, he claimed, "was rife every time he went to the Salon Royale."

According to one of the accounts, the "last testimony bore on the government's contention that Miss Guinan, if not the actual owner of the Salon Royale was at least the directing spirit, and so liable for infractions there."[56] By demonstrating that Guinan acted as would an owner, the prosecutors hoped to eliminate any potential gray areas surrounding culpability regarding the charges.

Judge Edwin Thomas, brought in from Connecticut to conduct the highly publicized trial, faced a constant battle in maintaining order in the courtroom. By all appearances, Guinan was immensely enjoying the attention. As the trial stretched into the third day, anticipation was high as she was sworn in as a witness in her own defense, and "men and women fought with court attendants to gain entrance to the room."

As to her costuming on the day in which she would take center stage, Guinan toned it down "until it was no more than a Fourth of July celebration in Peoria." Gone were the opening-day pearls; on her head was a "poke-bonnet,"[57] an old-fashioned hat in the shape of a hood with laces that tied under the chin. The hair she displayed in the first two days of the trial was modestly "poked up" inside the bonnet. Still, there were the diamonds.

She began in the "straight man" role, answering questions from Special Attorney General Norman Morrison in a terse, sparring style.

She, "personally, was an actress," she said, in answer to Morrison's initial probing into the nature of her employment. In her hands she kept a bottle of smelling salts, which she visited on occasion, though less often than her smiling glances to the all-male jury.

After a series of questions, to which Guinan answered with curt "yes" and "no" answers, Morrison "gallantly informed her" that she was welcome to elaborate as far as she liked in response to his queries.

"Oh," she said, brightening and feigning naiveté. "You mean I may talk all I want to?"

"Yes."

"Thanks very much. You are so kind," Guinan replied.

Morrison forged on, gathering from his table a paper regarding Guinan's work at the Salon Royale, which guaranteed her a minimum of $1,000 per week.

"Did the lawyer draw this up out of the blue sky?" asked Morrison, directing his question to Guinan while holding up the employment contract for the jury to see.

"No," Guinan replied. "He drew it up in his office."[58]

The capacity crowd, sampling at last a taste of what it had hoped to find in her testimony, "roared with mirth," sending Judge Thomas into a gavel-banging frenzy.

"This is a trial and not a show," Thomas admonished, threatening to expel spectators who continued to respond with laughter from the crowded benches. His gavel-banging had little effect.

Guinan, under examination by her own attorney, established that she lived in a small place at 17 West 8th Street, "with my old father and mother for whom I provide." Morrison immediately objected to the depiction.

Her attorney, Maxwell E. Lopin, brought her along slowly, intent on giving Guinan ample opportunity to impress the jury. At one point, Morrison objected again, arguing, "We don't want her whole life," in hopes of limiting the length of her testimony. Still, Lopin persisted, bringing the chronology of her life to the point of her work at the Salon Royale, and asking what, exactly, she did.

"See that everybody had a good time and came often," she answered.

Were there occasions when persons had drinks?

"Well, perhaps."

She was reminded of Agent White's testimony in which he stated he had been introduced to her as an oil man.

"Oh," she quickly answered. "I've been done in oils before."

Guinan offered that White had gone so far as to send her batch after batch of flowering orchids. "I finally had to tell him to stop sending them; that I had orchid fever."

About a missing piece of paper that Morrison had pestered White about during the opening testimony, Guinan was specific.

"Do you mean that slip of paper I was supposed to have written my address and telephone number on when Mr. White said I invited him to my house?"

"Yes."

"Oh. Well, I never in my life invited him to my house. He wouldn't be at home if he got there."

Her exchanges with Morrison were more pointed, a reporter noting, "Miss Guinan is one of those women who need opposition to be at their best."

White, according to Guinan in answer to Morrison's questions, was "a wolf" in pursuit of her "little girls," and the nightclub was "a great philanthropic institution," one in which she made "plenty of money."

"Then you are rather mercenary, Miss Guinan," Morrison jeered.

"I always have been," she replied. "But I am not grasping. It's just a matter of business. Sometimes I haven't even known what my share was. It was just turned over to my attorney and he invested or saved it for me while I was out of town."

At the end of Wednesday's round, Morrison promised that his corner would continue that hard-line questioning when the trial resumed in the morning, but scoring the punches might have been difficult. Thursday, the "Queen of the Night Clubs" took a philosophical approach, explaining her tactics for the jurors, none of whom had ever set foot inside the Salon Royale.

The more she talked during Thursday's session, when the government had little left to call into account, the more comfortable Guinan became.

Morrison inquired about Guinan's pet phrase, "Hello, sucker," a line that began with her teasing of big spenders. By painting Guinan as a mercenary who dispensed illegal alcohol in hopes of separating a man from his hard-earned money, the attorney might score points with the all-male jury.

"Why," Guinan replied, in a surprised tone, "you don't understand. Everybody's a sucker. Why, I'm one of the biggest suckers in the world. When I say, 'Hello, sucker,' it's just like saying 'Hello, pal.' I've seen my friends of the press be suckers too." (That may have been an allusion to the printing of many of her far-fetched life stories.) "A sucker is one who does something and then the next day wants to kick himself around the block for it. We're all suckers. See?" This brought another round of laughter from the crowd. In "a final flurry and roar," Morrison thundered at Guinan, inquiring if "anyone has ever told you — you should address your remarks to the jurors and not the press."

"Most certainly not," she answered just as quickly, and then slowly turning to face the panel, she smiled and purred, "but they are not hard to look at."

Morrison, perhaps by now behind on points and sensing himself on the ropes, dropped the verbal sparring, "at a point where the gallery of observers seemed to think he was running a poor second."

It took the jury one hour and four minutes to deliberate, and when the "not guilty" verdict was announced, the entire assembly erupted in cries and shouts of joy. Guinan raced across the room and bestowed kisses on the faces of the entire middle-aged jury and stated that her only regret was that "by her acquittal, she lost $50,000 offered to her by a newspaper syndicate to write a series of articles on life in jail."[59]

Turning to Special Assistant Attorney General Morrison, she said, "I want to thank you. You were a perfect gentleman."

"Texas," he replied, "you were the toughest customer I ever had."

Not only was it a blow for Morrison, but the government's heralded crackdown on Prohibition violators suffered as well. The final count was ten, the associates of Texas Guinan who opted to plead guilty. At the sentencing the following Monday, Judge Thomas listened as Louis Jersawit, an attorney representing the ten, explained his position.[60] "Your Honor," he began. "We find ourselves in an embarrassing and somewhat paradoxical situation. A jury before your Honor acquitted one person who was equally guilty with these, her co-defendants. These men have violated the law and the only decent thing they could do was to plead guilty rather than attempt to impose upon the credulity of a jury."

Jersawit went on to explain how his clients had lost all profits and would have to borrow money to pay fines and the fines of the employees, and that the acquittal of their co-defendant on evidence that might have provided similar judgments for her fellow employees.

"I commend these defendants," Judge Thomas replied, "for standing by their plea of guilty and avoiding committing perjury. I am not going to send them to jail. Jail sentences imposed by me in the past have been based on the kind and character of the places operated. I am glad to hear that the proprietors intend to pay all fines in the case."[61] Thomas gave suspended sentences and fines that ranged to $400.

At word of the government's failure in the case, Assistant U.S. Attorney General Mabel Walker Willebrandt raced back from Washington in hopes of salvaging something from the wreckage of the Guinan case. The New York Times of April 13 noted the government's intention to pursue the following week the cases against Granlund, Helen Morgan, and others. Morrison would not be at the lectern. Instead, Special Deputy United States Attorney General Leslie Salter would represent the prosecution. Morrison was sent back to Washington in defeat.

Three days later, the blustering of the Prohibition enforcers fluttered and died. Judge Thomas, having taken an increasingly lenient position as the morning's sentence-hearings continued, eventually found himself swayed by pleas of waiters being "penniless" and unable to pay fines. Albert Berryman, who captained the waiters at the Frivolity Club, received a $150 fine. Five others from the club walked away free.

Having watched the activities all morning, Special Assistant Attorney General Leslie Salter conferred with Willebrandt and then told reporters that "the case against Nils T. Granlund, a radio announcer known to his air audiences as 'N.T.G.,' had been severed from that of his co-defendants of the Frivolity Club."[62] Although Salter did not say specifically that the charges against Granlund would be dropped, he told reporters the promoter "would never be brought to trial."

Guinan threw a "coming out" party, inviting the judge, lawyers, jurors, and spectators, and enough showed up to tax the capacity of the building. She arrived in a red satin gown with shoes and stockings to match, and walked to the stage while the orchestra played "The Prisoner's Song." The audience cheered a full five minutes after the music stopped. When it finally died down to the point where she could speak, she gave the crowd her familiar greeting: "Hello, suckers!"

Mabel Walker Willebrandt, the government's main Prohibition enforcer, may have missed Guinan's party, but she could not fail to see the implicit message. She still believed in enforcing the laws of the country, and believed she could personally make a difference.[63]

"Give me the authority and let me have my pick of 300 men and I'll make this country as dry as it is humanly possible to make it," she said in a newspaper profile. In truth, her rigid prosecution of the nightclubs became almost half-hearted after the Guinan verdict. "I have no patience with this policy of going after the hip-pocket and speakeasy cases," said Willebrandt. "That's trying to dry up the Atlantic Ocean with a blotter."[64]

Anti-Prohibition forces gathered momentum, but it was still another four years before Americans saw a change. Franklin D. Roosevelt, the newly elected president, had campaigned with a pledge to repeal the Prohibition and almost immediately made good on his promise. Determining that the Volstead Act, the law that defined which spirits fell under the Prohibition, could be changed much more quickly than a repeal to the constitutional amendment, Roosevelt signed an act on March 23, 1933, declaring spirits less than 3.2 percent alcohol to be classified as "non-intoxicating." Said Roosevelt after signing the bill into law, "I think this would be a good time for a beer."

Granlund would have declined the beer, but did pose with comedian Henny Youngman in a post-repeal ad campaign for Schenley's Red Label Blended Whiskey. The nightclub-setting photograph has him sitting between a cigar-smoking Youngman and floor show producer Wally Wanger, whose half-burned cigarette can be seen in his left hand, a big bottle of Schenley's in front of them.

Ironically, of the three, Granlund was the only one smiling and looking into the camera, the tips of his fingers touching an empty glass on the table in front of him.

"My mother's stern influence, no doubt," he said later, noting his personal preferences. "I am not a drinking man ... nor do I smoke."[65]

SIX

The Wenzel Sisters

A man who is known to be strictly honest may be ever so poor, but he has the purses of all the community at his disposal.
— P.T. Barnum

The newly-arrived eighteen-year-old Greek immigrant named Spyros Skouras caught his first view of the United States on the morning of July 27, 1910, when the liner *Athinai* steamed into New York.[1] He had hopes of quickly tracking down his brother Charles "Pete" Skouras, who had made the passage three years earlier and had just married an American girl from Missouri. Charles had joined the thousands of young Greek men who immigrated to Utah in search of employment. A labor agent named Leonidas Skliris[2] was recruiting heavily from his home country to fill mining, mill, and railroad jobs in Utah and other western states, and Charles found work as a railroad trackman in Salt Lake City.

Like so many others from his country, Charles arrived alone and without a sponsor. By 1925, one out of every four of his former countrymen had left Greece for America, and for many of them, securely sewn into their underwear was the meager silver wealth collected by their families.

After Spyros joined Charles in Utah, the two began working together in an effort to save enough money to pay for the passage of younger brother George. It took the better part of a year to collect the ticket money for George P. Skouras to make the crossing. He arrived in 1911.

The Skouras brothers, sons of a poor Greek sheepherder in the town of Skourohorion,[3] and more recently residents of the state of Utah, packed up their belongings and headed for St. Louis and the home of Charles' in-laws. William and Ida Souders ran a boarding house on Page Street. The brothers took jobs in downtown hotels, working as busboys and bartenders. When William Souders died, the extended Skouras family gave up the big boarding house and took up an apartment at 5750-A McPherson Avenue.

It was a time when the movie industry was struggling to a start, and cities and towns were seeing the first movie houses, or nickelodeons—the latter name stemming from the priced charged to view a one- or two-reel film. Vaudeville acts scheduled in between showings filled the balance of the day's offerings.

With their frugal expenditures, the Skouras brothers managed to save some $3,500 in cash, with which they constructed a small movie theater at 1420 Market Street. It was completed in 1914, and they named it the Olympia. Within five years, the brothers were no longer working in the hotels; they listed themselves as "Motion Picture Exhibitors,"[4] opening several additional houses and even employing the widowed mother-in-law Ida Souders as a cashier. By 1920, the Skouras brothers' collection of theaters constituted a regular stop for some of the vaudeville acts that shared the theaters with the short-running films, and the brothers envisioned the opening of a lavish St. Louis theater, one they hoped would stand as one of the great entertainment houses in the United States.

Their Ambassador Theatre Building opened in 1926 at the northwest corner of Locust and 7th streets. It was a seventeen-story, five-and-a-half million dollar project, designed by noted architects Rapp & Rapp, with a 3,000-seat theater occupying the lower six floors.[5] In the entertainment world, it might have been the crowning achievement of a lifetime, particularly in the rags-to-riches case of the sons of a Greek shepherd. For the St. Louis Skouras Brothers Company, it was only a start.

The brothers ultimately sold to the Warner Brothers, but later took over the Fox–West Coast theater operation and, as a result, operated the largest chain of theaters in the United States. Fox eventually merged with Twentieth Century, and the major film company was run by Spyros P. Skouras for twenty years. Charles Skouras later headed National Pictures and in 1952 built the St. Sophia Church in Los Angeles as a "tribute to God" for his business success. Brother George headed United Artist Theatres, the historic group founded by Douglas Fairbanks, Mary Pickford, Charlie Chaplin, and D.W. Griffith.

Those same Skouras brothers hired a fourteen-year-old dancer in 1920. They paid her cash; as a result, Rose Wenzel would claim years later to have worked as a professional dancer since the age of fourteen.[6]

Rose was born in St. Louis, the daughter of Otto Wenzel, an electrician for the telephone company whose parents had immigrated from Germany. Her mother Anna was Irish, and the family, including Rose's younger sister Eileen, lived in an Irish-German area on Vista Avenue several miles west of downtown and just north of the railroad tracks.

The Wenzel sisters had aspirations, plus the sort of good looks that gave them an edge in any face-to-face interview. Within a few years of Rose's dancing on the Skouras theater stages, she and her family relocated to New York, hoping to hit the big time. It was not a matter of instant success, but Rose did find work. It came in a roundabout fashion, and it was for a man who was striking out on his own search for Broadway success.

In his circle of acquaintances, Nils Granlund regularly encountered a mod-

erately successful songwriter named Earl Carroll, who had penned the popular "Dreams of Long Ago," "Give Me All of You," "Isle d' Amour," and "Just
the Way You Are," in addition to musical scores for several Broadway shows.[7]

Carroll announced in 1921 that he intended to open his own theater, a
pronouncement that the New York Times appeared to view with some degree
of doubt, reporting that Carroll "contemplates the replacement of the old three-
and four-story buildings at the southeast corner of Seventh Avenue and 50th
Street, with a theater, store, and office building, the cost of which is estimated
at $500,000."[8]

In truth, Carroll leased the 100 × 140 foot site for a period of sixty-three
years at a total cost of $4,700,000 which was paid over the course of the lease.
It was no grand palace, and certainly no threat to the elaborate houses being
constructed by Marcus Loew. The brick building favored the block-shaped
office buildings of the time, a five-story structure with a taller first floor that
resembled a series of store fronts that might accommodate drug stores and bar-
ber shops. Carroll attached his name at several spots on the outside walls of the
building, and renovated the interior.

Champagne, of course, was illegal in 1922; the Times rued the fact that a
bottle of it would be given over to the formal dedication of the new Earl Carroll Theatre in an afternoon ceremony. On February 17, Carroll hosted a lunch-
eon at the Lambs Club, New York's professional theatrical club founded in 1874.
Some three hundred "Lambs" followed Carroll in marching down to the theater, where "Mrs. Carroll smashed to smithereens a bottle of champagne against
the walls of the edifice she christened."[9]

Ten days later, in the evening of Monday, February 27, Carroll hosted
his first performance. The play, which he had penned himself, was entitled
Bavu, described as an "ingenious and somewhat archaic melodrama of the revolution in Russia."[10] Those were about the kindest words to be found in the
review by Alexander Woollcott, although he allowed that the theater interior
itself was "ambitiously and intelligently equipped." The reviewer also gave
credit to the lead actors in the piece, William H. Powell and Maude Eburne,
both "artful and canny," and proving "once again that nothing can perturb
them any more."[11]

The follow-up stage presentations at Carroll's theater were also savaged
by the critics. The bad press was not only confined to the theater pages of the
newspapers: The use of his building on one occasion to accommodate a "meeting hall" audience — perhaps in an attempt to offset some of the monthly rent —
resulted in a front-page report of an Irish "donnybrook."

A gathering of Irish Republican sympathizers at the Earl Carroll Theatre
on November 27 erupted into a "Broadway riot" in which New York police and
firemen were routed by a mob of some three thousand angry Irish who had been
refused admittance to the already full theater.[12] In the course of the full-fledged
melee (in which an effigy of England's King George was set afire), an officer

stumbled to the side and encouraged the fire battalion chief to "turn a hose on the crowd or help in the effort to clear the street by driving the trucks through."

"Do it yourself,"[13] replied the fire chief, who had witnessed the fully charged Irish mob pulling his men from the sides of their vehicles. Apparently considering the advice to be sound, the officer took up a car with a sergeant and driver inside. Clinging to the vehicles running boards, an "extra crew of club-swinging policemen" drove headlong through the crowd gathered in the intersection.

It was not the kind of press coverage that Earl Carroll had anticipated.

Early the next year, Carroll decided to change his own tactics regarding the theater. Granlund recalled his skepticism at hearing that the playwright intended to break in on the monopoly held by Florence Ziegfeld and his *Follies*. "I want to do a big musical like Flo's and call it the *Vanities*," he told Granlund. "Earl Carroll's *Vanities*."[14]

Granlund recalled asking whether Carroll had sufficient financing to undertake such a project, knowing from personal experience the cost of outfitting a revue. Carroll claimed to have the money, but was worried about finding chorus girls.

As Granlund remembered it, the casts of the shows, including Ziegfeld's *Follies*, were all comfortably set, and he believed that he had enough contacts through his vaudeville circuit with Loew's to put together a uniform chorus line. He settled on eighteen dancers, including a few who could perform solo routines, and brought them over for Carroll's approval.

"He hired the lot just as I had picked them," said Granlund. "That was the first of Earl Carroll's *Vanities*."[15]

Even then, Carroll faced an uphill battled. No sooner did Granlund's cast of dancers begin rehearsals than the Actor's Equity Association issued a notice that forbade any members from appearing in Carroll's production.[16] The opening salvo was an indication of the impending warfare between the Actor's Equity and the Producing Manager's Association, a battle over the lock held on bookings in many of the theaters. According to the Actor's Equity Association, the *Vanities of 1923* had been represented as a vaudeville production, and as such was exempt from the association's requirements that the cast be members of the group.

When the Equity officials determined that the show "was not to be a vaudeville show at all, but a regular revue," they informed Carroll that he would be required to hire a 100 percent Equity cast. Carroll responded by telling his dancers that they could either renounce their Equity membership or "consider themselves discharged."

Equity reported that more than "sixty principal actors and nearly ninety chorus people have refused offers by Mr. Carroll since learning that he had discharged his Equity players." Carroll called it all a "mess of lies," and to some extent laid the blame on Granlund.

Carroll told the *Times* that the situation was "caused by the fact that a number of the actors engaged for his production were recruited from the vaudeville ranks and were members of the National Vaudeville Artists' Association, an organization bitterly opposed by Equity."[17] Carroll would have preferred to have a "100 percent Equity membership for his cast," but said it was impossible "in the case of vaudeville actors."

The battle continued, with Carroll even resorting to the auditioning of more than 100 Columbia students for roles in the production, hiring a dozen of them whom he felt could fit the bill. In the end, considering the glowing review that Carroll finally received for a performance in his theater, he emerged as the victor.

According to one reviewer, *Vanities of 1923* was "gorgeous" and "fast-moving,"[18] including everything from pratfalls to singing and dancing. The "eager Earl Carroll" could read at last that he had become a "lavish producer," with a "good and serviceable revue on his hands." The reviewer went so far as to hope that the inclusion of the year in the title meant that it was simply the first in a long-running series. The article also pointed out that the evening "brought forth other vaudeville comics—[and] perhaps it should be noted that the players have been largely recruited from vaudeville." It concluded with the observation of "evidence throughout that Mr. Carroll has poured forth unstintedly, and he is entitled to a genuine success."[19]

Granlund insisted that Carroll pay the dancers $100 per week,[20] the same rate that Ziegfeld paid for the chorus minimum, a considerable amount in 1923. (The *Times* noted in their Equity Association story that Carroll offered to pay $75 a week to dancers who would rescind their Equity membership, although Carroll later denied having made the offer.) Granlund also found the lights and staging effects personnel for Carroll's new production.

An offshoot of popular recognition was requests for gratis appearances, and Carroll's success with the *Vanities of 1923* immediately placed demands on his cast under the pretence of benefit performances. Carroll finally opted to keep a select group of dancers who could appear in benefit shows, and would receive a special incentive pay for their specialty acts. Carroll relied on a young man named Herman Hover to escort the girls to their performance locations. Hover was in the employ of both Carroll and Granlund, working as a stage manager for Granlund at the Silver Slipper for $25 per week.[21]

At a 1923 benefit performance, Hover introduced one of the new dancers to Granlund. She was Rose Wenzel, a seventeen year old who had just arrived in New York with her family from St. Louis. By 1923, Granlund already considered himself something of an expert when it came to judging entertainment talent, whether it was singers, comedians, musicians, or tall, leggy, showgirls; he recognized something in Rose, and what's more — he "fell madly in love."[22]

The two suffered through differing schedules, and both worked odd hours at odder locations, but Granlund was successful in his courtship. When Rose

Earl Carroll on May 6, 1924. His show *Vanities* was a competitor to Ziegfeld's *Follies*, and his Hollywood nightclub battled Granlund's Florentine Gardens (courtesy Library of Congress LC-F81-30305).

turned eighteen in 1924, the two were married. Granlund's best man was Joseph Vogel, an executive with Marcus Loew who later became president of the $220 million corporate empire that included MGM film studios. Herman Hover, the young man who introduced the two, found his way to Hollywood as well, and by 1948 was profiled in *Time* magazine as the owner of the immensely popular Giro's nightclub. He had supplanted both of his former bosses as operator of the trendiest nightspot in Hollywood.

From his position as publicity manager and his increasingly high-profile work on WHN, Granlund had the contacts to generate press opportunities for himself, Rose, and her sister Eileen. The Wenzel sisters had not been in New York long before both were employed on Broadway, despite their young ages. On Christmas Eve of 1927, a photograph of Granlund appeared in papers across the country documenting his search "for the most perfect ankle on Broadway." The caption noted that many of his "difficult" tasks were of a "self-imposed" nature, and although the term "self-serving" was not included, it may well have been inferred. (His selection, by the way, was one Jean Murray.)

The borderline-scandalous *Art & Beauty Magazine for Art Lovers and Art Students*, in 1928, featured dancers from both Earl Carroll's *Vanities* and the Ziegfeld *Follies*. The women, clad mostly in flowing silk scarves, draped themselves over divans, or reclined in innocent but beguiling poses. The publishers of such magazines had nothing but the highest ideals, allowing no doubt that "in the realm of art the undraped body is an essential," and that "copies falling into the hands of utter laymen should not be misunderstood."

Rose Wenzel was one of the undraped essentials in 1928.

She continued dancing for a couple of years after their marriage, appearing in Carroll's *Vanities* with her sister Eileen, and in a revue with Lillian Roth, a singer and actress who appeared in the first three versions of *Vanities* and in Ziegfeld's *Midnight Frolics*. Eventually, though, she gave up the stage for the business end, taking a troupe of dancers organized by Granlund to Buenos Aires and Rio de Janeiro, accompanied by her sister Eileen.

Between the two, money was good. Nils and Rose kept an apartment on West 67th Street at Columbus Avenue, just west of Central Park, and in late 1927 the two began searching for a second residence that would allow them a chance to get away from the bustle of the city. They found a suitable place in Bergen County, New Jersey, with stone walls built in the Revolutionary War era. It was located in what was then an unincorporated borough called Ramsey, later incorporated but considered part of the New York Metropolitan area. In 1928 it was only slightly removed from the wilderness of the Revolution era, and was about an hour's drive from Central Park.

The Ranch, as Granlund called it, consisted of eighteen acres of land with a wooded area and two small lakes that could only be accessed by a narrow dirt road. He and Rose later bought an adjacent 150 acres.

Clark Kinnaird, a King Features Syndicate writer who later penned the

preface to Damon Runyon's posthu-
mously published *Poems for Men*
(1947), depicted Granlund as a world-
wise adventurer, now gentleman
farmer. In his May 4, 1928, syndicated column "The Daybook of a New
Yorker," Kinnaird called Granlund
"the man who is, among Broad-
wayites, the best-known man on
Broadway and who is most likely to be
identified as the 'typical Broad-
wayite.'"[23] He devoted the entire
article to Granlund, pointing out
that his work for WHN was only "one
of his multiple interests and activities."

"Like most Scandinavians," Kinnaird wrote, in an account that must
have greatly pleased Granlund, even if
his eyes rolled occasionally in the
process of reading it, "he was born a
sailor, and in his teens he was a man-
sized fisherman on a Portuguese ship
off Labrador, but he yearned for better things, and he shipped on a craft
that enabled him to come to the
United States. The ship made port in
New England, so that was where the
youthful Nils sought his fortune. He

Rose Wenzel appeared in 1928 in *Art &
Beauty* magazine, along with other *Follies* and *Vanities* showgirls, clad in
shawls and scarves (courtesy McHuston
Archives).

obtained a job writing about fishing and yachting for a Providence newspaper.
When the famous old Australian convict ship came to Provincetown Harbor,
Nils, who knew the treacherous waters around the promontory as few others
did, he was asked to pilot it."

Kinnaird touched on Granlund's work for Marcus Loew in New York as a
publicity specialist, noting,

> He's been a Broadwayite ever since. By day he is an executive of a vaudeville
> circuit. Evenings, he is radio station manager and announcer. At midnight, he
> tours the nightclubs, not as a pleasure seeker, but to supervise the shows he owns,
> at the Silver Slipper, Frivolity, and other resorts. Then, around 3 or 4 he motors
> over to his farm in New Jersey to supervise the work of milking the cows, making
> butter, sorting eggs, dressing chickens, and such things, for his farm supplies many
> Broadway restaurants with milk, butter, eggs, and other food products. Frequently,
> Granlund is the deliveryman himself.

In answer to what many readers must have been wondering by this point, Kinnaird noted; "He sleeps afternoons."[24]

"The street knows him as a remarkable discoverer of stage talent," the writer concluded. "Scores of girls owe their places on the stage to their luck in being noticed by NTG behind a 10-cent counter, or in a restaurant, or around the farm down in Jersey."

Having a getaway spot an hour's drive from the hectic New York scene allowed Granlund and his wife to establish closer relationships with some of their key contacts. The first guest to visit the rural New Jersey house was Ruby Keeler,[25] a dancer and actress whom Granlund had hired to aid in the publicity campaign for the movie *The Jazz Singer* starring Al Jolson, whom she later married.

More frequent on the guest list were Broadway celebrities, chorus girls, and the newspaper scribes who covered the entertainment scene — writers like Ed Sullivan, who wrote for the *Daily News* (and became better remembered as a CBS variety show host), *Daily Mirror* editor Jack Lait and *Mirror* writer Lee Mortimer, who joined forces to produced a series of crime-related books including the *Washington Confidential* (a 1951 bestseller) and *New York Confidential*, which was adapted for a feature film in 1955.

Granlund became particularly close with Mortimer, who penned a widely read Broadway gossip column and maintained a correspondence with the show producer even after Granlund moved his act to California. It was the syndicated connections of Mortimer and Lait that allowed lengthy columns about Granlund and his associates to be carried nationwide on a regular basis. Many of those on the Broadway beat kept odd hours, and Mortimer was among those best described as a "night owl."

"He came only because there was no other place to go at four or five in the morning," Granlund recalled of Mortimer's first visit, an early morning exploration of the rural home site that ended with Granlund firing a .22-caliber rifle at imaginary snakes. "Lee told everyone on Broadway how I had bravely protected his life in the wilds of New Jersey."[26]

Even royalty could navigate the dirt road drive to the Granlund Ranch. The brother of King Fuad of Egypt, Mohammed Ali Ibrahim visited often enough to have the formal salutations dropped in favor of the nickname "Deco." Granlund remembered the prince as being about twenty-five years of age, well-educated and wealthy.

Members of the Swedish royal family made regular visits to New York City. Prince Gustaf Adolf, the eldest son of the crown prince of Sweden, sailed back home on December 9, 1928, after making an appearance along with Prince Sigvard at the wedding of "Miss Estelle Manville to Count Folke Bernadotte of Wisborg."[27] Bernadotte was nephew of the king of Sweden and brought an army of Swedes for the marriage of their relative to a wealthy New York heiress on December 1.

The following February, Eileen Wenzel danced with Prince Gustaf,[28] the grandson of the king of Sweden, under the supervision of club hostess Texas Guinan, in the "white light district," the area of New York given over to entertainment consumption, luxury, and success, and so-called because the area was among the first to be outfitted with exterior lighting. Gustaf, it was reported, "had a royal time for a mere 35 cents."[29]

"He gave a cigarette girl 25 cents for a bag of almonds," the Coshocton, Ohio, *Tribune* reported February 25, 1929, in a syndicated story, "and a doorman 10 cents for hailing him a cab. His adventures included dances with Eileen Wenzel, Norma Taylor, and Dottie Justin." Norma Taylor danced in Broadway shows such as *Here Comes the Bride* (1931), then headed to Hollywood where she landed chorus line assignments and played opposite cowboy star Gene Autry in 1935's *Tumbling Tumbleweeds*. Dottie Justin danced for Ziegfeld in the *Follies*. The report credited Texas Guinan with keeping costs down for the prince by refusing to accept payment.

Younger sister Eileen Wenzel held her own against Rose, who should have had the publicity advantage through her marriage to Granlund. Much of Eileen's press diverged from the soft-sell stories that featured Nils and Rose Granlund. It was her showgirl good looks that got her noticed by the press, the same good looks featured in a syndicated story on July 16, 1930. Eileen's portrait, along with photographs of Frances Joyce, Dorothy Britton, and Irene Ahlberg, highlighted the story under the headline "Show Girls Taken in Raid."[30]

Earl Carroll, for whom the girls worked, appeared before a New York magistrate on charges of producing an "indecent performance," in which one girl was "accused of dancing with only an ostrich fan for clothing."[31] The United Press account of the arrest noted that Carroll faced charges of "exposing too much female epidermis on the stage of the New Amsterdam Theater," the venue offering the current *Vanities* revue. His attorney immediately asked for more time to study the charge which depicted Carroll's show as a "vile and indecent theatrical performance."[32]

The arrests came less than a week after the show's opening; comedian Jimmy Savo and eight showgirls were taken into custody following a matinee performance. Carroll, the "small, rather delicate-appearing rival of Ziegfeld,"[33] was out of town, but his attorney promised his appearance by the court date.

Police Captain James J. McCoy, who had provided the main prosecution testimony in an indecency case against Mae West and the cast of *Pleasure Man*, had attended the *Vanities* production, and — with a writing tablet balanced on his knee — "discovered enough material for several notebooks full of shorthand evidence."[34] His agents entered through the backstage door, crossing under the painted sign proclaiming that "through these portals now pass the most beautiful girls in the world," exiting without undue fanfare through the same doorway minutes later. The reigning Miss America, Irene Ahlberg, was among those escorted out and transported to the precinct house.

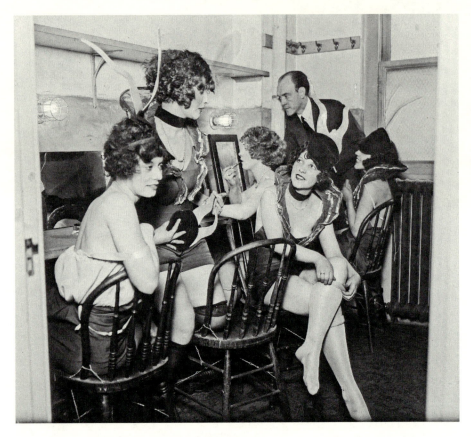

Earl Carroll backstage with dancers in his production *Vanities* on January 26, 1925 (courtesy Library of Congress LC-F8-34095).

Scalpers had a heyday following the raid, selling tickets for sold-out shows for upwards of $20 apiece, and the newspaper noted that "publicity will assure a long run."

The publicity also assured additional coverage for Eileen. The magazine section of the *Syracuse Herald* of Sunday morning, August 17, 1930, included a full-page article with the byline of Eileen Wenzel under the headline "Don't Try to Be a Beach Beauty If Your Type Really Needs a Night-Club Setting."[35] She had a long list of hints for American housewives hoping to improve their summer looks.

"All this talk about the wholesome, suntanned girl being the prime beauty of the world has rather irritated me," she wrote. "I like summer all right, but I like the winter, too. A girl can wear a lovely sable coat worth $20,000 or $50,000 in the winter time."[36]

Money and beauty went hand in glove, for Eileen Wenzel, or perhaps hand in purse. "As for me," she declared, "I believe that beauty—expensively got up—is beauty intensified."

In September, Eileen appeared nationwide again in another edition of the syndicated magazine insert, in which Herman Hover, "famous dance instructor of Broadway beauties," introduced America to his "New and Amazing System of Exercises" that allowed chorus girls to keep their "boyish figger."[37]

Eileen left Earl Carroll's show for the stage of the B.S. Moss Broadway Theatre and Monty Woolley's production of *The New Yorkers*. The show opened December 8, 1930, and ran for 168 performances, closing in early May 1931, just in time for auditions for what would be Florenz Ziegfeld's final production of *Follies*.

Eileen made the cast for Ziegfeld's show that opened on July 1, 1931, at the Ziegfeld Theatre. In it, Ruth Etting delivering the signature version of the song "Shine On, Harvest Moon." *Follies of 1931* ran for 164 Broadway performances before ending its New York run on November 21.

By the time it closed, Eileen was well-known to Florenz Ziegfeld and remained in his employ for the next production, a springtime musical called *Hot-Cha*. Then the front pages of the nation's newspapers carried the story of the tragic disfiguring of her beautiful appearance, the first of a series of accidents involving Granlund and his immediate family. Eileen's ordeal perhaps began as a result of the attention she paid to the "millionaire admirers" noted in the 1930 exercise column.

A socialite named Louis Ehret regularly made the Broadway rounds, attending shows and benefits, and spending his part of the family fortune generated by his grandfather George Ehret, who founded Manhattan's Hell Gate Brewery. When successor George Ehret, Jr., died in 1928, his industry was also dying.[38] The family managed to keep the facility open through the eighteen years of Prohibition to date, making "near-beer" in hopes that the beer and wine regulations might eventually be changed. *Time* magazine reported in their "Lost Hope" article on July 15, 1929, that employees "had thinned to 123 [and] their sales to 100,000 barrels per annum," and as a result, the remaining heirs to the brewery fortune "decided that theirs was a hopeless plight." George Ehret's son Louis had announced earlier in the week that the brewery would close on August 1 and would be "sold, torn down."[39]

Louis Ehret, grandson of the brewer, was perhaps more comfortable in the role of Broadway playboy than that of a brewery executive. A decade earlier, he was written up in the *New York Times* for a large box party at the Winter Garden, for a benefit performance sponsored by the Knights of Columbus War Fund. During the intermission, Ehret gave a substantial donation to the fund drive workers stationed in the theater lobby.

He called for Eileen at the Ziegfeld Theatre on June 19, 1932, after the final performance of Ziegfeld's penultimate show *Hot-Cha*,[40] in which Wenzel appeared. The cast intended to celebrate the successful run of the less-than-critically-acclaimed show with a party at the Central Park Casino, which had been originally designed in 1870 as a Ladies Pavilion, but had evolved into a rendezvous point for the Roaring Twenties café society. There was energy and excitement in the air; champagne flowed freely and the cast members wound down from the evening and the concluding run of the show.

When the party in Central Park dispersed, Ehret headed back to his car with Wenzel, walking in the company of Vera McDermott, the "divorced wife of a wealthy Canadian steel man,"[41] and Francis R. McDonnell, a broker who lived on Park Avenue. Eileen took a spot on the front bench seat with Ehret, the driver; with McDermott and McDonnell situated in the back, the four set out for the drive to Wenzel's home.

Leaving Central Park, Ehret rounded the bend on Central Park East Drive near 87th Street when, according to the report, "an unidentified automobile sideswiped his car while both were going north on East Drive, causing him to lose control." The car veered wildly off the roadway and slammed into a lamp post. Wenzel was thrown forward and the impact of her face against the glass shattered the windshield.

McDermott received facial lacerations and suffered a concussion, while her escort McDonnell reported a minor leg injury. Ehret, the driver of the car and listed as sharing in the fifty-million dollar estate left by his father, was uninjured but suffered the insult of being charged by police for "damaging park property."[42]

Wenzel and McDermott were rushed to the Fifth Avenue Hospital, where the twenty-one-year-old Wenzel received seven stitches to stem the trauma, and then was transferred to Park East Hospital, where reports indicated a "grafting operation was performed on her nose and thirty-seven stitches taken in her face." For the next couple of years, Eileen, unable to work, relied on her mother for lodging, staying at her apartment at 25 East 68th Street, and looking to her sister and brother-in-law, Nils and Rose Granlund, for financial support.

Seeking reparations for her loss of employment stemming from the wreck, Wenzel filed a $250,000 lawsuit against Louis J. Ehret, Jr., and Madeline Ehret, listed as the owner of the car.

In the summer of 1935, before the trial, Eileen accompanied her sister as part of the cast of a Granlund revue heading for South America.[43] Granlund had already staged productions on both the American and European continents and organized a tour in June to Buenos Aires and Rio de Janeiro.

The driving force behind the South American shows was Martín Máximo Pablo de Alzaga Unzué, an Argentinean playboy originally from Buenos Aires. He had inherited a family fortune and spent much of it on luxurious autos and racing cars.

He headed an all–Bugatti team at the Indianapolis 500 in 1923, and on one occasion walked into a Paris showroom and bought every Fernandez & Darrin car on the floor. He eventually bought twenty-six of the custom-built French luxury cars. He raced in the Italian Grand Prix in 1923, failing to finish, but in 1924 he led from start to finish in winning the Coupe de l'Autodrome near Marseilles, France, driving a 4.9 Sunbeam.

Better known as simply Macoco, he displayed his fast moves on Broadway as well.

Macoco loved New York City and, in particular, New York showgirls. He was a regular companion of Bill Leeds, an American heir to a manufacturing fortune, with whom the Wenzel sisters took a Mediterranean cruise in 1932. When the United States entered the Great Depression, Macoco returned to Argentina, where a similar financial crisis was underway. He then contacted Granlund with an idea for bringing Broadway to Argentina.

Granlund asked Rose to manage the tour, and sent an entire floor show to the Atlántico, a Buenos Aires nightclub with whom Macoco had made arrangements. Jack Naples, one of Granlund's assistants, did most the work for the productions but Rose got most the credit. An NBC publicity release included a photograph and story about the two celebrating a "reunion dinner"[44] in New York following the tour. The release went so far as to claim that Rose had listened to her husband's radio show on the network affiliate by short wave and then "cabled her husband her comments and criticism" from South American while she was away, and at her return, "Mrs. Granlund takes a front row seat at each of the NTG and His Girls programs broadcast each Tuesday night at 9:00 P.M., E.S.T., under the sponsorship of the makers of Bromo Seltzer."[45]

By fall, Eileen Wenzel, back from a restorative tour, was ready for court. Moses Feltenstein, her attorney, wasted no time in pointing out that — before the accident — Wenzel was "probably the best-known, best-glorified, and best-publicized show girl in New York," with "exceptional charm, beauty, and certainly 'it.'"[46] (In the parlance of the Roaring Twenties, a girl possessing "it" was one having that character trait later described as "sex appeal.")

For her courtroom appearance, Eileen selected an outfit described as "somber black," something to set off the pallor of her complexion.[47] It was a fashion statement met with skepticism by the defense counsel. "Makeup can make people look beautiful or ugly," Frederick Mellor told the jury. "She has an oily substance on her face to make her look sullen and sad. Don't be fooled."

On the stand on Wenzel's behalf was another acquaintance of Granlund, photographer Murray Korman, who had produced Granlund's publicity photographs that regularly appeared in print. Feltenstein asked Korman, as a photographer of beauty, to define that quality described as beauty.

"Well," he responded from the stand, looking out to the jury, "it's perfect features, plus complexion and charm," the last of which he described as "an expression — an expression you can't acquire. You are born with it, but may lose it." Korman told the jury that as a model or movie player, Wenzel had, "at present, no value whatever."[48] It was all too much for Eileen to hear. She raced from the courtroom when the topic of her appearance came under frank discussion.

Almost cruelly, newspapers carried "before and after" pictures of Wenzel, with the post-accident photographs displaying a raised eyebrow, a drooping lip and a skin condition that resulted from the accident. It was the entering as evidence of those same photographs that ended the trial.

When Wenzel's attorney lifted the two pictures for viewing as exhibits, John A. Witt, one of the jurors whose courtroom seat was directly behind the standing Feltenstein, suddenly reached forward and shoved the attorney in the back. The courtroom erupted into confusion, and the judge banged his gavel trying to restore order. Under questioning, Witt apologized, claiming that he was merely trying to get a better look at the pictures. Justice Aaron J. Levy suggested that the trial continue, but the defense attorneys refused.

The $250,000 lawsuit ended in a mistrial.[49]

Months later, a second jury was seated and the suit came to trial once more. Earl Carroll appeared on October 2, 1935, as the chief witness for Eileen, testifying as to her beauty. "She had lustrous hair of fine texture," Carroll purred, "a forehead like a snow peak and eyes that made men swoon."[50]

"Strike that out," called Justice Ferdinand Pecora, hammering an end to Carroll's description. "Please be more specific."

The account of the trial has Carroll leaning back and looking toward the jury while testifying, "Miss Wenzel's eyes were bright, her teeth and mouth regular, as was her chest, her throat lovely and her lips inviting."

He pointed out under questioning that a featured showgirl, a position he described as requiring "poise, vivacity, and beauty," could expect to receive $100 a week, and that Eileen had been employed in that capacity previous to the accident.

Ehret took the stand and, in what might have been the chivalrous declaration of a former suitor, told the jurors that "he had seen Miss Wenzel twice since the accident and each time she had appeared to him to be as beautiful as before the accident."[51] His claims may have been closer to the truth than the jury believed. Subsequent operations made an astounding difference in Eileen's facial appearance, to the point that later photographs displayed no disfiguring at all, but the jury made determinations based on the evidentiary photographs.

Ehret claimed that his efforts had been to avoid hitting another car which had cut in front of him, resulting in the accident, but he was forced to admit that "they had several champagne cocktails at the Central Park Casino" before they had started away. The millionaire testified that his intentions were to pay Eileen's medical bills, but he broke his agreement to do so when she filed suit against him.

The jury, mostly businessmen who could have appreciated the situation of a manufacturer and financial heir, or the relative value of Wenzel's face and the financial setback as a result of her loss of assets, deliberated two hours and ten minutes before returning a verdict in her favor.[52] The award, though, was not returned in the amount Eileen had sought. Instead of the quarter-million dollars judgment she asked, jurors awarded a damage amount of $90,000 — a substantial portion of which she had already spent on reconstructive surgery.

According to a syndicated article that was carried in the *Salt Lake Tribune* on July 7, 1935, the accident and its aftermath could all be attributed to a cruise the Wenzel sisters took aboard a "cursed" ship. "There is a weird toll of tragedy and accident in the wake of the Leeds' sumptuous yacht, *Moana*,"[53] the story proclaimed, in reference to the ship owned by Bill Leeds, heir to the forty-million dollar estate of the late William B. Leeds, Sr. The elder Leeds made a fortune in manufacturing and married the former Princess Anastasia of Greece. The writer expressed doubts as to whether culpability for the unexplained accidents lay with the boat or its captain.

"Practically every craft afloat on which Bill has set foot has proved to be the scene of some mishap or escapade for the tin-plate princeling or a favored friend," related the account, a full-page spread that was syndicated nationwide and included photographs of both Eileen and Rose Wenzel. "In 1932, Leeds invited two outstanding beauties of stage and nightclub fame to accompany him on a Mediterranean cruise. They were Rose and Eileen Wenzel, sisters, and perhaps the best known show girls of Manhattan. Rose had married taciturn, lantern-jawed Nils (NTG) Granlund, celebrated master of ceremonies. Eileen was unwed."

Claiming that "Anastasia's Jewels," the diamonds, rubies, pearls, and emeralds in unrivaled quantities had been cursed after the death of the owner, and brought ill fortune to all who possessed or benefited from them, the writer speculated that the trip aboard Leeds' yacht brought bad luck to the Wenzel sisters: "The pleasure cruise was an immense success, but a few months after the voyage ended, disaster struck. Rose was thrown from her mount while riding near her home and seriously injured. She recuperated quickly, but some weeks later suffered a repetition of the accident."

The article went on to lay blame for Eileen's automobile accident on the same cruise. Meanwhile, a later trip to the *Moana* off the coast of Florida by Earl Carroll and Beryl Wallace, another Broadway star, ended when their small launch ran out of fuel en route. The two floated helplessly until they were discovered by a passing boat, but it was too late to allow Wallace to make her Miami performance that evening. Even a 1931 murder near the Leeds' estate near Northport, Long Island, was blamed on the proximity of the "cursed" yacht.

The court judgment came after the article's publication or no doubt it would have cited the "curse" for Eileen Wenzel's fortune, or lack of it. The jury award was challenged by Ehret, but a Christmas Eve hearing before New York Supreme Court Justice Pecora upheld the amount, holding that facial injuries affecting the prospects of a favorable marriage warranted extra damages. The amount, however, was later altered, cut to $40,000 on appeal in 1936.

At that point, Wenzel may have decided that the prospect of a "favorable marriage" might be the only solution to the problem of her personal finances. Granlund was presently making marriage announcements for his sister-in-law Eileen, who may or may not have been serious about the betrothal that made headlines on sports pages across the country in 1938. It certainly made for good press coverage.

A big Welshman named Tommy Farr, the pride of British boxing fans, entered the ring in Yankee Stadium on the night of August 30, 1937, for a show-down of champions.[54] Farr, the British and Empire heavyweight champ, entered the ring to take on American title-holder Joe Louis, then at the height of his career, in a fifteen-round match. Before the bout, Louis had knocked out eight of his previous nine opponents, and after the Farr match, he kayoed the next seven men he battled. When the final bell sounded at the end of his fight with Farr, the Welshman was still standing, but Louis retained his title by decision.

Farr's hard-hitting right hand was hurt, and his eyes were so badly swollen that he could scarcely see during the final round. Even his lips were puffed and red when he spoke to reporters.

"I came here to give them a go, and I did, didn't I?" he offered, and then pointed to his hand as the glove was cut away. "Please don't say much about this finger. I don't want them to think I tried to alibi.... Joe is a great puncher. I don't know if he's the hardest hitter I ever fought. But he hits hard enough. He hurt me a couple of times, but I never was close to being knocked out. They don't knock out Tommy Farr."[55]

That was the boxer's bold claim, but Eileen came close. When Farr announced his intentions to stay in the United States for a time, to take on a series of opponents in hopes of a rematch with Lewis, he ran into the showgirl and began a whirlwind romance.

Granlund was in Chicago for a production weeks later, and met his sis-ter-in-law and the boxer at the airport after they flew in from New York. Granlund immediately set to work on the publicity. Papers nationwide jumped on the story, filling the paragraphs with boxing-related puns relating to the couple's engagement announcement.

Farr came out of the corner quickly. "We will be married in a couple of months," he said, standing next to his smiling fiancée. "We haven't set the date yet."

"But we will," Eileen quickly added.[56]

Farr was coming off a March 11 loss to Max Baer. When the sportswriters continued to have a time with the marriage story, Farr played along, claiming that Baer only won the bout because he was fortunate enough to have a wife.

"Max is a family man now," Farr told the press in Hollywood. "Being a father has changed his entire attitude. He fought like a man who was determined to take care of his family when he beat me. If it did him so much good, it may be my remaking."

The Hollywood press naturally asked if he had come to try his luck in the movies.

"With a mug like mine?" he laughed. "Never."[57]

Within thirty days, Tommy Farr lost on points again. Arriving in New York from California, intent on heading back to his home in England, he told reporters asking about his marriage that he was "planning to fly the Atlantic to forget it all."[58]

"Are you married yet?" someone shouted.

"What are you doing?" Farr called back. "Joking again? Only one word stopped us from being married. She said, 'No.'"

If the British champ took it on the chin, he was a good sport about it, and continued to pose for pictures. The story played out for another month with headlines like, "Another Setback in the U.S. Wins for Farr the Title — 'A Good Loser.'"

Fortunes changed dramatically for the Wenzel sisters over the coming years. Columnist Walter Winchell reported that Rose was selling tickets in a New York City box office, not as a show producer, but vending to the line of customers waiting outside the theater. She was estranged from her husband by then and her association with the Broadway crowd was more closely associated with the audiences. A lawsuit judgment in her favor allowed some degree of comfort before the decade was out, and Rose was able to remain in her New York apartment until she died of cancer in 1983.[59]

Eileen outlived her sister by ten years. Unlike Rose, however, she found the spotlight again, although under completely different circumstances. She continued her appearances in the Broadway gossip columns, not as a showgirl, but as the socialite wife of millionaire Max Bamberger, a decades-long member of the New York Stock Exchange. The Philadelphia native had a long history of association with showgirls; Dorothy Kilgallen reported in her column "The Voice of Broadway" in 1942 that Hazel Forbes, "recently divorced from Harry Richman, is being wooed ever so ardently by millionaire Max Bamberger, who used to be married to Blanche Satchel." Bamberger had divorced Satchel, his second wife and an ex–Follies girl, in Reno in 1938 after a five-year marriage.

Perhaps for Bamberger, the third time was a charm. It worked out well for Eileen too. They lived lavishly at the Savoy Hilton until his death at the age of 66 in 1962. Four years later, Winchell still had occasion to report about at least one of Broadway's beautiful Wenzel sisters: "Eileen Wenzel, former Earl Carroll showgirl," he wrote in his August 26, 1966 column, "is the widow of Max Bamberger, Wall Street figure. An Aqueduct sportsman tried to interest Eileen in the thoroughbred breed field ... interest her money, that is." The "sportsman" was trying to entice Wenzel to back his knowledge with bets at the racetrack window, but as Winchell reported, after the running of the races there "was not a winner among them."

It was of little concern to Eileen Wenzel Bamberger. She had already hit her long shot.

• SEVEN •

Movies and Mobsters

If I shoot at the sun I may hit a star.

— P.T. Barnum

He was born Asa Yoelson, but made his fame as Al Jolson. He was to the Roaring Twenties what performers Michael Jackson and Madonna were to the 1990s; by the end of the decade he was firmly established as the most famous and highest paid American entertainer.[1] In September of 1928 there were rumors of a star-studded marriage — that of Jolson and Ruby Keeler, dancer, actress, and long-time friend of Granlund.

The start of the week brought immediate denials. Simply rumors, claimed Jolson, although he considered Keeler to be "an adorable kid."[2]

Keeler's response?

"Marry Al Jolson? Well, I'm sure I can't answer you right now. He's a very dear friend of mine, but I can't tell you anything more...."[3]

That was earlier in the week.

Jolson's comedic custom originally included blackface routines and he attained his popularity with the advent of talking pictures along with his signature performance of the song "Mammy."

Keeler had slipped into the El Fey Club at the age of fourteen, at the time when Texas Guinan could be found on that stage nightly, with Granlund producing the floor show.

"She was pretty," said Granlund of the dancer who was looking for work, "but she looked like she needed a friend. The heels of her worn shoes were badly run down, and her dress looked as though it had gone through many washings."[4]

Granlund put the girl in the chorus, but it was quickly apparent that she was star material. "She rated a top spot right away," remembered Granlund, who established Keeler as the leader of the chorus and in a front-and-center position in what would be an enviable rise to fame.

The young dancer quickly found notice and appeared in several Broadway shows before being spotted by Florenz Ziegfeld, who reportedly sent her roses and a note asking, "May I make you a star?" She would later appear in his production of *Whoopee!* but first, there was the matter of Jolson.

Granlund had expanded his floor shows to include the Pavilion Royal on Long Island, a place whose stage drew jazz luminaries such as Leon "Bix" Beiderbecke, a cornet player considered to be one of the legends of the Jazz Era. Before taking her career to Hollywood, Keeler performed there as well.

Granlund recalled the excitement in her voice when she declared she was marrying Jolson; she told him, "We want to come out to the Pavilion tonight and announce our engagement there."[5] He was ecstatic at the idea.

Later in the evening, the couple appeared in front of the Pavilion Royal crowd and Jolson was "coerced" into singing "Sonny Boy," one of the tunes from his first movie. Granlund called a couple of reporters, a move that later caused confusion in the printed reports. By the time the stories hit the wire service to be repeated across the country, Jolson and Keeler were already making denials of any impending marriage. As an afterthought to their announcement, they had hoped to be able to slip off and be romantically wed aboard the ship that would carry them across the Atlantic for their European honeymoon.

Jolson contacted White Star, the ocean liner company, inquiring as to whether they could be married on board the *Olympic*, on which Jolson had booked passage.[6] He learned that company regulations no longer allowed it.

The Oakland, California, newspapers were just printing on Thursday the initials reports of the Sunday engagement announcement, but included the denials of both Jolson and Keeler as well. The *New York Times* reported two days later that the couple had married on Friday.

It occurred in Port Chester, New York,[7] on Long Island Sound near the Connecticut line. Westchester County Surrogate G.A. Slater performed the private ceremony on Friday, and just before boarding the *Olympic* the two confirmed the report that they were man and wife. Captain W.H. Parker welcomed them aboard and escorted them to the Prince of Wales suite. The ship steamed out of port on Saturday morning.

It was to be a brief honeymoon, as Keeler was among the cast members to appear in the Florenz Ziegfeld–Eddie Cantor production *Whoopee!* which was scheduled to open December 4 at the New Amsterdam Theatre.

As a floor show producer, Granlund enjoyed his own honeymoon of sorts, in his continued ability to please crowds with his chorus lines and specialty dancers at the El Fey Club. The spot became increasingly popular, but was also so tightly associated with Guinan as hostess that — to many — the business was simply referred to as "Guinan's Club."

Working the El Fey stage with Guinan exposed Granlund to undercurrents of gangland activity at the many nightspots that began springing up to sidestep the liquor laws. To say that Larry Fay enjoyed his reputation as a flamboyant gangster is a misstatement: He enjoyed the attention and publicity, but worked hard to distance himself from the mob identity that he had acquired.

According to Granlund, Fay craved legitimacy and used bootlegging as a means toward an end, providing money for fine clothing and business opportunities such as the nightclub that employed Guinan. Granlund described Fay as "lantern-jawed"; others described the club owner as "horse-faced." He tried to make up for his appearance by dressing sharp, reportedly traveling to Europe to outfit himself in an impressive wardrobe. He liked loud ties worn over indigo blue shirts, sometimes under a leather jacket. His nails were manicured and his hair styled by professionals. It was his look that writer Damon Runyon chose to portray the gangsters in his stories. Fay's tale was told in the movie *The Roaring Twenties* (1939) with James Cagney playing the part of club owner "Eddie Bartlett."

The title of that movie may have come as a play on columnist Oscar Odd McIntyre's descriptions of the music playing Broadway nightclubs situated from 39th to 49th streets, a particularly popular club district he called the "Roaring Forties." McIntyre, whose folksy gossip column "New York Day by Day," was carried by more than 500 newspapers, in May 1925 tagged Fay as a former waiter who "has amassed money enough to buy the late Charles Murphy's big estate at Good Ground and also the building that housed the Automobile Club. The latter was turned into a midnight club which was in Broadway parlance a flop. It needed a Texas."[8] He described Guinan as "a famous personage in the hectic night life" who "is now paid a straight salary of $1000 a week and other nightclubs have asked her to name her own price. She is of Amazonian build, with hair of Titian tint and is a dynamo of activity."

Although Fay had financial interests in several successful operations including the LaVie, the Parody, the Silver Slipper, and the Cotton Club, he never again reached the degree of success he enjoyed with Guinan fronting his business, and was "virtually penniless"[9] at the time of his death. During his height, he kept an office in Manhattan and became involved in the New York Milk Chain Association, an affiliation of independent bottlers that he organized to try to combat two dairy giants that between them controlled most of the New York City market. He made millions and worked continually at achieving the appearance of an honest businessman. He produced a Broadway show, but the theater burned before opening night.

The El Fey was shut down during the Prohibition raids and the dapper dresser tried his luck at other locations under other names, without an affiliation with Guinan and Granlund. The Del Fey was opened next door to the padlocked El Fey,[10] with the change in the name as a tribute to chorine and actress Irene Delroy, with whom Fay had a longstanding infatuation. Despite the honor, Delroy declined to marry Fay, but—like so many of the plots in which she acted—ended up married to a millionaire. By the time Fay landed at the Casa Blanca he had no investment at all. The golden touch that brought money rolling in for Fay in the early days seemed to vanish,[11] and he was eventually brought in to the Casa Blanca club as a working partner.

The Great Depression was well underway at the time, and even those with money were being affected. Fay, in charge of the hiring and firing at the Casa Blanca, announced that he was cutting wages by forty percent[12] in an effort to help make ends meet. Times were tough.

The Casa Blanca, at 33 West 56th Street, hosted a New Year's Eve party on December 31, 1932. Fay was in the club the following day, overseeing the clean-up after the festivities. He had given a man who was out of work a chance to earn a little money, helping sweep up the floors.

About eight-thirty in the evening, Edward Maloney,[13] one of the club door-men, showed up and began to argue with Fay over his loss of wages. Maloney had been drinking all day and had worked himself into a state of courage for a showdown with the boss. After a brief, heated exchange, Maloney pulled out a pistol and fired five times, at nearly point-blank range. Four of the shots hit Fay and he died on the spot.[14]

In a report of the shooting, the *Times* noted that Fay, who was acknowledged to have made a fortune in his various business enterprises, died with "three thin dimes"[15] in his pocket. The story also made mention of the consensus that it was Fay's early nightclub, the El Fey, with its highbrow attitude and Texas Guinan as hostess, that had totally changed New York's style of entertainment. The combination of Fay, Guinan, and Granlund certainly brought a highbrow legitimacy to the former "clip joints" and speakeasies, in which customers might later find themselves knocked on the head and relieved of their wallets. The death of Larry Fay, "racketeer, gangster, and boss of strong-armed thugs,"[16] did not end the association of Granlund and New York mobsters, but it marked a delineation of the types of businesses with which he was associated, clubs in which the mob ties were kept in the background.

It was Lee Mortimer, columnist for the *New York World*, who gave credit for the major change in nightlife presentation to Granlund and the opening of his grand cabaret, the Hollywood Restaurant, a mantle of success that Granlund was more than willing to accept. Granlund eventually produced floorshows that ran simultaneously in a dozen nightclubs, more than a few of them owned by shady operators who came to know him through Fay. He was employing nearly one hundred girls in the various revues, vaudeville appearances, and radio programs. His success had to be partially attributed to the 1924 pairing of Guinan and the El Fey, but it was not his only accomplishment of that year.

Granlund was approached by Lee and Jacob Shubert to serve as stage manager for their production of *The Passing Show of 1924* at the Winter Garden Theatre.[17] The Shuberts' offerings were blatant copies of *Follies* and *Vanities*, but tended to be more risqué and feature scantier clothing (if possible) than the stage shows of Ziegfeld and Carroll. They were lavish revues, however, and featured some of the top names of the time, performers like DeWolf Hopper, Ed

Granlund in a publicity photo by Murray Korman, circa 1925 (courtesy McHuston Archives).

Wynn, and Fred Astaire. It may have been the influence of the Shuberts and their conviction that nudity could sell a show that later pushed Granlund in that direction.

As it turned out, the 1924 edition was the final outing for *The Passing Show*, which had kicked off in 1912 with a name borrowed from a late 1800s musical. Dancing in the chorus in its final outing was a desperate twenty-one year old named Lucille LeSueur, who had come up the hard way.

She was born in San Antonio, Texas, to Thomas LeSueur and Anna Bell Johnson, and almost immediately her father abandoned the family. Relocating to Lawton, Oklahoma, Anna Bell married Henry Cassin, who later encouraged his stepdaughter in her efforts at dancing.[18] The family moved to Kansas City by 1916 and ran a rundown hotel. After dropping out of school, LeSueur, an attractive amateur dancer, was hired by a traveling dance troupe that worked a circuit from Oklahoma City to Detroit, with some questionable after-hours entertainment in between. It was in Detroit's Oriole Terrace cabaret room[19] that Jacob Shubert saw her perform and offered her a job in his 1924 Winter Garden show *Innocent Eyes.*

Following a performance of that show one night, LeSueur — sobbing backstage on Granlund's shoulder — asked if he could help her find extra work to assist her ailing mother in Kansas City. "I only get thirty dollars a week," she said as she continued crying, her shoulders heaving. "Can you give me work after my show at the Winter Garden?"[20]

LeSueur needed the money immediately. Granlund knew it would take too long to work her into one of his own productions, but realized that his friend Harry Richman could put her to work at once. Richman reluctantly agreed. But LeSueur immediately returned to Granlund after her visit with Richman, again crying, claiming that Richman insisted she wear an evening gown for her performance. Granlund gave her twenty dollars and sent her up Broadway to a dress shop at 42nd Street. LeSueur presently returned with a suitable dress and six dollars in change. She wanted to try it on immediately, and Granlund stepped out of his office to afford her some privacy. She was partway into the dress when Marcus Loew opened the door and entered Granlund's office.

"He was embarrassed," said Granlund, who recalled that his employer was a shy man who would not understand the idea of a woman changing clothes in a business office. "I searched frantically for something to cover my confusion, to fix up the situation. Suddenly, I remembered, and I reminded him that when he had bought Metro, he had asked all of us to be on the lookout for new stars to replace fading Metro names."[21]

He pitched the idea of Lucille LeSueur as a film actress, and suggested to Loew that she be considered for a screen test for a Metro Pictures contract.[22] Loew agreed to the idea and directed Granlund to take LeSueur to meet Edward "Major" Bowes, who was in charge of conducting film tests on the East Coast.

Bowes ran the Capitol Theatre and also worked for Loew as a talent appraiser of sorts. (In April of 1934, Bowes replaced Granlund on WHN radio[23] and ran radio's best-known amateur show for more than a decade.) He filmed LeSueur on several occasions, but each test returned with the same disappointing results.

LeSueur, meanwhile, continued to dance for Richman and eventually became romantically involved with the entertainer,[24] and her pay increased to the point that lifted her out of her earlier desperation. She managed to save enough money to buy a ticket to Kansas City to visit her mother at Christmas. Granlund, in the meantime, had been in contact with Harry Rapf, one of Metro's producers (and later head of production at MGM), hoping to pull strings for LeSueur, but as the year-end approached, nothing had come of it.

At the Loew's Christmas party at their Broadway headquarters, Granlund was in Nick Schenck's office[25] when one of the New York Metro employees came in to deliver a telephone message that "Hollywood" wanted to sign LeSueur to a contract. The New York office had been searching for her all day. Granlund was given $400 as expense money to wire to LeSueur.[26] He penned a telegram right away: "You are put under a five-year contract at seventy-five dollars a week. Leave immediately for Culver City California."[27] Granlund wired the traveling money to MGM's Kansas City office and heard back from LeSueur the day after Christmas.

"This is the happiest day of my life," LeSueur wrote in reply. "Leaving for California."[28]

She boarded the train for Hollywood on New Year's Day, 1925, and never returned to Kansas City as Lucille LeSueur. It was an era when film executives held the idea that certain names sold tickets more quickly than others. The same mindset that turned Marion Morrison into John Wayne determined that a similar change was in order for the former New York dancer after her first two movies were completed, and they transformed Lucille LeSueur into Joan Crawford.

To his Metro Pictures studio ownership, Loew added the studios owned by Samuel Goldwyn and Louis B. Meyer, and under her MGM contract, Crawford led the life of a true film star over a 45-year career that rated her in the top ten of the American Film Institute's 25 Greatest Male and Female Screen Legends.

It was a career that began with a $14 gown, slipped on in the office of Nils Thor Granlund.

In the second half of the twentieth century, Americans grew up hearing, on a weekly basis, a steady tone that replaced the programming on their radios and televisions. The tone was followed by a series of usually terse instructions about what actions should be taken in the case of "an actual emergency." Later, the Emergency Broadcast System was replaced with an Emergency Alert System[29] with a similar tone and somewhat less dire set of messages.

When Granlund sat in the security of his Loew's WHN studio in 1925, no such system existed. The industry was still working out the growing pains of new technology and its regulation. There were no protocols set up to pass along information in dealing with emergencies, since nothing of the sort had presented itself. At the time, installations such as WHN were true "stations," having the ability to send and receive. Companies such as the *New York Times* had also taken to outfitting their buildings with transmitting and receiving equipment.

The British steamer *Fenchurch*, a 7,335-ton freighter built at Sunderland, England, in 1909, lifted anchor at Philadelphia on May 28 for the Atlantic crossing to Marseilles, France. In two days' time, the ship had reached a point about "400 miles southeast of Sandy Hook in the vicinity of the Gulf Stream."[30] Granlund was seated before the microphone in his studio providing his regular nightly programming, when, shortly after nine o'clock, he was advised that a distress signal had been heard over the station's wireless.[31] It was an SOS from the *Fenchurch*, on fire at sea.

Immediately understanding that an emergency was at hand, and fearing that the radio broadcasts of WHN and other stations might interfere with the ability to receive further wireless reports, Granlund picked up the telephone. The *New York Times*, in its front page article, reported that Granlund contacted the Naval Communications Office and "all radio broadcasting from this vicinity was at once stopped."

The steamship *Cheldale* responded, giving a location and "stating that she was putting on all steam and should reach the *Fenchurch* by midnight."[32] At WHN, Granlund and his engineer could hear the confident captain of the *Cheldale* asking the *Fenchurch* to "be ready to send up rockets about 11 o'clock," so that he could more easily find the ship in the darkness.

The *San Blas*, a freighter owned by United Fruit Company, picked up the distress signal as well, but its captain apparently determined that his ship was too distant to be of any aid. He radioed the captain of the *Fenchurch* at 9:55 P.M. and said that he was "resuming course toward England. Best of luck."

An Associated Press report indicated that the ship was in no immediate danger. The wireless station at Southampton expressed that assurance, although without evidence, and indicated that the *Cheldale* was standing by to render aid.

Unbeknownst to the officials at Southampton, the *Fenchurch* was racing for its life, trying to return to shore under its own power with a blazing fire sending clouds of thick smoke billowing into the sky. Thirty-nine crew members worked to beat down the flames while manning their positions as the *Fenchurch* turned and headed for New York, five hundred miles away. It was a three-day ordeal.

When the weary crew entered the harbor at New York on the night of June 1, flames could be seen rising above the outline of the ship.[33] Officials sent out fire boats at once, and tugs towed the freighter to the Red Hook Flats off 59th Street where it was beached. Throughout the night, tons of water were pumped into the burning hold, and by the evening of June 2, the fire was believed to be under control.

For its effect on local radio broadcasters, Granlund had triggered what amounted to the first Emergency Broadcast System, a call to discontinue regular programming to allow for the communication of vital information. Even the *Times* report of May 30, 1925, mentioned that all radio activity in the area had immediately ceased. In the only enactment of the U.S. EBS system — a false alarm in 1971[34] that triggered the activation — WSNS-TV in Chicago was the only United States broadcasting station to follow mandated procedures and immediately halt all broadcasts.

The "all-clear" on that event came fifteen minutes later, without smoke and without fire.

With an energy level that could only be described as indefatigable, Granlund not only managed the operation of the radio station, his hundreds of dancing showgirls, and his New Jersey farm, he also shook hands with a man named Jim Redman and sealed a deal to transform the seedy Club LaVie,[35] a spot where a gangland ambush had left a man dead by the front door, into a respectable nightspot (renamed the Parody Club). Redman was just one of the club's owners, and investors included mobster Owney Madden.

He hired the clarinet-playing jazz band leader Ted Lewis for a two-week engagement at $3,000 a week to kick off the entertainment at the new club. Lewis was one of the leading players of what was then called "hot jazz," a style that became dated, but one that Lewis could never shake.[36] He recognized good clarinet players, though, and hired musicians of the emerging style to take center stage for his band, including Benny Goodman, Don Murray, and Jimmy Dorsey.

From Atlantic City came Cliff Edwards, known as "Ukulele Ike" at the time, but perhaps more widely recognized in later years as the voice of Walt Disney's Jiminy Cricket in the animated feature *Pinocchio*. Edwards was already well-known when Granlund inked the deal for his week-long performance, but he hit the big time after leaving the Parody Club. "Ukulele Ike" appeared in George Gershwin's *Lady Be Good* in 1924, introducing the song "Fascinatin' Rhythm," a huge hit for him, one that contributed to the public perception of the Broadway-of-the-Twenties crooner with a uke and a song. His career encompassed 107 motion pictures,[37] Broadway, and a collection of hit songs, but he died penniless and alone in Hollywood. His death was announced the same day as that of Granlund's longtime Hollywood bandleader Ted Fio Rito, who penned "Toot Toot Tootsie" and other hits.

Granlund paid Ukulele Ike $500 for the week, a huge sum at the time.

Joe E. Lewis was once a singer, but his run-in with Al Capone's henchmen ended with his bones broken, his throat slashed, and his tongue cut. He was lucky just to have survived, much less make a return to show business. He left Chicago for New York and felt he was sufficiently recovered to take the stage. Granlund put him on the night the Parody Club opened. "Joe's debut on Broadway was the most heartbreaking thing I ever witnessed," Granlund remembered.[38] He lied to Lewis about the quality of his performance and encouraged him to continue his comeback.

Lewis, the little comedian who overcame the violence of the Chicago Mafia, did get better, as Granlund predicted. His stable of jokes about heavy drinking became some of the most memorable of all time, lines like: "You're not drunk enough if you can still lie on the floor without hanging on," "I went on a diet, swore off drinking and heavy eating, and in 14 days I lost two weeks,"[39] and "I distrust camels, and anyone else who can go for a week without a drink."

When Frank Sinatra read the 1955 Art Cohn biography of Lewis, *The Joker Is Wild*, he was so taken with it that he had it produced as a 1957 film in which he played the part of Joe E. Lewis.

Between the two music acts alone, Granlund had promised the payment of an immense amount of money which offered little chance of bringing an immediate return, but he was intent on altering the shady reputation of the locale. "We figured that if the Parody lost five or six thousand dollars in its first two weeks, we would still be all right," Granlund noted in his memoir.[40] "It was worth that much to dry-clean the LaVie. But the Parody showed a profit from the moment it opened."

It went a long way toward establishing Granlund as a savvy operator who could make money in addition to entertaining the audience. An argument over chorus costumes with Redman soon sent Granlund across the street to the Silver Slipper at Forty-eighth and Broadway.

Frankie Marlow ran the Silver Slipper,[41] and Club Rendezvous as well. He was a former partner of Larry Fay in the Les Ambassadeurs Club. He was a part-owner at Club LaVie, along with Link Mitchell of the Hudson Dusters gang. Frank Marlow was a known gambler and race horse owner, a one-time boxer, and boxing promoter, and one of the men the papers called a "reputed racketeer," either because there was no rap sheet on the desk in front of them, or they wanted a little "wiggle room" in case they later had a run-in with the subject of the article. The *Times* described him as "an intimate friend of the late Arnold Rothstein and George A. McManus," two of the top figures of the New York mob syndicate.

On June 24, 1929, Marlow was sitting comfortably with several companions at a table at a speakeasy called La Tavernelle, one of the less-than-glitzy clubs on West 52nd Street.[42] The bartender called him to the phone, he talked for a couple of minutes, hung up, and walked to the front door. As he stepped outside, he was immediately met by two men who hustled him into a car that sped away. Later that night, his body was found beside a country road, in a clump of bushes opposite the cemetery in Flushing, New York, with gunshot wounds to the temple, neck, and jaw.[43]

In canvassing the neighborhood, detectives found that no one heard any gunshots at all, leading police to believe that Marlow had been shot while in the car, and his body tossed out of the moving vehicle.

He had been "taken for a ride"[44] by rival gang members.

First reports claimed that Marlow had been dining alone when he was called out to his death, but Police Commissioner Whalen later arrested three of Marlow's dinner companions. They were now material witnesses.

It was December before Ciro Terranova, Daniel Grosso and Nicholas McDermott were brought in for questioning in the case of Marlow's execution.[45] Terranova, a native of Corleone, Sicily, was the one-time leader of the Morello crime family in East Harlem. Although there was evidence that he had promised to pay $30,000 for the killing of Frankie Marlow, he was never charged with the murder.[46]

Despite the gangland connections, some of the big names of the day got their start in appearances for Granlund at the Silver Slipper, along with others who were already established, like Ruby Keeler. Comedienne Imogene Coca, Jimmy Durante, Walter O'Keefe, George Raft (at one time a driver for Larry Fay), and torch singer Helen Morgan could all credit paychecks to Granlund and the Silver Slipper shows he produced.

Granlund was able to slip back in time in 1927, revisiting his days as a newspaper writer and penning an article that first appeared in the *New York World*. Carried over the Associated Press wire service, it also made the *New York Times* and the front pages of newspapers across America.

Granlund had only just recently turned down adventurer Richard E. Byrd's offer to have him broadcast reports on Byrd's attempt to cross the Atlantic to Paris, when Charles Lindbergh went from unknown to world-famous by completing the trip non-stop in his custom plane "The Spirit of St. Louis." It was an attempt by Lindbergh to secure not only a spot in the record books, but a $25,000 prize being offered by hotelier Raymond Orteig.

Lindbergh came home to a nationwide hero's welcome, the extent of which is difficult to imagine in modern times. Just as he was mobbed in Paris, the pilot met with parades and tickertape on his return to American soil. Through Granlund's connection with Charles S. "Casey" Jones (ace pilot, vice-president of Curtiss Airplane Manufacturing Company, and the same airfield operator who had loaned him a plane and pilot for a flight to Atlantic City), he was able to secure a seat in the car taking Lindbergh from New York to a reception in Washington. Granlund later claimed that the shared Swedish ancestry played a part.[47] Lindbergh had hoped to travel to Washington in a government plane that would allow him time to return to New York for a meeting with schoolchildren in the early afternoon. Bad weather eliminated that possibility; the visit to the school was cancelled, and the trip would have to be made by car. Jones was driving.

The wire service account carried in nationwide papers on June 16, 1927, featured Granlund's typical low-key slang.[48] "'Slim' wants that ship here so he can start with it to St. Louis," said Granlund in the article, substituting his own nickname for the pilot over the more widely used "Lucky Lindy." Lindbergh's airship, the Spirit of St. Louis, had been his sole companion the length of the flight. "He does not want the ship brought here by anybody else. He wants it here right away so that he can fuss over it and tune it up."

"This is the first time I have been my own boss since I got to Paris,"[49] the pilot told Granlund as the crew in the car made their way through the pouring rain. Earlier, Lindbergh had Jones, the car's "pilot," stop to allow two motorcycle-riding policemen serving as their escorts a chance to "ditch their motorcycles" and ride in the automobile.

He was asked by Granlund about the paperwork he carried to France.

"Did you really think you had to take letters of introduction and tell them when you came down on the field that you were Lindbergh?" Granlund asked.[50]

"That was one laugh on Ted Roosevelt," Lindbergh replied, grinning. "I mean, about the letters. I didn't say anything when they came to the side of my plane in Paris. I was scared speechless for fear the crowd would get up against the propeller which was still spinning and get their heads cut off."[51]

Granlund related in the article Lindburgh's own account of the landing in Paris and his return to the United States, including a flying stunt Lindburgh performed for the first time while nearing Philadelphia. "I saw some of the boys doing that at Bolling Field Saturday," Lindburgh told Granlund. "I figured I could do it."

Lindbergh was not the first famed pilot to come under the Granlund interview. In 1926, in a newspaper account that could have written by the publicist himself, the novelty of radio celebrity interviews included mention of Charles Nungesser, the man usually described as "The World's Greatest Living Ace," who shot down 44 enemy airplanes in World War I. Captain Nungesser managed to convert his aviation fame into a film appearance in *The Sky Raider* and visited WHN for a Granlund interview, "but was so rattled before the microphone that he had to be constantly prompted."[52]

The wire service article included a number of Granlund interviews including Gene Tunney, "heavyweight champion of fistiana," who was also "extremely uneasy" during his first efforts at broadcasting.

Granlund's observations included Al Jolson's "chummy" attitude regarding the microphone (Jolson advised his adopted son it was bedtime), an entirely opposite approach from Charlie Chaplin's "declining invitations to broadcast his voice."[53]

The newspaper article also pointed out another Granlund innovation, one that still features greatly in the reporting of sports figures and events. "In July 1925," the writer stated, in pointing out the first time use of radio technology in connection with a sporting event, Granlund "held the microphone to Dave Shade" before his boxing match with Jimmy Slattery.

"'I am going out there to win as quickly as I can,' Shade said, and ten minutes later he was back to tell the world, and particularly Mrs. Shade, that he had knocked out Slattery in the first round."[54]

It wasn't ESPN, but then again, the television network dedicated to sports coverage that debuted fifty-four years after the Shade-Slattery bout has changed little in principle from Granlund's early example.

In a demonstration of the affinity among the press agent corps, Granlund paid tribute to one of his associates in a plane over Broadway. Walter Kingsley, longtime press agent for Florenz Ziegfeld and the *Follies*, had become a good friend of Granlund over the years. In 1915, Kingsley authored a tongue-in-cheek article for the *New York Times* entitled "How to Sell a One-Act Play,"[55] writing it as a script and including a part for himself in which he played the "Author–press agent."

Kingsley "had given the best years of his life to the business of making Broadway famous,"[56] and asked that after the cremation of his body, his ashes be scattered over that famed Great White Way. In the company of Kingsley's widow in a plane piloted by John Wager, Granlund upturned the urn and the "ashes of Walter Kingsley whirled in a mad dance as they were caught in the gale created by the speed of the airplane. Then, separating, invisible against the infinite blue, they drifted downward, slowly and gently."[57]

In his flowery summation of an event the writer considered to be of the sort "press agents dream of," he ironically noted that Kingsley's request that his ashes be scattered over the roofs and sidewalks of Broadway would only be partially successful, since "a crowd that gathered to watch a man demonstrate a reducing belt in a drug store window quite blocked the sidewalk."

If pilots and planes were not enough, Granlund could fall back on the hot air balloon, or the new-fangled zeppelin, as another opportunity for press.

Loew's MGM studios, in a partnership with the Hearst newspaper chain, released in 1929 a "three-reel talking motion picture" entitled *Across the Atlantic Via Zeppelin*, in which NTG appeared along with Lady Drummond Hay, "the only woman who ever crossed the Atlantic from east to west by air."[58] The film, a behind-the-scenes accounting of the dirigible flight, included such highlights as the picturesque French countryside passing below, a "merry" first meal aboard ship, "scenes of animation and unflagging watchfulness" from the control cabin, and Knut Eckener, "the handsome and stalwart son of the commander," who set out to repair a damaged stabilizing fin by "clambering up a crazy ladder, fighting every step as the force of the gale almost tears him away."[59]

Things were flying high for Granlund in the producing business as well. His Atlantic City acquaintance, Enoch "Nucky" Johnson, the liquor-smuggling political boss for whom Granlund had flown into town for a beauty contest, bought New Jersey's version of the Silver Slipper Club and gave Granlund a "blank check" to stage an elaborate show there.

It was gangster money that had financed the transformation of New York's Silver Slipper as well. Arnold Rothstein was the New York crime boss who turned the neighborhood thugs into an organized big business. It is widely believed that Rothstein was also behind Major League Baseball's "Black Sox Scandal" in 1919, involving gambling and the World Series.

Farther up Broadway from the Loew's office was Lindy's Restaurant, at the time located at 49th Street next to the Rivoli Theatre. Rothstein used the place as his office, and could be seen regularly outside, surrounded by bodyguards.[60] It was a place also frequented with some regularity by Granlund and his friend Damon Runyon, who preferred a table to the right of the front door.[61] Later, they sat there discussing the "dealings" that ended in the dramatic events of November 3, 1928. Granlund's version was a Manhattan poker game at the Park Central Hotel a week earlier, a three-day high-stakes game with Nick the Greek and George "Hump" McManus, a big Irishman whom the *Times* described as a "Broadway card game operator."

Rothstein hit a cold streak and walked away leaving $312,000 in I.O.U. promises. When the debt was called in a few days later, Rothstein decline to pay, claiming that the game was rigged.

The gambler took a seat at Granlund and Runyon's table at Lindy's on November 3, and had not been there long when the telephone situated on the stairs landing began ringing.

"That's for me,"[62] Rothstein said, and jumped up to answer it.

After a few minutes had passed, Rothstein returned, grabbed his coat and tipped his hat at his companions as he hurried outside. Granlund and Runyon were still seated at the table when word came that Rothstein had been shot. He had stumbled into the lobby at the Park Central Hotel asking for a taxi, when the attendant noticed Rothstein was bleeding. He was rushed to Manhattan's Polyclinic Hospital with a gunshot wound to the abdomen, and died the following day. He had six thousand dollars cash in his pocket at the time of the shooting.[63]

Runyon, who was writing for the *New York American* at the time, got better mileage from the story than did Granlund. He was able to include actions just before the shooting as part of his report, and perhaps more importantly, he turned the real Arnold Rothstein into the fictional character Nathan Detroit in *The Idyll of Miss Sarah Brown* which was the basis for the long-running Broadway success *Guys and Dolls*.

Although Granlund believed the Silver Slipper the most spectacular club of the era, it was the Hollywood that truly revolutionized the cabaret scene. When it was time to find financing, Granlund initially believed that the money would come from the hard-hearted enforcer Owney Madden.

Author T.J. English, in his exhaustive treatise on Irish-American gangsters *Paddy Whacked*, called Owen Victor Madden the "preeminent mobster of the Prohibition era." Madden was born to Irish parents and was sent from England to New York following his father's death in 1903. His relatives lived in what was then the predominately immigrant area of Midtown Manhattan called Hell's Kitchen, which had all the attributes of the Five Points district previously infamous for its violent gang activities.

Owney, as he was called, quickly fell in with the Irish Gopher gang, known as much for their infighting as their frequent clashes with the rival Hudson Dusters. English notes that Madden "developed expert proficiency with all the tools of the trade: the revolver, blackjack, brass knuckles, and especially the lead pipe wrapped in a newspaper, a favorite weapon of early twentieth century gangsters."[64] He was arrested a total of fifty-seven times before his career was over; by fourteen, he was already called "the Killer" by New York police, and was feared for his exuberant fierceness. This was exemplified in a fatal attack on an Italian merchant[65] near Madden's home after which he reportedly stood in the street and shouted, "Owney Madden, Tenth Avenue!" A year later, a mortally wounded store clerk named Willie Henshaw on his deathbed identified Madden as his assailant, but by the time the suspect was captured and questioned, no one wanted to come forward against him — including the prosecutors. All charges were dismissed.

Years later, a case against Madden fell into place, and he was sentenced to prison for his involvement in the death of Pat Doyle, one of his own gang members. Madden served eight years before his release in 1923, but the

Gangster Owney Madden, released from Sing Sing prison in 1923, backed Granlund at Club La Vie and held financial interests in other Prohibition-era nightclubs (courtesy McHuston Archives).

gangland activity had continued in his name even while he was incarcerated.

Seventeen-year-old James Lawlor, a member of the Owney Madden gang, was shot and killed on January 8, 1922, by two members of the Hudson Dusters Gang in what was described in the newspaper report as a "war between rival gangs in New York's underworld."[66]

Larry Fay, who had entered into the agreement with Granlund and Texas

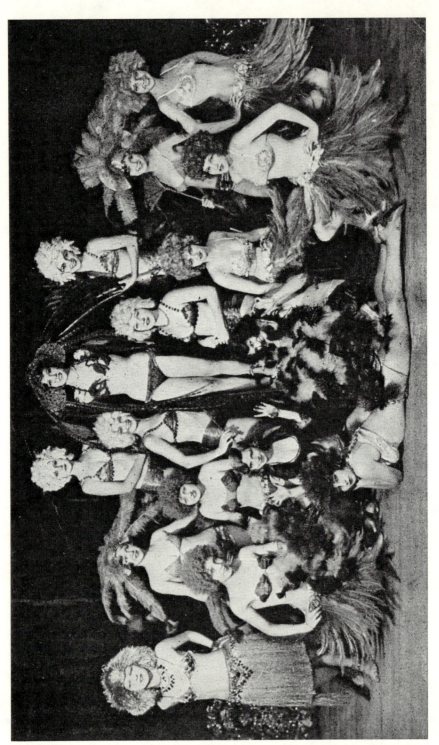

Period postcard featuring the chorus girls from Granlund's Hollywood Restaurant at Broadway and 48th Street (courtesy McHuston Archives).

Guinan for the El Fey Club, had been a member of Madden's early gang. When Madden was released from prison, Fay gave him a job as an "enforcer" in his liquor-smuggling enterprise that centered around his taxicab company.

It wasn't long before Madden was again in a position of money, the kind of cash that could finance a ritzy night spot. What Granlund envisioned was a new sort of club, one that could appeal to the common man rather than target the high-rollers, and turn a profit by dealing in a volume-trade rather than the commonly found high-priced venues. Where the cafés to date were cramped hideaways tucked away in lofts and basements, Granlund wanted a grand-scale room with a large dance floor and a cabaret — a spacious affair that could easily accommodate the lavish chorus line productions he intended to produce.

Madden bumped into Granlund one evening and repeated his appreciation for the turnaround at Club LaVie, in which he was a part-owner.

"Tell you what," Madden said. "I'll back you up to a hundred grand for a place of your own."[67]

When Granlund described to the mobster his cabaret idea, though, Madden expressed doubts. Granlund's plan was to make money on food instead of illegal liquor sales, an idea that Madden described as "nuts," pointing out that cabarets made money on cover charges and liquor sales.

Granlund sought advice in the expertise of Jake Amron, who had run the food and beverage operation for the then-stylish Knickerbocker Hotel on Broadway, describing his idea of charging for food, but offering — in addition to the menu — a floor show. Shortly thereafter, he contacted Joe Moss, one of the Jewish entrepreneurs on Broadway who, alongside Billy Rose, owned several East Side cafés.[68] Granlund found willing partners in Moss and Amron, and the three formed a partnership to open just such a night spot. It was to be called the Hollywood Restaurant[69] and located on the second floor of the former Rector's Restaurant. Granlund used his Hollywood connections to decorate the cabaret with a film theme à la the Planet Hollywood chain restaurants that launched in 1991. With all the glitter and glitz of its West Coast namesake, the Hollywood, unfortunately, was off to less than spectacular start.

Nils Thor Granlund was all about the promotion.

The *New York Times* reported on November 20, 1927, that the competition among Broadway nightclubs was so intense that club owners were soliciting business in front of their competitors' establishments. Arrested were James De Lucca, Benjamin Cohen, and Daniel Barnes, who could not explain to police why they were loitering about the entrance to the Strand Roof nightclub.

Patrolman William C. Wilson made a search of their pockets and discovered cards with the names of competing clubs. In the pockets of De Lucca were cards "bearing the name of the Hollywood Restaurant."[70] The three were fined $15 each for soliciting the patrons of the Strand Roof and explaining the merits of the other clubs. The official charge was disorderly conduct.

Later, promotional efforts were slightly more upscale, and included such things as photographic postcards featuring the dining area or the chorus line in costume.

The Hollywood Restaurant had certainly achieved success by 1930. Writer Paul Harrison, in a piece carried in the Lowell (MA) *Sun* in June 1934, gave credit for the entertainment format to Granlund, "who started the first of the modern types of cabarets." Lee Mortimer of the *New York World* worded it a little more strongly: "N. T. G. is the conceiver, inventor, and creator of modern night life," he gushed, "and the Hollywood was the daddy of practically every cabaret in the business today."[71]

Entertainer Ozzie Nelson, who with his wife and two sons starred in the long-running television series *Ozzie and Harriet* (1952–1966), commented in a *Redbook* magazine article during the run of that show that "anyone not familiar with midtown New York at that time would find it difficult to realize how glamourous this place [the Hollywood] was. I don't believe there ever were as many beautiful girls in one room at one time as at the Hollywood Restaurant that year."

Part of the impetus for Granlund's striking out on his own may have been the death on September 5, 1927, of his longtime employer, Marcus Loew, the man Granlund described as more of a father to him than his own father had ever been. Granlund turned off WHN[72] radio as a gesture of respect, keeping the station "dark" until just before the 2 P.M. funeral ceremony was to begin.

"To know Marcus Loew was to love him," Granlund broadcast when WHN signed back on, in a memorial address that clearly indicated his affection for his boss. "He was a man without an enemy. He lived his life in gentleness, peace, and humility, beloved of his fellowmen as few have ever been."[73]

The funeral was held on Long Island. The *Times* reported that messages had been received from politicians, businessmen, and entertainers from Europe to the West Coast. More than 2,500 arrived to attend the ceremony; most had to be turned away. A flower wreath with the words "The Last Curtain" came from the Loew's Theatres managers, and others were sent by David Warfield, Nicholas Schenck, and William Randolph Hearst. Two hundred cars lined for the funeral procession and pallbearers included the biggest names in American business and entertainment: David Bernstein, Adolph Zukor, John Golden, Lee Shubert, Charles M. Schwab, Edward F. Albee, and others.

There were already three thousand people waiting at the cemetery gates, but they were not allowed to enter. The family and mourners were escorted by fifty policemen to the gravesite, and when the casket was brought from the hearse, there were more than a thousand gathered around the tomb when the body was placed in it.

Eight

Prosperity at the Paradise

Money is a terrible master, but an excellent servant.
— P.T. Barnum

The medium known as radio had become a success. It was not exactly the communications tool that its earliest promoters had been envisioned, since predictions were that the wireless radio sets in the homes of Americans would eventually be used to talk to neighbors and relatives, thereby replacing the telephone. Wireless communication of that sort — the cellular telephone with its wide-ranging technologies—came much, much later.

On the heels of the overwhelming public acceptance of the radio, however, came a second line of products promising pictures to go along with the radio sound. Though the idea was dramatic, the actual product was less than impressive in its most primitive versions, which offered televised images about the size of a business card. Before 1930, General Electric and others introduced mechanical sets that were hints of what might eventually be possible, but developments in true "electronic" imaging came later.

Granlund was there to help provide a formal demonstration to the New York City public on April 26, 1931.

In conjuring the newspaper account of the event, the *New York Times* writer tried to explain exactly what was to be presented, in terms that any layman might readily understand — even if the expression made little sense in accurately describing the technology. He settled on the eminently illogical phrase "radio talkies," which he reported were "officially inaugurated last night in New York by the union of the microphone of WGBS and the television 'eye' of W2XCR, an image transmitter at 655 Fifth Avenue."[1]

Special television and sound receivers had been set up in the Aeolian Hall at Fifth Avenue and 54th Street. Several thousand people gathered in the area,[2] hoping to catch a glimpse of the miraculous new technology which — unlike the movies— would present pictures and sound *live*— at the very moment the activities were being enacted clear across town. Viewers had to be close to the screen to appreciate the performances; the television screens were about twelve inches square and the images filled only about half the screen.

Granlund introduced a number of the acts during the course of the event, which inaugurated the regular television broadcasting schedule for the station. WGBS, the flagship station of the broadcasting chain begun by the Gimbel Brothers department store, was later sold along with the rest of what became the General Broadcasting System chain to William Randolph Hearst's newspaper empire. The television station announced, as part of its first show, a regular schedule to commence after the demonstration, with four hours of films and live entertainment each weekday and two hours of live performances on the weekends.

Appearing on the special demonstration were a host of Broadway stars: boxer Primo Carnera; actor Lionel Atwill, who performed an excerpt from the show *Silent Witness*; Felix the Clown from the Ringling Circus; and dancers Maria Gambarelli, Patricia Bowman, and Fay Marbe.[3]

In late September, in a second demonstration that was somewhat more flamboyant, Granlund, three of his Hollywood Restaurant showgirls and a television camera, settled into the cockpit of an airplane that was to buzz over the skyline of New York City while — at the same time — broadcasting their showgirl antics, albeit in cramped fashion, to the thousands gathered in the darkened Madison Square Gardens.[4] At times the noise of the plane drowned out the audio, but the estimated 45,000 people attending the "television talking moving picture" demonstration at the Gardens witnessed a comedy sketch performed by the "Hollywood Club Troupe" as introduced by Granlund. The airborne performers used a piano outfitted with a radio receiver in providing the accompaniment, which also allowed those aboard to monitor the broadcast as it aired.

Granlund had staged what was the first broadcast of a televised image from the air, and the first occurrence of radio programming originating from an airplane. The signal was carried over WGBS and its experimental television transmitter W2XCR.[5]

Although the ten-foot images projected onto the huge screen at Madison Square Garden highlighted the show, the gathering was actually part of National Radio Week, sponsored by the National Federation of Radio Associations. President Herbert Hoover extended his "heartiest greetings to all those participating in the observance."[6]

Granlund was in the air, on the air, on the stage, and in the press. Increasingly, he found his name among those regularly dropped in the Broadway gossip columns, benefiting from the success of his Hollywood Restaurant. Walter Winchell, a writer who could always squeeze in a line about Granlund, had begun his New York tenure as a vaudeville performer, but is credited by many as the inventor of the newspaper gossip column. Granlund knew Winchell from the old days, when the writer worked the Loew's theater circuit as half of

Winchell & Green, a husband-and-wife vaudeville act. The duo appeared in 1918 at the Loew's American roof, in an act in which Winchell sang and his wife danced.

"His act was not particularly good,"[7] recalled Granlund, "but it was attractive enough to get him in a few small theaters and finally into Loew's."

The Palace Theater was one of the premier stages in New York City, opening in 1913 at 1564 Broadway with a performance by Ed Wynn. For any performer, "Playing the Palace" was an experience that could not be topped; the sidewalks always bustled with actors and actresses who could look up at the towering edifice and dream of their big-time shot. The Loew's State Building was nearly next door, at 1540 Broadway, and in between was a business where an aspiring star could get a cup of coffee and a big square of cake for fifteen cents. The cake at Yohalem's Restaurant was big enough to make a meal, and the between-work performers who lingered on the sidewalk near the Palace became known as "cake-eaters,"[8] filling up on cheap food while trying to find work in the entertainment industry.

Granlund described Winchell as one of the cake-eaters whose ambition took him from the performance stage to the pressroom, landing an early job with *Variety*, reporting the vaudeville news. Winchell later found work with *Vaudeville News* and then joined the *New York Graphic* for whom he began reporting Broadway gossip. The best source for *new* news of the sort Winchell liked to report came from the conversations in the better speakeasies, but club owners had no desire to allow newspaper writers into their establishments. It was Prohibition, after all, and the liquor that freely flowed behind the doors of the society cafés was not something that an owner wanted to read about in print.

In addition, clubs with ties to the New York underworld had no desire to see their names or the names of their clientele in the pages of the newspapers. Granlund knew that the clubs would keep the reporters out, and would eject the ones who slipped in.

Even with his ties to the mob-run nightclubs, Granlund had a difficult time getting past the front door when in the company of writers such as Lee Mortimer, Damon Runyon, and Winchell. He began a campaign on their behalf,[9] promising those behind the speakeasies that the gossip column writers could keep the owners' names out of print while gathering material about Broadway notables.

Larry Fay relented first, and through Fay's association with Owney Madden and others, the writers soon were able to slip into the speakeasies with their pencils and notepads, surreptitiously gathering the gossip of the evening. Winchell's columns would eventually be carried in more than 2,000 newspapers nationwide, and some fifty million Americans either heard his weekly radio show or read his syndicated newspaper column.[10] He was in the clubs often enough that he became close friends with Madden, who by 1931 was one of the primary figures in the New York underworld. Winchell's fear of gangland reprisals caused him to flee to California,[11] where he collected his health and self-confidence before returning to Broadway. Madden, after continuing police harassment, left New York for good in 1935, heading for Hot Springs, Arkansas,[12] where he opened a spa and casino.

With the company they kept, it is no surprise that Granlund and Winchell remained friends, and that the writer would find a spot to flatter his companion.

"Nils T. Granlund, perhaps, has the greatest address book on Broadway, if not in the world," Winchell wrote in his May 22, 1931, "On Broadway" column. "[He] can supply any producer with the shapeliest, the prettiest, and the blondest persons." Winchell claimed it to be only a legend that Ziegfeld, White, and Shubert had more attractive dancers, and that all the showmen came to Granlund to fill their chorus lines, claiming "only the other day Mr. Ziegfeld recruited a dozen of them from the Granlund floor show."[13]

The girls from the Hollywood Restaurant, the same group from which Granlund selected three to accompany him in the television-demonstrating flight above the city, were said to be unmatched in beauty. Lee Mortimer of the *World* wrote that Granlund's girls were the most beautiful "this side of heaven."[14]

"I built the whole show around them,"[15] said Granlund, who called the Hollywood policies a revolution that changed the face of Broadway, with "a six-course dinner and floor show for a dollar and fifty cents. We served no liquor and we had no cover charge. It was the best bargain in New York."[16]

Unsurprisingly, there was liquor being consumed at the tables of the Hollywood Restaurant.[17] Granlund's spot suffered the embarrassment of a raid, but it came toward the end of the Prohibition years and Granlund himself was not charged. The price for a dinner had risen from the initial dollar-fifty to five dollars by the time postcards were printed in 1930.[18] All along, the Hollywood offered more expensive dinners along with the house "special." It remained a popular dining spot even following the stock market crash of 1929.[19]

James Aswell, another syndicated columnist, found space to praise the operation in 1931. "Nils T. Granlund," he penned in "My New York," "that tall, frail, nightclub impresario ... remember, he was the ace of sports reporters in the early radio days before Graham MacNamee crackled into fame." Aswell called the Hollywood the "only first-rate nightclub in town where two can dine, see an elaborate floor show and dance for five bucks."[20]

For Granlund, though, three-plus years at the Hollywood were enough. His one-third ownership provided plenty of income, but the decision-making process as to what direction the restaurant should follow was stifled by differing views, particularly those of partner Joe Moss. "We had built a little gold mine,"[21] Granlund remembered. "He wanted to bring in big names in show business, spend more dough on one or two people, and let the rest go."

Unbeknownst to Granlund, he was being hunted by a fellow named

Charles Sherman, another shady figure with ties to Waxey Gordon, a bootlegger who bought up breweries, distilleries, and nightclubs with his exorbitant rum-running profits. Gordon ran all of the East Coast operations for mob syndicate head Arnold Rothstein,[22] and Sherman's fortunes rose along with Gordon's. Sherman was known to have money at his disposal, but no one seemed to known where or how he had acquired it. Rumors that it had come through dealings in opium resulted in his being nicknamed "Chink" and "The Chinaman."[23]

One evening, Sherman and a companion entered the Hollywood Restaurant and took a table. The man with Sherman was Mark Hellinger, a writer who won celebrity of his own for his *New York Daily News* column, and later moved to the *Mirror* to cover the Broadway beat. It was said that Hellinger had accompanied Al Jolson and Ruby Keeler aboard the cruise ship *Olympic* to keep America apprised of their honeymoon news; in 1929, when Hellinger wed *Follies* dancer Gladys Glad, he reported on his own nuptials,[24] describing the happy couple as "the highest paid and most beautiful showgirl" who had married "hardly the highest paid and certainly not the most beautiful columnist." When he brought Charlie Sherman around to meet Granlund, Hellinger had just published a collection of his short stories, entitled *Moon Over Broadway*. He later penned the screenplay for the 1939 film *The Roaring Twenties*.

Hellinger was already well known to Granlund, and the writer had been sought out by Sherman for an introduction to the man behind the success at the Hollywood.

Sherman wanted legitimacy, and believed that the quickest way to acquire it would be by owning the biggest and fanciest cabaret that could be situated on Broadway. He wanted the Hollywood Restaurant, only larger-scale. He wanted Granlund to run it. "You build the place,"[25] Sherman told Granlund, "and I'll give you $250 a week and 25 percent ownership."

It was a no-strings attached offer, and one that would allow Granlund to continue operating his cabaret without a dependency on illegal liquor sales. He decided to take Sherman up on the proposition.

He gave his partners thirty days' notice of his intentions, and spent his off-hours during that time searching for a suitable location for the new cabaret. Thirty days later, after his replacement emcee at the Hollywood Restaurant took the stage, Granlund still had no location. Finally, he looked closer to home and discovered a vacancy that eventually accommodated 750 customers on the second floor of the Brill Building at Forty-ninth and Broadway, sitting catty-cornered from the Hollywood and "perhaps glaring a little in a competitive way."[26]

When Granlund crossed Broadway in 1932, he had no way of knowing he would spend the rest of his life trying to recapture the magic he had created at the Hollywood Restaurant.

The *New York Sun* carried an announcement of Granlund's plans on

May 12, 1932, indicating that the Broadway Swede, "who for three years has been a fixture at the Hollywood, has decided to take a fling on his own and he will open his club at Forty-ninth and Broadway in early December, which will be known as the Paradise. It will run along the same lines as the Hollywood, with one of those stupendous and extravagant revues at the dinner and supper hours, and featuring some well known orchestra."[27]

As promised, Sherman provided the money. The renovation of the Brill Building space cost him some $175,000[28]—an amount roughly equivalent to 2.5 million in 2007 dollars when adjusted for inflation. Additionally, he provided Granlund with the idea to one-up the Hollywood, by bringing in real Hollywood showgirls from California. Granlund agreed it was a great idea. He had just seen the Eddie Cantor movie musical *The Kid from Spain* and determined that the beautiful chorus line that the show featured had exactly the girls he needed at the opening of the Paradise.[29]

In a deal typical for a lifelong promoter, Granlund found a way to make arrangements to everyone's benefit. He knew William Wallace Atterbury, the rail executive whose Pennsylvania Railroad owned the precursor to TWA Airlines. Atterbury agreed to furnish Granlund with a Ford tri-motor for the flight to California and back, in exchange for positive publicity for his company. Busby Berkeley, who choreographed *The Kid from Spain*, helped track down girls from the film, which was made for Samuel Goldwyn's studio. Goldwyn agreed to help as well, as did Eddie Cantor.

Sitting in at the auditions with Granlund was his friend Jean Harlow, whom he had helped advance from "naïve and guileless"[30] amateur to a Hollywood movie star. Harlow, a contract actress for MGM, starred in four films in 1932 alone and made the list of the American Film Institute's list of Greatest Movie Stars of All Time. She died, tragically early, of kidney failure at the age of 26.

One hundred and fifty hopefuls appeared for the audition, but few would commit to the offer, which included a six-month contract at $100 a week to work the Broadway chorus line. In addition, Granlund promised to fly the girls back to California whenever they liked, should they decide to quit the show for any reason. Harlow addressed the showgirls on Granlund's behalf, insuring them that "if any of you take this job and find that Granny has broken his promise, I'll personally make good on it."[31] Granlund recalled that Harlow's pitch on his behalf was the deciding factor.

Granlund managed to get publicity shots of the showgirls beside the plane from the airport in Los Angeles to the runway in New York. "N. T. G. will fling the doors of his Paradise Club open and let you angels in December 23," the *World-Telegram* declared on December 10, 1932. "He brought his twelve beautiful Hollywood girls in yesterday and appointed Abe Lyman and his Californians to the bandstand. Energetic nightclub grammarians who passed by the Paradise Club on upper Broadway have phoned in to correct Mr.

Granlund's prose on the big sign. The sign, they assert, reads 'The World's Most Loveliest Girls' and they wonder why Mr. Granlund has been tampering with superlatives."[32]

For the first production, called "Continental Night," Granlund hired Lina Basquette as the headliner. Basquette had danced for Ziegfeld and appeared in her first film at age nine before making movies for directorial legends Cecil B. DeMille and Frank Capra.

There was no shortage of press for the opening of the Paradise. The *New York Sun* critic called it "a spot you mustn't miss if you're exploring Manhattan night life."[33] The Paradise made the proclaimed December 23 opening date, and the *New York Sun* critic was impressed. "In addition, there is a score of lovely girls, including a dozen beauties transported by plane from Hollywood, where they graced the filming of Eddie Cantor's *The Kid from Spain*."[34] The paper reported that in the first week, the Paradise was jammed to capacity, with five hundred would-be patrons turned away on an opening week night.

Granlund, meanwhile, had continued his regular rounds to the Loew's theaters, taking his chorus girl revues in tow, making his first appearance with the new "Paradise Revue Stars" at the Loew's State Theatre in the first week of 1933.[35] The January 6 appearance also featured the Yacht Club Boys, an acrobatic troupe, and headliners Madelyn Killeen and Bert Frohman.

The revues were different only in the names of the chorus girls' affiliation. Paul Harrison wrote in his "In New York" column of the similarities between the Hollywood Restaurant and the Paradise Cabaret, and the way they both catered to the out-of-town trade. "Another reason they're so alike," Harrison declared,[36] "is that [Granlund] was master of ceremonies at the Hollywood before he went to the Paradise. Granlund is a tireless and voluble fellow from Providence, R. I., who crashed the big town as one of the pioneer radio announcers and soon went to work in one of the night spots owned by the late and violently deceased Larry Fay."

James Aswell also could not resist a comparison. "Then there are my old friends,"[37] he wrote in "My New York," "the Paradise and the Hollywood." Aswell made a note of the additional female clientele attracted by entertainer Rudy Vallee, who at the time was still on his way up the success ladder.

"The Paradise," Aswell continued, "is the place I would suggest for substantial business men who know a pretty girl when they see one. [Granlund] has an uncanny eye for beauty; he is one of the town's born pickers, and this is no common talent.... [T]hen — here's winking at you — Miss Sally Rand is currently the attraction at the Paradise. On opening night I recognized a couple of officials from the department of licenses hanging around in the background there, and I was filled with trepidation. They had heard that Sally Rand was going to do the fan dance which got her into trouble in Chicago this past summer and they were on hand to guard the morals of the town, but Granny fooled them and posed them a problem."[38]

"WHO'LL BUY—
WHO'LL BUY?"
It's a Little-Realized Fact
That Glamorous Claire
Luce's Start to Stage
Fame Was As a Cigar-
ette-Girl in a New York Night Club—
and Nils Granlund Saw Her and Got
All Smoked Up.

Caricatures of Granlund and Claire Luce in an August 11, 1935, King Features Syndicate story titled "When a Millionaire Sues a Showgirl" (courtesy McHuston Archives).

Rand was a burlesque dancer and actress who was born a Missouri girl as
Harriet Helen Beck. Director Cecil B. DeMille changed her name to Sally Rand,
and she became infamous for a dance she performed using ostrich feather fans
to strategically hide her body while she danced.

"It is true that Miss Rand does her dance in the same costume, or lack of
it,"[39] Aswell wrote of her appearance on Granlund's stage, "but the lights have
been so dimmed that it is almost impossible to see the other members of your
party, much less Miss Rand. This lends a ghostly glamour to the proceedings,
a weird spice, and prosperous brokers rise at the rear tables and peer frown-
ing into the gloom through which Sally flits."

It all contributed to the allure of the Paradise, which Granlund considered a triumph. "The Paradise was a tremendous success from the day it

opened," he said.[40] "It paid back its original cost within the year, and a Depression year, at that."

It was late 1935 when Paul Harrison reported in his column that Granlund "plans to go from nudes to dudes with a yippee ranch in New Jersey."[41] Lee Mortimer, Granlund's late-night comrade and frequent visitor to that New Jersey ranch, summed up in florid fashion what patrons might expect at the Paradise: "Nightly, the headwaiter's heart was gladdened by big spenders, Wall Street Blue Sky artists, and scions of what was known as the 'idle rich.' Most of the show cuties had sables to cover their minks, and at least two of them rode to work in chauffeur-driven Rolls-Royces."[42]

Lee Mortimer shared Granlund's affection for the "dumb Dora stories," the malapropisms attributed to certain dancers in the chorus line. Vera Milton was often the butt of the Dora jokes; Mortimer reflected in his *New York Mirror* column that "one night while driving through the park in a taxi, her new boy friend let his arm rest negligently on her shoulder while he gave her the old buildup. 'You have marvelous potentialities,' he said. 'Hush,' Vera cautioned. 'The driver might hear you!'"[43]

Granlund claimed that Milton was studying the schedule backstage at the Paradise when he drew near, and she pointed out one of the lines in the order of the night's show: "I can't do that number. I didn't rehearse it."

"Which one?"

"That one," she answered, laying her finger on the word "Intermission."[44]

Such was the humor that was the mainstay of Granlund's stage routine. He continued drawing from that well for years, despite increasing criticism from patrons and newspaper critics. Granlund heckled both his audience and his performers, although it was never mean-spirited; one critic noted that Granlund had never received a "punch in the nose"[45] from any victim of his sometimes caustic comments. It was the only style of humor he knew, and the only line of patter that came easily for him onstage. It was only in his final years, when he was no longer making stage appearances, that he would admit that the "Dumb Dora" routine had become politically incorrect.[46]

Some things never changed. Granlund's penchant for women began following the Shubert philosophy early in Granlund's run at the Paradise. It was Jacob Shubert's more risqué *Passing Shows* at the Winter Garden that served as Granlund's indoctrination in 1924, and Shubert's belief that a nude or nearly-so chorus girl could make a mediocre show into a hit. Such thinking became Granlund's trademark. At the Hollywood Restaurant, where he expected a man and his wife to come have a low-priced good time, the chorus line costumes were daring but decent.

"In New York" columnist Paul Harrison pointed out that while the amount of clothing decreased at the Paradise Cabaret, the price of the experience went the opposite direction, although he seemed to express little objection to either. "For pure Broadway flavor," he wrote on October 18, 1934,[47] "noisy, crowded, clattering, speedy, tuneful, and unclothed — there's the Paradise. Mr. Granlund ... picks the prettiest gals in town. It's a long show, and costly, with an amazing juggler, a tap-dancing miss named Theo Phane, and other specialties. As one who never cared much about Messrs. Jimmy Durante, Lou Clayton, and Eddie Jackson, I am not one to sentimentalize over the madcap comeback of Mr. Jackson in this show. Measured by the applause, though, he is either terrific, or colossal, or maybe both."[48]

Among his later innovations at the Paradise, Granlund took a sixteen-year-old Brooklyn girl named Rose Zelle Rowland (a 1937 newspaper article spelled her name as Roselle Roland,[49] and another called her Rosie Rowland) and "covered her in shimmering coat of gilt paint" and nothing else. The girl was underage, but it should be noted that she was already performing at the Irving Place Theatre on 14th Street, and Granlund had viewed her act there as a favor to a talent agent. At the Irving, Rowland was wearing silver paint and a G-string. When he brought her to the Paradise, he promised to build a production number around her; Rowland assured Granlund that she already knew how to put on a coat of paint. He found a space in the storeroom for her — undressing room.[50]

"We got a huge tin tub,"[51] Granlund explained, "and I tipped a bus boy each week to see that she had three pails of hot water at the end of each performance, to remove the paint."

In December 1933 (Granlund remembered it as 1934), he was contracted by Clifford Whitely of London to duplicate Granlund's Paradise floor show, then called "The International Revue," to be staged in a tour of European capitals.[52] The show would play the Dorchester Hotel in London and Whitely insisted that the show include Granlund's painted chorus girl.

"We must have her,"[53] said Whitely, determined to reach a contract. Granlund believed the act would fail in London's Dorchester Hotel, where he expected "The Golden Girl" would have to be clothed, ruining the effect. Whitely persisted, however, and Granlund washed his hands of the responsibility. He auditioned the girls and negotiated each a contract with Whitely, remembering that "Goldie" was paid $200 a week for her show-all part of the show. News of his Paradise "Golden Girl" soon was being reported all across Europe, not necessarily for the floor show, but for the European royalty it attracted.[54]

Arthur "Bugs" Baer remembered the scandal in his 1937 column for Hearst newspapers. "The Golden Girl was just Rosie Rowland before Baron Empain took her off the standard. Now she is a Belgian baroness with a guest card to the Paris subway." Baer reminded his readers that Rosie was a former burlesque dancer, doing so in his own inimitable style, concluding with, "[W]e fear when the Golden Girl is 40, the Baron will change her for two twenties."[55]

The Belgian baron, whom Baer claimed had an income of "ten million waffles a year," was one of the wealthiest men in Europe and took Granlund's glittering dancer on a well-publicized, if scandalous, cruise aboard his yacht, the *Heliopolis.* Rowland became pregnant and Baron Jean Empain agreed to marry her, but died a short time afterward in Spain during World War II. The Golden Girl, who—when Granlund hired her—had been near penniless and living in a cramped New York City hotel room with her mother and two sisters—inherited the baron's financial empire and an elaborate estate at Chateau Bouffmont near Paris. She married again in France, to the baron's cousin Edouard Empain, who adopted her son.

"About half the girls I took to the Dorchester married and remained in Europe," said Granlund.[56] "It was the best indication of our popularity I can mention."

In a July 1935 report headlined "And No Wonder London Cabaret Girls Couldn't Take It," the competition of American showgirls was put to rest by British John Bull and the Ministry of Labor when he told them they would be required to "leave the country when their contracts expire."[57] The caption under the showgirl photographs identified Nancy Lyons and Louise DeForrest as members of Granlund's Paradise Restaurant show in New York.

Belgian barons and London nightclub clientele made up only part of the audiences during the Paradise Revue years. Granlund staged a show at the maximum security Sing Sing Prison for the benefit of Owney Madden, who was behind bars, as Granlund remembered, "to serve out his sentence like a gentleman, for a perfectly justifiable homicide."[58]

"It is highly doubtful that he was the one who fired the shots," Granlund said of Madden, who was convicted in the murder of a gang rival.

It is not difficult to imagine the sort of reception the scantily clad showgirls received at Ossining, New York, a penitentiary first called Mount Pleasant when it opened in 1828.[59] The prison was neither on a mount, nor was it ever pleasant. When Lewis Lawes took the job as warden in 1920, 33 of the 795 male prisoners were missing from their cells and never accounted for, and 20 of the 102 women. Another prisoner, behind the bars for five years, had no record of ever being admitted. He was declared to be a "volunteer," and immediately set free.[60]

The show at Sing Sing preceded the trip to London; Granlund took Clifford Whitely and his associates to the prison revue, for a taste of the traveling act they would accompany in their tour of the European capital.

Francis Towle, a Whitely associate, was concerned at the appearance of several women aboard the bus taking the show to Ossining and asked Granlund if they were part of the dance company. "Oh, no," Granlund replied. "They're just friends of some of the prisoners. They're going up to see their boy friends."[61]

Granlund situated Whitely and his associates on the second row of the prison auditorium, where they were surrounded by gang members, murderers, and thieves. Whitely was impressed by the reception the show received, but it is probable that that entertainment-starved prisoners would have cheered any act inclined to take the stage.

The prison patrons of that Granlund revue included Little Moe Sedway, who worked for mobster Meyer Lansky in New York, and George Jean "Big Frenchy" De Mange. Sedway began traveling to Las Vegas on Lansky's behalf in the early 1930s and is credited with accurately predicting that the resort town would boom with the postwar demand for entertainment.

De Mange was a former member of the Irish Gophers with Owney Madden; *Time* magazine described him in his October 2, 1939, obituary as "a cagey onetime hoodlum, highjacker [*sic*], and bootlegger, latterly a millionaire Broadway restaurateur (The Club Argonaut, Park Avenue, Silver Slipper)." He died of a heart attack eight years after Madden "scraped up $35,000 to ransom Big Frenchy when itchy-fingered Vincent Coll kidnapped him and threatened his life." *Time* noted that Owney was the chief mourner at Big Frenchy's funeral, "complete with six cars dripping with flowers."

Whether staged for hardened criminals or London's social elite, the work of running shows kept Granlund in the pages of the nation's newspapers. A syndicated piece in June 1934 noted it was "N. T. G. who started the first of the modern type of cabarets eight years ago."[62] Prohibition had ended by the time of the article's appearance, but Granlund was quoted in an another article as saying the drinking among college students had actually fallen off. "They do drink a lot less," he admitted. "During Prohibition they'd bring flasks and bottles and wouldn't stop until they'd finished every drop. Today they know they can't drink the bar dry, so they don't try."[63]

According to Granlund, attitudes changed after the repeal. "When Texas Guinan used to yell: 'Here's a college boy!' that was a signal to get him out of the place. Well, we still spot them and still put a captain or headwaiter to watch them. But they don't try to wreck the place any more — except maybe during football season."[64]

The reporter asked Granlund about his showgirls, and how they might have changed. "In the last few years," he replied, "an entirely new type of chorus girl has come along. They're clever, decent kids, interested in show business and ambitious enough to take dancing and vocal lessons so they can get better jobs. They have a strenuous routine, which means guarding their health, staying away from liquor and getting plenty of sleep. They are never permitted to sit with customers, or even to meet with them. In fact, the tragedy of their lives is that they scarcely meet any men at all."

Granlund's remarks indicate some awareness of the changing of his attitude toward some of his employees. He was no longer the tall, slim, and dapper "Broadway Swede" of his earlier days. He was 45 years old at the time of the interview, old enough to call his dancers "kids" with some legitimacy, although his age did not slow his affection for women in general, or — specifically — the showgirls who could be constantly found in his company. There were dancers in his shows, though, with whom he took a strictly patriarchal attitude. Toward the end of the college-student-as-nightclub-patron interview, the reporter noted that Granlund did not smoke or drink, having "no use for their sophomoric vices."

Granlund admitted as much himself. He was not a gambler, a smoker, or a drinker. But long-legged showgirls remained the one vice he would never shake.

Seventeen years— the amount of time Granlund spent working for the corporate entity founded by Marcus Loew — would have ended his run as publicity manager for the film chain in 1929. The work toward the latter part of his association amounted to less and less as time went on. "I was making so much money out of one job that what I made working for Loew was hardly worth mentioning," he said of the time leading up to the end of his association with the organization.[65] "I stuck with the Loew organization because I loved Nick and Joe Schenck and all my coworkers. There was never a definite break with them. My outside work occupied more and more of my time and less and less was given to Loew, and finally my time and my paycheck at Loew's stopped."[66]

He was replaced on Loew's WHN, but did not stay out of New York radio for long. In July 1935, an NBC press release[67] announced his return to the broadcasting studios: "[The initials N.T.G.] have come to denote one of Broadway's outstanding producers of nightclub revues and favorite masters of ceremonies. Now he is giving dozens of Broadway showgirls their first chance to become microphone entertainers in a new series of broadcasts over NBC networks."

Granlund, described in the release as "six feet tall, lean and spare, his hair thinning slightly at the temples," was by now carrying a slight amount of extra middle-aged weight, visible in the photograph that accompanied the announcement of his return. In addition, the media announcement took the opportunity to repeat Granlund's many "finds," including "Irene Delroy, Barbara Stanwyck, Claire Luce, Mae Clarke, Ruby Keeler, Frances Upton, Joan Crawford, and Alice Boulden." Added to that list are dozens of others who owed Granlund a debt for early career boosts, including Gwen Verdon, Jimmy Durante, Ethel Merman, Martha Raye, Sheree North, Ray Bolger, George Raft, Walter Winchell, Lee Mortimer, Clara Bow, Texas Guinan, George Jessel, Earl Carroll, Harry Richman, Yvonne De Carlo, Imogene Coca, Walter O'Keefe, Lili St. Cyr, Harriet Hilliard (of Ozzie and Harriet), and Jean Harlow, among others.

The NBC biography mentioned Granlund's studies at Brown University and his dramatic reporting work for the *Providence Tribune*, as well as his brief stint as a professional boxer "just to fill up his spare time." Under the name Kid Yelle,[68] Granlund boxed as a bantamweight, taking on Jimmy Fasane in a 1914 match[69] in which the lanky Swede's height "gave him a long left jab" and helped to keep him "in the ring despite his lack of punching power." Granlund also managed Frank Mantell, a middleweight contender, and Young Dyson, another prizefighter, and worked as the New England representative for James

J. Johnston, of Madison Square Garden, and also the two boxing Dans, McK-
ettrick and Morgan.

His return to the air, in presenting amateur-acts among the chorus showgirls, was called "N.T.G. and His Girls" and was broadcast each Tuesday night
at nine over NBC's WJZ. It was a time when radio networks scheduled programs on a weekly basis and had a programming lineup in the same manner
that television would later. Writer Paul K. Damai said the network viewed the
show with "mixed emotions."[70] NBC's president Merlyn H. Aylesworth called
Granlund's show "a capital idea, if it isn't carried too far. Remember, we cannot countenance scantily clad girls traipsing around the studios."[71] Damai
reported, tongue firmly in cheek, that Aylesworth's edict meant "no nudios in
the studios." Engineer Joe Blotz, whose position required him to monitor all
activity from the glass booth, described his participation as "a pleasure," but
James Wallington was skeptical, deciding that to announce the program successfully, "one must keep close concentration on the script."

By July, Damai had little good to say about the new radio show except for
Granlund's own portion. He wrote of the announcer whom he called an "old
showman":

> He opens and closes the half-hour with "Somebody Stole My Gal," played in
> stop-time by Harry Salter's band and accompanied by the tapping of a chorine
> line. Granlund has a smart kidding chatter and this is the one good thing on the
> program. It seems that before each broadcast NTG makes the rounds of the honky-
> tonks, picks up all the BVD blonds and sets 'em to coon-shouting with a "Sic 'em
> darling." (He calls all the girls indiscriminately "darling." And how they do shout.
> In fact, we think that there should be a B. L. added to NTG: then it would stand
> for Not Too Good but Loud!)[72]

Damai was not the last to associate such words with Granlund's often used initials.

In 1935, Granlund sat with his benefactor Charlie Sherman at a table in
the Abbey Club, an establishment originally opened by Texas Guinan after
leaving Larry Fay. Presently, a group sat down at the table near them; even in
the dimly lit room, Granlund recognized one of them as mobster Dutch Schultz.
The notorious gangster was entrenched in the Bronx, and lately had begun
moving his racketeering operations into Manhattan. From restaurant owners
in Manhattan, Schultz and his enforcers demanded money in exchange for
"protection" from beatings and vandalism. The attacks would come from his
own henchmen if the owner refused to pay. Sherman was among the Manhattan operators facing the extortion tactics employed by Schultz.

Sherman told Granlund to get up, as most of the customers in the club
had already done, quietly but quickly moving toward the exit. "Charlie, they've
planned this," Granlund said.[73] "They're going to get you. Let's call the police."

Sherman urged Granlund to get out through the kitchen to avoid a beat-
ing from Schultz and his men. Granlund never used the term in describing his

backer, but Sherman was widely known as "Chink" and "The Chinaman," and was armed with a pistol as he sat at the cabaret table. Before being beaten down, Sherman got off a shot that hit Schultz in the shoulder. Both gangsters survived, but the Chinaman's hand was irreparably disfigured.

Several months later, in October 1935, Schultz was gunned down at the Palace Chophouse in Newark, New Jersey.[74] The assassin, Charles "The Bug" Workman, forced his way past a bodyguard to gain entry to the tavern, opened the door of the toilet, saw a man, and shot him once. The Bug managed five years before he was sentenced to life in prison for the killing. Schultz managed twenty-two hours after the bullet-removing surgery was performed, then suc-cumbed to the effects of his infection-ravaged abdomen.

During those hours, Schultz — under the influence of morphine and a high fever — kept up a steady stream of rambling, one-sided conversations, which were taken down by a police stenographer. Among his babblings were references to Granlund's backer "Chink" Sherman. "Crack down on the Chinaman's friends,"[75] muttered Schultz at one point, and later, "Don't let the Chinaman get me."[76]

Several days later, Sherman was seated with Granlund at his regular table at the Paradise, when the headwaiter approached with a message for Sherman. Sherman mumbled, "This is it," before shaking Granlund's hand and walking out of their nightclub.

Charles "The Chinaman" Sherman was taken for a ride after stepping out of the Paradise Cabaret, leaving his partner Granlund sitting alone at the table in the back. It was the last time anyone at the Paradise saw its financier alive. Granlund later liked to describe how Sherman's "crumbling skeleton was unearthed under the dirt floor of a barn," and the only way it could be identified was "the tip of one little finger, a deformed, twisted little finger, pressing against the palm of the hand."[77]

A *New York Times* report offered another version of the discovery of Sher-man's body near the Catskill Mountains resort town of Monticello, New York, indicating that "a few days after Schultz's death, the body of Sherman was found, covered in a compound of earth and quick lime, in an abandoned barn." It was true that — in identifying the body — police were forced to use fingerprints "of fingers not yet destroyed."[78] The report also reported that, in their attempts to locate the barn's owner, police had uncovered a basement full of slot machines, and that the gang war had dated to 1930. Along the trail came the "discovery of the body of a man known as Davey (Frisco) Gordon" and well as the body of small-time New York hoodlum Samuel Medal (or Medow), the body of "Chink" Sherman, the body of a man known only as Jack, and the body of "a man named Sol Goldstein, who walked out of a Glen Wild boarding house in the summer of 1937 in answer to a telephone call and has not been seen since."[79]

The circle of violence in which Granlund operated the Paradise contin-ued for nearly two years and involved a number of mobsters being called on the phone before being "taken for a ride."

The barn in the Catskills was owned by a man named Jack Drucker, and from the confessions of two Brooklyn hitmen that came a full five years later, police hoped to include Drucker — who was questioned at the time, but released — in the indictments naming those believed responsible for Sherman's 1935 murder. Drucker, along with associates like Charlie "The Bug" Workman, were part of the group that the press dubbed "Murder Inc." and "Murder Incorporated," that carried out hundreds of killings on behalf of the mob from the 1920s to the 1940s.

Gone along with Sherman's presence was the protection that Granlund had enjoyed against the rival syndicates, and the clientele immediately began to change. Louis "Pretty" Amberg, given the nickname for strictly ironic reasons, was among the first to claim a front row table after Sherman's assault at the hands of Schultz's gang. Amberg, who — along with his brothers Joseph and Hyman — ran a racketeering operation in Brooklyn, would not trouble Granlund for long. The same day Schultz died, Pretty Amberg's body was found in a burning car, after he had been hacked to death with an ax.

The death of Charles Sherman came in much the same way. The November 5, 1935, wire service report in the *Syracuse Herald* carried a front-page banner headline proclaiming "Another Slain in War of Gangs."

Bloodstains on the highway led to the discovery of "a newly beaten path through the underbrush and to a deserted barn," which stood on the property of a former member of the Brooklyn Amberg gang. Sherman's body lay under four feet of earth, and examination showed "his head was crushed by an ax and he had been shot in the right arm." Police theorized that his death was a continuation of the efforts of "a powerful gang, supposedly headed by Charles (Lucky) Luciano, New York gangster, and Johnnie Torrio, onetime associate of Al Capone, to clear the metropolitan area of rivals."

The report did not mention Granlund or their nightclub, only the business address; and noted that Sherman's body "was found almost 100 miles from Broadway, where Sherman cut a conspicuous figure as an associate at one time or another of such underworld leaders as Waxey Gordon, Jack (Legs) Diamond, Owney Madden, and Arthur (Dutch Schultz) Flegenheimer."[80]

Granlund admitted later that the Paradise was "never the same" after Sherman's death. The business operation of the Broadway restaurant was almost immediately turned over to attorneys for Sherman's estate, a move that impacted Granlund's control of the enterprise.

"They weren't willing to give me the free hand that I had had with Sherman," said Granlund.[81] "It soon became pretty obvious that the Paradise had fallen on evil days. I had had over three big years in the merriest play spot on Broadway, but now the handwriting was on the wall."

Several months later, Granlund donned his brown fedora and walked out of the Paradise Cabaret for good.

· NINE ·

The Touring Season and the Sun

> Those who really desire to attain an independence have only to set their minds upon it, and adopt the proper means ... and the thing is easily done.
>
> — P.T. Barnum

The independence that Granlund experienced as a cabaret operator came after nearly twenty-five years of various associations, and he found himself at last, from a financial perspective, completely on his own. Dating back to his earliest days in Providence, he had enjoyed the security of one of the largest entertainment firms in the United States in providing for his room and board, his contacts, and his notoriety. Marcus Loew, in hiring Granlund as a publicity manager and giving him the confident backing — and media platform — that allowed him to grow into the ever-changing position, also served as an emotional security net for all of Granlund's endeavors. If something was less than successful, he could try it again, knowing that his employer would give him a free hand to try until Granlund achieved the level of success he and his boss expected.

When his ties to Loew's company diminished, other figures filled the gap, again providing security, even if — in the case of Charlie "The Chinaman" Sherman — it was security of a more literal kind, the sort that kept racketeering figures from preying on restaurateurs on Broadway.

With the deaths of Loew and Sherman, Granlund lost the financial and emotional support that had carried him into middle age.

Unlike many Americans, Granlund did not suffer during the Great Depression, and was actually in a position to provide assistance to many of the show business unemployed who came to him. Granlund walked away from the Paradise Cabaret with an enviable amount of money, and his revue income insured that he was not wanting in providing for his needs.

In addition to the nominal amount he received from NBC, Granlund collected from the advertising agency J. Walter Thompson, on behalf of Bromo Seltzer, a weekly $1,000 — an amount of money equivalent to over fifteen thousand a week in 2007 dollars. Granlund continued to collect for his floor show productions, and the demand for his appearances had never fallen off.

For the girls in the chorus line, there was no question as to loyalty. They had been hired by Granlund, and if he wanted them to continue in his employ, they were more than willing to leave the Paradise. Not every dancer did.

What Granlund had in mind was a coast-to-coast tour with the pick of the showgirls from the Paradise. His shows regularly merited coverage in the trade publication *Variety*. "N. T. G. parades his bevy of gorgeous girls in the usual nightclub setting here this week," the writer noted in the November 24, 1937, coverage of the show at New York City's Loew's State Theatre. "Atmosphere is created by shifting the house pit band on stage and fronting it with showgirls seated at a half dozen tables."

The critics were not always kind when it came to Granlund's style of humor. "N. T. G. (Granlund) makes himself seen and heard from the time the foots go up till they fold. His continuous 'beautiful but dumb' theme when introducing the beauts becomes rather tiresome and isn't overly funny."[1]

The critic did note, however, that seats were filled and the "Biz good." Granlund was compared to the "better *Follies* shows" regarding the showgirls and their costumes. The comment "Unit on the whole is entertaining" presumably includes *High, Wide, and Handsome*, the film scheduled on that evening at the State Theatre. The railroad tycoon movie was released by Paramount and starred Irene Dunne, Randolph Scott and Dorothy Lamour; it constituted 110 minutes of the 190 allotted for the entire evening's show, including Granlund's revue.

Criticism of the "girls aspect" of his new radio show *N.T.G. and His Girls* had the effect of changing the direction to include some non-amateur elements, a move Granlund made almost immediately after the show's initial broadcast. His July 23, 1935, show featured Mae Murray, a headliner of Ziegfeld's *Follies* by 1915, who had also made appearances in movies with Rudolph Valentino and other top stars for MGM. By the time she appeared with Granlund on NBC, her career had been in a steady decline. By the early 1940s she was appearing almost nightly at Billy Rose's Horseshoe Club, as part of the throwback nostalgia atmosphere he cultivated.

His inclusion of such personalities is evidence of Granlund's desire to cling to that period of Broadway history in which he was most comfortable, during the time-frame in which he enjoyed his greatest success. Network radio programming notes stated the obvious nature of Granlund's interview, describing the two as "Broadway chums in pre-radio days"[2] who "probably will discuss old times along the Gay White Way."

Even Granlund's health made the newspapers. Seated before the WJZ broadcasting console on the evening of September 10, 1935, Granlund faltered and then "collapsed before the microphone."[3] About halfway into the thirty-minute show he began to feel ill, and nearly made it through the program when he blacked out. He was quickly revived by studio personnel, and "insisted upon going on with the program," which he did, and only then was taken to the Medical Arts Sanitarium for observation. His condition was described by medical officials as not serious, having all the symptoms of gastroenteritis.

George Tucker, in his column "Man About Manhattan," still identified Granlund as a young man, although the Broadway Swede in 1935 was firmly entrenched in middle age at 45. Tucker called him "a quiet, tall, thin-faced, sandy-haired fellow. He is a veteran in the amusement field and has quietly and without telling about it nudged more young talent into stardom than usually falls to the lot of one man, however shrewd and energetic he may be. Joan Crawford is his masterpiece."[4]

Tucker noted Granlund's association with the Paradise Restaurant and credited him as the person responsible for the "superior entertainment." Clearly, Tucker was not as familiar with Granlund as other gossip columnists such as Lee Mortimer and Walter Winchell who often made reference to Granlund as the "Swede" or the "Lanky Lapplander." Tucker recognized that Granlund's voice differed from the typical New York accent, noting that although it would be "impossible to associate him with any place other than Broadway, he has a curious drawl which might easily identify him as a Texan."[5]

Tucker may have been fooled as to Granlund's origins by his frequent usage of such slang and casual introductions as "Let 'er go," a phrase noted by an early radio audience member who expressed his critique in a letter to the editor. The phrase is also preserved in a musical introduction in Granlund's onscreen appearance in the wartime film *Rhythm Parade*. The diction and vocal affectations of Granlund, raised in a Swedish-speaking household before spending his early adult years wandering the theaters of Brooklyn, the Bronx, and Manhattan, had a hard-to-define quality that would have easily been mistaken for a regional dialect. He may also have been affected by his time with the drawling Texas Guinan.

"His real value," Tucker continued, "may be conned from the fact that when the West Coast sent Jean Harlow east for a tour of personal appearances — long before she became a star — they looked the field over very carefully and then importuned Granlund to ally his revue with her act, so that she would at least have a capably arranged and fitting debut."

Harlow, the original "platinum blonde," hailed from Kansas City and initially gave up a fortune for a $55-a-week movie contract. According to Dan Thomas, whose column was syndicated by the Newspaper Enterprise Association, in her home town "Jean was a society belle and one of the few who would one day share her grandfather's wealth," but then she "got the movie bug."[6]

When Harlow was offered a $55 weekly contract by Hal Roach, "Grandpa burned up the wires with protests and ravings. But Jean stood firm." Thomas reported that Harlow called the contract offer "an opportunity I am not going to pass up on. I have tried the movies and I love them."

Grandpa had a change of heart when his lovely granddaughter caught the attention of Howard Hughes, who offered her the leading role in his film *Hell's Angels*. When she signed a five-year contract, her grandfather also reinstated her position in his will, although — ironically — he would outlive his movie-star granddaughter.

Harlow loved the movies and the movie audiences loved her. It might have been a match made in Hollywood heaven if not for the film critics, who somehow managed to look past her stunning physical beauty in almost universally panning her acting skills. Millionaire film producer and director Hughes owned Harlow's contract, but began loaning her out for appearances at other studios, and she had just finished playing a supporting role in the 1931 MGM release *The Secret Six*. It was also early work in the career of Clark Cable, another film newcomer at the time; his name did not rate a mention in many of the early ads for the Wallace Beery vehicle.

Granlund remembered his efforts on behalf of Jean Harlow as a favor to MGM executive (later company president) Charles Moskowitz, who had remained a friend since the New York days in the office of Marcus Loew.

"Charlie's call came at the weird hour of 10 A.M.,"[7] said Granlund. "Nightclub characters are sound asleep at that hour, or should be, so his call woke me up." Moskowitz was calling on behalf of Nick Schenck, who was afraid that Harlow was bombing in her tour of the Loew's-owned theaters, and he needed someone to work with her to polish her routine. Moskowitz offered Granlund $600 a week ($8,000 in 2007 dollars) to bring her back into favor with American audiences.

The trouble, Granlund believed, was the sexual tone of Harlow's movie appearances, which had drawn the attention of the Hays Office, a motion picture watchdog that predated the film rating system. Will H. Hays, an attorney who headed the Motion Pictures Producers and Distributors Association (which later became the Motion Picture Association of America), was cracking down on film content which he believed reflected the loose morals widely believed to be held by the residents of Hollywood. The Production Code, also known as the Hays Code, had been enacted in 1930 as a set of industry censorship guidelines, spelling out what filmmakers could and could not include as they addressed issues of morality and decency.

The critics took up the cause as well. Maurice "Red" Kann, editor of *Motion Picture Daily* and leading trade journalist, wrote in a "Special Dispatch" to the *Syracuse Herald* that Harlow's film *Red-Headed Woman* "carries sex into the open."

His July 2, 1932, report described the film as "very hot-cha" and added,

"[T]he picture is a 24-sheet argument for the primal urge, camera-angled so you can't miss the idea by MGM."

Harlow, by 1931, had already earned descriptive references in print as the "Blonde Bombshell" and the "Platinum Blonde," but for her appearance in the film's starring role, was required to make a cosmetic change, which Kann derisively noted: "Jean Harlow, no longer platinum, is supposed to have dipped her hair in henna for the title role. The picture is in black and white and so you can't prove it by us. We do know, however, that the platinum is gone in favor of something a trifle closer to the brunette and makeup has changed as well."[8]

Kann minced no words in delivering his opinion: "Lurid from beginning to end, *Red-Headed Woman* is no picture for family trade. For big town first-runs where audiences like their pictures plenty scorching, this looks ready-made."

In addition to the other monikers, Harlow had already been dubbed "the most dangerous blonde in pictures." The harsh press coverage that began with *Hell's Angels* continued unabated with *Red-Headed Woman* and Harlow's fans began reading on a regular basis articles that inferred that the actress was of low moral character. In an attempt to show another side of her, Harlow was booked into a series of public appearances at East Coast theaters at $3,500 a week. A four-week tour through houses owned by Warner Brothers was to be followed by six weeks in Loew's venues.

The Mastbaum in Philadelphia marked the final appearance in the Warner portion of the tour. Granlund found himself in the gloomy old theater, seated in the midst of an uninterested audience that had tolerated a chorus line presentation before Harlow's introduction. Granlund remembered her call to the stage as being "filled with innuendo about her sex and her voluptuous figure,"[9] and that the audience scarcely cared about the film actress who had appeared in some of the year's most widely publicized films. The slight applause generated by the act quickly died out.

After her portion of the act, Granlund found her backstage, already in tears and dreading the remainder of the tour. Although he had misgivings, Granlund expressed confidence that her performances in the Loew's theaters would be better received. The first show was scheduled for Loew's Metropolitan in Brooklyn, and he explained that his plan was to introduce her to the audience and then follow with a series of questions and answers, staged as though they were from filmgoers.

The two worked out the framework of a routine and field-tested it on radio announcer Major Bowes and Louis K. Sidney, an MGM executive, figuring that if the two conservatives were not offended by the content, then the routine was clean enough for a family audience. The dry run presented no reasons for change.

Granlund took the stage in front of a huge staircase which he had arranged for Harlow's entrance. It was an idea borrowed from Florenz Ziegfeld. "Take my word for it,"[10] Granlund told the restless audience, "she doesn't steal husbands like they make out in the movies. No, and just between us, she is scared to death because her whole future depends on what you think of her."

They thought she was great.

After the show, MGM executives Nicholas and Joseph Schenck greeted her backstage and offered congratulations. The tour continued with Granlund and the "Platinum Blonde" for the remainder of the six-week contract. When the RKO theater representative offered a ten-week follow-up deal to take the act through their chain, the Swede declined.

On September 6, 1932, Harlow's husband Paul Bern committed suicide at their home in Hollywood. The death came just days after the actress had penned a letter to Granlund. "Hello, N.T.G. Darling,"[11] she wrote in the note recalling their time together on stage. "I long for the five-a-day. Enjoying my first vacation ... I'm heading for New York as soon as I can."

Granlund believed that Harlow belonged to the bright lights of Hollywood, not the footlights of the former vaudeville stages. Her last film, 1937's *Saratoga*, was completed six years after Maurice Kann declared that she was not suitable as family fare, and just days before she died of uremic poisoning from kidney failure at age 26.

While George Tucker was reminiscing about NTG and Harlow, others were marking Granlund's tenure on Broadway. Friends threw a party for his thirteenth anniversary as a radio announcer in New York City, a career that the news columnist said began "with the cats-whisker sets when you strained an earphone to get a whisper across the wave-lengths."[12] Weeks after the party, Granlund renewed his contract with the Skouras Brothers, formerly of St. Louis, who extended his tour of the Fox-Skouras Theatres for an extra ten weeks.

One of the girls in his touring company, a moody dancer named Delores Dawn, met with a tragic demise that filled a full page of the newspapers of the King Features Syndicate. A beautiful girl determined to make a show business career for herself, she landed a job in George White's *Scandals* shortly after she arrived in New York, but according to her co-workers she was never happy. "At one time," the writer pointed out, "she entered the Paradise Restaurant nightly for two weeks. She would say hello to Nils T. Granlund, then the manager, but never utter another syllable. Finally, Granlund became curious. He asked her what in the world she wanted."[13]

"Please don't be angry, Granny," she answered, "but could you lend me five dollars?"

Always willing to lend a hand, Granlund immediately came to her aid. He had no place for her in the Paradise show, but he offered her a job with his touring revue company. When the show returned to New York City, however, she quit and found work in a New Jersey night spot. Later, she talked Granlund into writing a letter of introduction on her behalf, something she could present to Joe Moss at the Hollywood. "Noting a striking resemblance between

Delores and the famous showgirl Marian Martin," wrote the King Features Syndicate writer, "Moss hired Delores to understudy the latter. It was her last job."

On New Year's morning 1936, Dawn leaped from the window of her sixteenth-floor room at the Hotel Wellington, distraught over her dismissal at the Hollywood.[14] Moss had told her she was too moody.

Not all of the full-page press was depressing. Still managing his flair for publicity, Granlund staged a "Queen of Radio" contest, but he could not pare the field to a single winner. "Helen Marshall, Harriet Hilliard, and Dorothy Lamour, all singers, have been adjudged by Nils Granlund, noted beauty authority, as co-holders of the title of 'Miss Radio of 1936,'" wrote Lilian Campbell, whose syndicated column was carried nationwide, in February.[15] There was no indication in the story as to what prompted the selection, or who deemed Granlund as the final arbiter of the contestant's qualifications to hold the title. Marshall was a soprano described by Granlund as "a true beauty of the outdoor type." Lamour, he felt "typifies the classical beauty much in demand in Hollywood," and Hilliard, a "blues singer with Ozzie Nelson" the band leader, was "the perfect example of showgirl beauty." She became better known to television audiences later, when she was part of the long-running series *The Adventures of Ozzie and Harriet.*

Granlund began casting on a Monday afternoon in March 1938 for a new show, taking interviews at his office at the Hotel Des Artistes, a Gothic-style building off Central Park West at 67th Street. Hopefuls had the first part of the week of March 15 to make an impression. The touring company was to open at the Hippodrome in Baltimore on Friday.[16]

On the swing that took him through Chicago, Granlund collected a dancer named Claire Powell, whom he brought back to Broadway as his latest discovery. He described her as "one of the most beautiful girls he has ever seen."[17] He billed her as an "added attraction" for his Radio Girl Revue, which featured the Slate Brothers and Rita Rio, the leader of an all-girl orchestra who performed regularly with NTG before making a film career for herself in the 1940s and early 1950s.

Claire Powell did not fare quite as well. She left Granlund's revue almost immediately and took a spot in the *Follies*, but that employment was short-lived. By March of 1937, she was appearing for two nights at the Grand Theatre in Oshkosh, Wisconsin, where she would demonstrate the recent national fame she had achieved by appearing in a "series of instructive portraits" in a recent magazine issue. Her "special engagement" at the Grand was to demonstrate to "women the intimate details of how to undress properly before a husband."[18]

As for Granlund, he would be playing at that Broadway pinnacle, the Palace Theater, in a return to that heralded house of the revue-style shows that had been absent for some time. The reviewer, erroneously claiming continuing links between Granlund and the Hollywood and Paradise restaurants, might have been brought to that idea by the Swede's stage setup. His staging included "a cabaret set-up on the stage, with tables at which the performers are seated, and the theater orchestra on the boards also, forming both a musical and visual background for the various numbers."[19]

Granlund had to have been satisfied with the results. "The opening day audience was especially pleased with Rita Rio," the reviewer noted. "She opens with a blues version of 'Solitude,' which she breaks in the middle to 'swing it,' combining a great deal of hotcha dancing."

The revue included the Three Slate Brothers, an acrobatic comedy team; Wally and Verdyne Stapleton, tap dancers; and Sonya Katliarskaya, a "Gypsy-Russian" singer, as part of the hour-long bill.

In June 1936, with handkerchiefs mopping at the brows of members of the Fourth of July crowd at the pavilion, Granlund stood nattily dressed in front of his line of Palisades Park beauty contestants on the New Jersey side of the Hudson River.[20] For newspaper columnist James Aswell, seated at the judging table, this was one of the perks of his association with Granlund. To his left sat NTG's wife Rose and Lee Mortimer, another newspaper writer and long-time associate of Granlund, described as a "White Way man-about-town and newspaper raconteur."

More than likely, the account, which was distributed as a syndicated feature, was penned by either Mortimer or Aswell, and the column inches were enough to fill an entire page of any national newspaper. References to Granlund by name or initials managed to make about every fifth paragraph.

Following the death of Florenz Ziegfeld, the two Broadway names most closely linked with beautiful chorus girls were Earl Carroll, founder of the *Scandals*, and Granlund, the tireless touring impresario. That is not to say they were the only two offering chorus line entertainment. The Shuberts bought the name *Follies* after Ziegfeld's death and continued the tradition, and George White's long-running *Scandals* served as a launching stage for a number of later stars. It was Carroll and Granlund who found the lion's share of the newspaper press coverage, perhaps much of it at their own instigation.

When Miss America pageant officials placed the crown on twenty-one-year-old Marilyn Meseky, parading the Miss Ohio banner, Granlund and Carroll were outraged.[21] The two New York showmen shared the belief that the title should have been awarded to Miss California, nineteen-year-old Claire Jones of Los Angeles, who had been runner-up in the Atlantic City pageant. Taking matters into their own hands, Granlund and Carroll brought Jones to New York City and staged their own coronation in a lavish hotel ballroom, and presented the California titleholder with her own crown and an elaborate trophy.

The revues continued non-stop through the autumn and winter, and Granlund was described as the "non-stop talker" heading the program at the building that housed his publicity office for so many years. The day after Christmas, he brought his "Broadway Midnight Follies" to the Loew's State Theatre.[22] His enchantment with the Shubert plan for success called for his chorines to, as the reviewer put it, "confine their theatrical efforts to displaying expensive furs."

Fifty singers, dancers, comedians, and specialty acts filled the bill; still tap-dancing their way into the hearts of the audience were the Stapletons, who followed old-time variety player Frank Gaby, a voice-throwing, cigarette-smoking comedian. Rita Rio had exited in favor of Ruby Zwerling and the "State Senators," who provided the music for the evening's program that wound toward its completion while "Douglas and Magma, midgets, dance[d] engagingly."

It was as if Granlund would single-handedly preserve the ways of the Albee vaudeville stages of old.

Despite his earlier remarks regarding the new breed of chorus line dancers, Granlund had no desire to tamper with the formula that had brought him a degree of fame and financial security for so many years. In what should have been a dramatic lesson as to the changing tastes of the nightclub audiences, he was given a chance to return to the scene of his biggest success to date.

Things were not well at the Hollywood Cabaret. In fact, things were not well all along Broadway. (The year would later be judged as the most disastrous ever[23] suffered by the nightclub industry, in the city that invented nighttime entertainment.) Still under the ownership of Joe Moss, the Hollywood had become a sole-ownership when the second of the three original partners, Jake Amron, left in 1935 for an association with heavyweight boxing champion Jack Dempsey. For Amron, it was a fortuitous move — Dempsey's Broadway Restaurant, on 8th Avenue and 50th Street, became an institution across from Madison Square Garden and remained open until 1974.

Moss, who had assumed the entertainment directorship at the Hollywood when Granlund departed, was looking for anything that might bring back the crowds he had once hosted. It had been Moss's desire to change the direction of the Hollywood entertainment that provoked Granlund's departure, and it was with some swallowing of his pride that Moss contacted Granlund.

At age 47, Granlund pulled out all the stops in attempting a revival of his former crown jewel. His suave good looks graced the pages of the *Brooklyn Daily Eagle* on April 16, 1937, with the news that he and his revue would make a return appearance at the Hollywood. The picture of his dapper self was dated, showing the lean and debonair Granlund of an earlier decade.[24]

It was billed as "The Triumphant Return of N. T. G."[25]: Moss sprang for a series of extravagantly designed newspaper ads announcing "Gaiety Back on Broadway," in the form of a revue that would open Monday, April 19. It would be a special new show, the *Hollywood Revels of 1937*, with "Never Before Such Girls," and "Never Before Such Fun!" The "Event of the Year" would introduce new policies at the Hollywood, and a special ten o'clock show, in addition to shows at seven-fifteen, midnight, and two in the morning. Prices would be rolled back for dinner and supper, only $1.50, excepting Saturdays and holidays, down from the five-dollar-plus check amounts recently imposed. Experienced food service operators routinely note that the introduction of all-you-can-eat buffet-style dining, and dramatic reductions in prices for the same menu items, are often the betraying signs of impending failure.

At the Hollywood, there was "Never a Cover Charge."

Moss promised that the "Gay White Way will reach a new high in frivolity with the return to the Hollywood Restaurant of Nils Thor Granlund, the Whoopee King."[26] The *New York Evening Journal* writer, perhaps taking up the midway barker, vaudeville style that best suited an introduction of NTG, pointed out that "to uphold his unchallenged reputation as today's peer of pulchritude pickers, the beloved N. T. G. has recruited fifty radiant new faces and slim new figures from the hinterlands to make their Broadway debut in his show. These young, breathtaking new belles were discovered by 'Granny' during his recent vaudeville tour of the country, in which he broke all box office records. Most of them are college co-eds who decided to forsake the campus for bright lights and theatrical careers."

The "Sparkling Springtime Revels" offered Mitchell Ayres a chance to put his "Fashions in Music" orchestra through its paces while "masterpieces in magnificent beauty" would wear little else besides their looks. To his credit, Granlund selected a solid performer in Ayres, who—as violinist—fronted the group that was sometimes described as comprised of members looking more like mousy lab assistants than suave band members. Ayres was later music director for Columbia Records and worked on a number of television shows before being fatally struck by a car at a street crossing in 1969.

There were highlights, of course. Columnist James Aswell admitted that on the subject of nightclubs, he "cut loose and peeked into one the other night, for the first time in weeks, after much delightful hooky from the 'rounds.'"[27] The writer complimented Granlund's "clowning" in a particular skit that he believed belonged in a "big revue" such as Shuberts, and hoped that Moss, "who owns the tinkly Hollywood, won't mind the tip to a rival."[28]

For all his efforts, Moss was unable to keep his sinking ship afloat. After struggling through the summer and fall, the Hollywood filed a bankruptcy petition on December 26, 1937, listing $260,000 in liabilities,[29] a debt equivalent to 3.7 million dollars in 2007. A. & S. Restaurants, Inc., under which the Granlund-less corporation was operated, asked for time to reorganize in the face of mounting demands by creditors, a request granted by Federal Judge John C. Knox.

If the reorganization plan had hopeful backers, the New Year's season brought to them a tease of success. An extravagant evening party on New Year's Eve at the Hollywood Restaurant filled the tables to capacity, but the disarray that permeated the house the following morning might well have described the financial picture as well. Compelled by the court to meet the current business expenses on a cash basis, Moss was forced to admit a few days after the New Year's Eve party that he "could not go on under the reorganization."[30]

Described as "one of the first of the more lavish Broadway cabarets," the Hollywood Restaurant remained locked on Friday evening, January 7. The following day, *The New York Times* reported that the night spot "failed to open its doors," resulting in the loss of 150 jobs.[31] Moss outlasted two of his competitors in surviving beyond the demise of the French Casino, which shut its doors on November 22, and Mori's, a well-known restaurant at 144 Bleecker Street in Greenwich Village, which the Hollywood bested by only a few days.

Even if he could not save his former business associate, Granlund took the grand publicity that commenced with his return to the Hollywood and rode a wave of continuing press coverage for his personal endeavors. The *New York Mirror* posted the Swede's initials in bold print at the top of the page and above a photograph accompanying an article describing his opening on Friday, July 16, 1937, at the Brooklyn Fox Theatre.[32] Perhaps realizing that the once readily recognizable initials might have fallen from their peak of identification among readers, the caption noted "in case you don't know, it stands for Nils T. Granlund, popular master of ceremonies." The Broadway Swede, in his starched white shirt and tie, and vested three-piece suit, is seen smiling down at his showgirl "sweeties" Noel Carter, Ann Peterson, and Jessie Schambers. Carter, one of Granlund's regular touring dancers, married bandleader Gray Gordon, whose Tic Toc Rhythm Orchestra became famous at the Green Room, a night spot at the Hotel Edison.

In the same week, *Mirror* columnist Robert Coleman devoted a lengthy story to Granlund and his observations on the Broadway scene. "There's nothing wrong with the theatre," said Granlund. "Give the public what it wants and your box office will be kept working overtime."[33] The story-leading quote had a golden truth about it, with which no critic could argue. It was, though, a reality that Granlund suffered to achieve in its application. In his reliance on the type of entertainment that had worked well for him through the years, NTG was more inclined to tell the audience what it wanted, and then deliver those goods, which usually amounted to his often-repeated formula consisting primarily of scantily clad women. "Vaudeville, the old stereotyped vaudeville," he proclaimed, "is washed up, but a new form of entertainment has replaced it. This new form relies on speed, fun, excitement, novelty, and human interest to pack 'em in."

Although his description sounds suspiciously like the very vaudeville he had just declared to be "washed up," his seventy-week tour of northeast vaudeville houses with his troupe was a success after all, so much so, he claimed, that "eight people fainted in one day from overdoses of laughter in Cleveland."[34] Coleman, in his article, adds, "He has affidavits to prove it."

For Coleman and his readers, Granlund rolled out an extensive pipe dream, one that would have his philosophy of entertainment offered coast-to-coast, with Granlund perhaps envisioning himself as the heir to Marcus Loew's theater building ability. "Between playing vaudeville, appearing at the Hollywood, and running a New Jersey farm," Coleman wrote, "he is working out plans for a chain of amusement palaces to span the country."[35]

The plan, as Granlund explained, would have the shows opening in New York City, then heading around the country playing his private circuit, filling houses that would be redecorated by him to appear as gaudy as possible. Stages would extend into the auditoriums, and the orchestra pits would take to the wings to keep the performers closer to the audience. He would have tables and chairs to accommodate parties of two, four and six patrons near the stage. Those in the audience could smoke and talk as much as they liked while the players went through their paces.

If it sounded a lot like the Hollywood and Paradise restaurants, no one should have been surprised. Granlund could recognize that his highest level of success had come in those venues, and he was determined to use the formula to repeat his previous achievements.

He did manage a few astounding promises of legendary proportion, even for Granlund, proposing games of all types, swimming pools built under stages, and aquatic acts that would perform during intermissions. This, he believed, would combine all the features that the entertainment-seeking public wanted: vaudeville, music revues, amusement parks, and a nightclub atmosphere.

Readers were led to believe that Granlund had already sought the help of financial backers for the idea several years previously, and that the principals were told that the headliners for the initial touring show would be Jean Harlow, Bing Crosby, and Milton Berle. When one of the investors claimed to have never heard of the headliners, Granlund tore up the contract proposal and stormed out of the office. There is no evidence that such an investor's meeting ever occurred, but even if it didn't, the story made for good press.

As 1937 wound down, the newspaper ads pledged to deliver that grand-scale style of entertainment that Granlund kept promising, things like "Real Broadway brought to you by the man who rules Broadway — the king of New York Night Life!"[36]

Along with the daring photograph of a scantily draped showgirl, the bold NTG initials overshadowed his name in offering his "all-new thrilling, amazing, girl-packed revue — Broadway After Dark." The international comedians "The Three Sailors" topped the bill, which also featured Charmion, the famous "Queen of the Nudists," and Heloise Martin, "College Humor's Shower Girl." There would be appearances by the "Great Ziegfeld Girls," plus "Famous Art Models" selected by the world's most famous artists.

The smaller ads simply mentioned his presentation of Broadway stars at such spots as the Washington Arms on Boston Post Road near Mamaroneck,

New York. The idea was the same, however. Women in a large quantity. Clothing in a small quantity.

It is hard to imagine Granlund's style of entertainment as progressive, despite his claims to the contrary, when one of the final shows of the year received a December 22, 1937, review in *Variety*. In its journalistically clipped style, the critic of the Lyric Theatre show in Indianapolis could scarcely get past the sheer noise factor of the show, in noting that the performance began with Granlund "passing out noise makers to audience members and introduction of clothes horse girls who assist him. Girls appear later in tableau called 'Spring in a Nudist Camp,' in 'Bathing Beauty Revue,' and as stars of Ziegfeld shows, wearing costumes made famous in those productions."[37]

The house, only three-quarters filled, witnessed the same "face-slapping, gags, knockabout antics, and work" of the Three Sailors, the "apparently unrehearsed" tap dancing of Lina Basquette, and three singers "heckled so much by the Three Sailors that their turns are secondary." Near the close, a feature dancer named Janice Andre made a brief appearance for a nearly nude interpretive dance with red veils called "Dance of the Harpies."

The typical Granlund show-closer featured an audience participation act, which he believed cemented the audience in his favor with the inclusion of several of their own on the stage. In Indianapolis, it was the Big Apple Dancers, a dance craze which Granlund purported to originate, although the step had been cited earlier in South Carolina. The called-dance was performed in a circle to swing-type music. As Granlund continued to present it through the course of his onstage career, he believed the act was best served when "stooges" — as *Variety* called them — were brought from the audience to join with the company for the big finish. In a later show in New Haven, Connecticut, the "customers were invited on stage to Apple with the N. T. G. girls, but the going got a bit rough and the stunt was killed."[38] A roller-skating act filled out the remainder of that show's running time.

Eventually, the Granlund revues fell into smaller towns and smaller venues. By March 1938, he was booking his show into houses like the Liberty Stage in Zanesville, Ohio—a tradition-rich house that no longer drew top-flight acts.[39] As a New York City–based revue, the two-day appearance was given a lush pre-sell in the local newspaper, pointing out that a "four-day break in Granlund's schedule —following his Cincinnati engagement and prior to his Chicago one"— allowed him to make the Zanesville appearance.

The "King of New York Night Life," the paper claimed, "is one of the truly great figures in the amusement world. Friend of every well-known screen, stage and radio personality, he has started many of them on their road to fame. Today, he employs more beautiful girls than any man in New York, and has the cream of the crop to choose from for his stage revues."

While his show may have impressed audiences in Zanesville, *Variety* and its stable of reviewers found the Granlund parade to be one that had lost its glamour. At the Hippodrome Theatre in Baltimore, the first act "ran a bit too long," and "some of the bumps and grinds" as put on by the rumba dancers were "a bit too strong for family patronage." The Slate Brothers act was "okay," before the "inevitable bathing beauty parade, a bit off the cob by now." Corny may have been the heart of his style of his vaudeville-style entertainment, but Granlund's heart remained in the cabarets.

"I hadn't seen much of Broadway," he remembered, claiming that by 1938 he was well-set financially from his touring, but remained homesick for Broadway and held "a yen to open a place all my own, no employers, no percentages, no weekly salary."[40] Granlund returned to New York City with the intention of opening his own establishment, finally settling on the Winter Garden building where he had staged his publicity stunt for *Pleasure Seekers* years before.

Nineteen thirty-eight also marked the 300th anniversary of the founding of "New Sweden," the first permanent settlement in the Delaware Valley, an event that spurred Congress to extend an invitation to Swedish royalty. On June 27, Crown Prince Gustaf Adolphus and Crown Princess Louise of Sweden arrived to be met by the president and be escorted up the Delaware by a Swedish man-of-war ship. Several states with strong Swedish ties offered a history of the early American events, a lesson recounted to the upper chamber by Senator Ernest Lundeen of Minnesota.

"Forty-four years before William Penn landed in Pennsylvania, and six years before William Penn was born, a permanent Swedish settlement had been founded," he reminded the Senate. "William Penn bought land from three Swedish farmers, the Swenson brothers, for the site of Philadelphia, including the land on which Independence Hall was built and still stands." To memorialize the historical event, a monument would be dedicated at Wilmington, Delaware, a "gift of the people of Sweden to the United States in commemoration."[41]

Granlund, the Broadway Swede, enjoyed the attention given to his homeland along with his many fellow Swedish nationals, but personally saw in it a chance to capitalize. He told Elliott Arnold of the *World-Telegram* that the Swedish royal visit inspired him to bring some of the beauty of Sweden to Broadway, in the form of a restaurant he intended to open called — appropriately — the Midnight Sun. Having come from that area of the world above the Arctic Circle in which at least one twenty-four-hour period is devoted to either complete daylight or complete darkness, Granlund figured there was plenty from his homeland that could appeal to those seeking a trendy spot on Broadway.

The *Herald-Tribune* reported on July 9, "N. T. G. can't stay away from Broadway for any length of time." Noting that Granlund's new spot would be located next to the Winter Garden Theatre, the paper added, "Granlund went to a White House party in honor of Swedish royalty and that gave him the idea for a 'good-will' nightclub with a Swedish motif."

Elliott Arnold, from the wording of his *World-Telegram* assessment, had apparently only recently returned from a trip to Stockholm, and his lengthy description of the "beautiful and fantastic Skansen Park" assumed that much of its foreign beauty would be incorporated into Granlund's new venture, although there was not a single quote in the story from the showman. Arnold wrapped up his Swedish travelogue with the expectation that "some of this atmosphere N. T. G. expects to provide in his new restaurant."[42]

Granlund hired Joseph K. Stauffer, one of Sweden's outstanding mural artists, to create a Swedish theme in the restaurant interior. For this venture, the money came from the pockets of Granlund himself. He paid for extensive alterations to the site of the old Montmartre in the Winter Garden theater building, and continued to sell the idea to anyone who would listen as a place that would appeal to the palate rather than the prurient.

To the uninitiated, it might have been more of the same, but Granlund believed that his Midnight Sun could be more of a restaurant than a nightclub, and simply feature a little entertainment for the late diners. He also hoped that he could draw some of the Broadway entertainers to his place after their own shows, and coax them up on the stage. It did happen, on occasion. Primarily, as might be expected, on the stage would be Granlund and the famous "Glamour Girls."[43]

Billed as "America's Finest Swedish Restaurant," and located on Broadway at 50th Street, Granlund offered that Swedish contribution to the American gastronomic spectrum called the Smorgasbord. The buffet-style dining experience, which traditionally features a multitude of hot and cold dishes, could be had for $1.25 with shows four times nightly.[44]

New York Amusements magazine hinted that "Old Triple Initial has a triple threat in fine food, fancy femininity, and furious fun," while Danton Walker in the *Daily News* wrote, "[I]t's a long jump from the ice-bound mountains of Lapland, lit by the midnight sun, to the blazing lights of Broadway. Nils Thor Granlund has made it, and in between has managed to follow a dozen professions and live a life of adventure that would make one of Horatio Alger's heroes a little envious."[45]

Walker included a blow-by-blow account of Granlund's life story before concluding that although Granlund was a "veteran of Broadway, the New Midnight Sun, just over the Winter Gardens, is the first nightclub he has ever owned."

Granlund's new spot opened Thursday evening, September 15, 1938, and to hear some accounts, it might have been concluded that the flow of the Hudson River changed directions. According to the *Journal-American*, "[T]he crooked lane that begins at the Battery and winds up at Albany became Broadway again last night when [Granlund] came back to the Great White Way with

the opening of his new 'The Midnight Sun.' It was a gala occasion; it was a welcome home; it was a triumph for a man known wherever entertainment exists
and who stands among Broadway's best-beloved."⁴⁶

Naming the acts and giving a brief word of praise to each, the article concluded that "[i]t was N. T. G.'s opening, N. T. G.'s night. Celebrities? They
ranged from Tommy Manville to Prince Mike, the last of the Romanoffs! From
Eddy Duchin to the Three Stooges. They were all there. Broadway was Broadway again, N. T. G. was back!"

Manville was well-known at the time, particularly on Broadway, where the
heir to a manufacturing fortune trolled for wives like fishermen chase big-
mouthed bass. Three years after the Midnight Sun's opening, Manville netted
his fifth wife, the daughter of a wealthy Chicago lumberman who said, in all
frankness, "I'm not in love with Tommy — I'm just infatuated. I hope to fall in
love with him after awhile."

The *Journal American* reference to Duchin named the gifted pianist who
began with Leo Reisman and later led the orchestra that played the Central
Park Casino for five years, from 1932 through 1937. The Three Stooges were
the stars of scores of Columbia two-reelers; the comedic trio had also appeared
in the Shubert's *Passing Show of 1932*. By 1938 standards, it rated as a great
turnout. Dale Harrison, in his syndicated "My New York" column, wrote that
he believed the place to be an unqualified success.

> The screwier the show, the better people like it. The sentence is mine; the senti-
> ment is Nils T. Granlund's. Mr. Granlund is the Broadway authority on insanity.
> The other night one of the gentlemen seated at a ringside table in Granlund's Mid-
> night Sun — a crazy house with a Smorgasbord — was a doctor from the psycho-
> pathic ward of Bellevue hospital. I don't say he was there professionally, but he
> might have been. Granny, which is what the Broadway bunch calls him, has had his
> finger on the pleasure pulse for nearly two decades. Known as an impresario of girl
> shows, he actually is the Zeus of zanies.⁴⁷

Harrison could well have been Granlund's publicity agent for the glowing
terms in which he continued to describe the owner of Broadway's newest night
spot. The columnist went so far as to propose that it was Granlund who
invented the "Hello, Sucker" insult that became Texas Guinan's instantly recognizable catchphrase.

Granlund, he wrote, "has made a fortune and spent it. If he makes
another — which is quite likely — he is sure to spend that too. Little things
like money don't bother him." Ironically, the case of fortunes won and lost
would prove to be a source of major concern for the showman in later
years.

The syndicated columnist recalled the tradition of Granlund's largesse that
began during the hardest years of the Great Depression: "[I]t is well known
around Broadway that NTG invariably carries a hip-pocket full of five dollar
bills. When show girls come to him for jobs and there are no jobs, Granny's

routine is to say 'Sorry, baby' and press one of the V-notes into her hand. It's a very poor way to get rich, but you'd be surprised how many broke and desperate chorines are grateful to the Broadway Swede...."[48]

The Midnight Sun would be one of Granlund's shorter-lived endeavors. He continued with his traveling revues while operating the Midnight Sun, changing only the name of his chorus line, and retaining many of the same acts that he had recently taken on tour. At the Loew's State show, his sister-in-law Eileen Wenzel was a featured dancer.[49] But unlike previous performance advertisements in which the Granlund review always dominated the upper portion of the print, the Margaret Sullavan-James Stewart film *Shopworn Angel* received topmost promotion.

More and more, the movies had begun to draw more than the live shows. In the Brooklyn Strand, the *Variety* reviewer noticed a reversal of the recent trend, pointing out that the combination of live shows and film had been "doing fair" since being reinstated some six weeks previously. However, the critic claimed it was not due to any higher entertainment value, but only "because NTG's informal stuff clicks better in a spot of this sort. Fact that most of his unit commutes from his Midnight Sun nitery on Broadway gives plenty of opportunity for plugs for his spot."[50]

Teddy King handled the emcee chores at the Strand, but stepped aside to allow Granlund to take center stage with "Collins and Peterson, pseudo-comedians. They work along the lines usually found in NTG units, heckling each other, the acts, the audience, and anyone in sight. Some of it manages to be funny, rest is windy but the crowd goes for it." The critic noted that Collins is involved in a trumpet solo when Granlund and Peterson apply a "double hotfoot," a practical joke involving the lighting of a match secretly stuffed between the sole and leather-upper of a person's shoe, usually resulting in a jumping, high-stepping reaction in trying to extinguish the flame. It was typical of the lowbrow humor of the Granlund stage act.

It was in the 1938 revue that Granlund began the spinning audience participation portion, in which "stooges from the audience" could collect cash from NTG by volunteering to be spun into a state of dizziness. As *Variety* noted, "Final volunteer is the usual 300-pounder."

Although the reviewer seemed to have deemed the Brooklyn audience appropriate for the nature of the review, there were others who claimed otherwise. In a letter to the editor sent to *Variety* magazine,[51] one audience member took exception to the language incorporated into the performance.

> Several weeks ago we read good old vaudeville is being resurrected, or trying to. Since it had gone into oblivion, radio broadcasts have been a blessing. They bring to our home many of our favorite musical comedy, vaudeville, and screen stars. However, it was a treat to welcome vaudeville back to the beautiful Strand theatre.
> It might interest Mr. Nils Granlund to know that we Brooklynites have a measure of self-respect and hope to set a good example for our offspring. I must confess our children of today are swing-babies, or shall I say jitterbugs, and it is a pleasure

to see them dance to the rhythm of Tommy Dorsey, Benny Goodman, and Russ Morgan's music.

However, the stage show was not fit for man, woman, or child to see, regardless of color or creed. The comedy team — if you can call it comedy — which Peterson and his partner sent over the footlights— every other word was either h — l or d — n and I was surprised to hear N. T. G. join in on that sort of language. The suggestive conversation that was carried onstage, I believe, was as embarrassing to those poor kids doing a four-a-day as it was to our group of ladies out front.

I remember when the actors' dressing rooms held a notice, "no profane language." I am not an old maid or religious fanatic. I laid my old gray bonnet away a long time ago and we join our small fry in all their festivities, but I was requested to write you. Please help us to enjoy the real vaudeville days....

The show at the Loew's State again brought proclamations from the *New York Enquirer* announcing that Granlund was "back" on Broadway. The Murray Korman publicity shot that accompanied the article offered a pre–*Casablanca* Humphrey-Bogart-as-Rick pose, complete with an upturned trenchcoat collar, fedora, and a "Here's looking at you kid" solemnity that infers more in the way of foggy Moroccan sendoffs than flights of New York festivities. It was the same dour expression that accompanied an announcement of his inclusion in the *Daily Mirror* Benevolent Society's dinner at the Hotel Astor.

Onstage, though, Granlund could loosen the neckties of even the stodgiest patrons. When the mayor and councilmen of a small Pennsylvania town traveled to New York on a junket that included time on Broadway, they filled up on the Midnight Sun Smorgasbord. According to the *New York Times*, five minutes after Granlund's appearance on stage the men "were wearing baby bibs, all of them, and cavorting about the floor like mad. If other Broadway joints afford relaxation to the tired businessman, the Midnight Sun is where he lets his hair back down."[52]

No one was above Granlund's needling, and he managed to keep most of his crowds laughing at his heckling and teasing. Most of the time his victims laughed right along, caught up in the general craziness of the atmosphere.

In a March 1939 column, *New York Times* critic Theodore Strauss noted that tired businessmen could seek out girls in a number of places, and at the Midnight Sun, "N. T. G. has girls, lots of them, but he seems to have something else and it seems to work." Strauss called the formula "Everybody join in!" and noted that Granlund's audiences seemed to follow the recipe, thinking nothing of the fact that Granlund "loudly admits his performers are lousy, though by no means as 'hammy' as he is. Standing at the microphone, he moans, groans, whistles, and chirrups insinuatingly: 'Now you see it, now you don't.'"

Onstage with the Swede at the time were Chiquita Estella, "climbing through her ruffles to do a rhumba," along with Yvette Dare, who with the assistance of "a salacious old parrot, divests herself of sarong, etc., while N. T. G. explains the significance of it all."[53]

That low-key cajoling displayed by Granlund onstage disappeared at his receiving word from old pal Lee Mortimer that the death knell had sounded for a member of the Broadway family. For all the events that would transpire in the following twelve months, it might have proven prophetic.

Auctioneers would officially sign the death certificate of the Hollywood Restaurant by offering for sale all of the fixtures, silverware, wall hangings, kitchen utensils, and appliances. Mortimer, in a 1939 column for the *Sunday Mirror* magazine section, memorialized the one-time Broadway landmark and featured photographs of showgirls, auctioneers, and portraits of stars who had performed there. Standing before a table of "expensive silverware" in the feature photograph were Granlund and Jake Amron,[54] described by Mortimer as "its first owners," along with three showgirls who had danced at the nightspot. Joe Moss was conspicuously absent.

"Those were the good old lusty days," lamented Mortimer, recounting the time when patrons smuggled in flasks of liquor to mix with the restaurant-provided "set-up," an ice-filled glass of cola, soda, or water. "During the Hollywood's first four years, Prohibition was still in effect. The club's largest seller was ginger ale. Three thousand bottles were sold nightly at a dollar a bottle. The stuff cost two cents wholesale." According to Mortimer, the Repeal brought about stiffer competition, and that—combined with Granlund's departure to open the Paradise, and Amron's partnership with Jack Dempsey—left a changed atmosphere in which Moss struggled to operate.

"Casts and employees couldn't be paid on the glories of the past—came the auctioneer," wrote Mortimer of the once-lively nightspot. "Requiescat in pace."

• TEN •

Ending a New York Era

> There's a sucker born every minute.
> — David Hannum (attributed to P.T. Barnum)

Financial recovery from the Great Depression took many forms, and a group of New York businessmen that included banker Winthrop Aldrich and Mayor Fiorello La Guardia supported the idea of creating a large-scale attraction that could draw crowds from abroad in addition to the U.S. attendees. The 1939 New York World's Fair remains one of the largest of the global expositions ever to be staged, and a tremendous amount of advance publicity insured that the event would be familiar to all.

In his May 24 column, George Ross reported on plans by oil millionaire and movie producer Howard Hughes to use his penchant for airplanes to promote the upcoming New York exposition, noting that Hughes "thinks he ought to chip in his talents toward helping the New York World's Fair, and so, leaving cinematic concerns behind, he proposes to get into his own plane some time next month, taking off from Le Bourget near Paris, and paying a personal call upon each European capital."[1]

Granlund would fly in the opposite direction. His intention was to hold his own personal exhibit at the New York World's Fair, the subject of which would be — to no one's surprise — beautiful showgirls. *Variety* announced his intentions in a brief note on April 12, 1939, that was datelined Hollywood, California: "Nils T. Granlund is due here tomorrow (Wednesday) from New York to line up 24 film girls, eight specialties, and four old-time picture names for his N.Y. World's Fair 'Congress of Beauty.'"[2]

On April 14, wire services carried the story of the return trip for Granlund and his "Eleven Beauties," who shivered in the wind, their "teeth chattering like castanets"[3] as photographers snapped away. "It wasn't modesty that caused the girls to shiver," the reporter noted. "Impresario Nils Thor Granlund shooed them out of their clothes in front of an interested gallery. Two of the girls demurred, but when it was explained that they had to weigh in for the flight, they capitulated."

"Just like a prize fight," said one of the girls.

"You bet," said Granlund. "The Department of Commerce is touchy about overloading a plane."

Not coincidentally, underneath the discarded clothing, the showgirls wore the exact costumes they would exhibit in their appearance in Granlund's "Garden of Eve" exhibit at the fair.

In Albuquerque, the costume was that of an Indian princess, and Granlund again garnered news coverage when his West Coast search for showgirls left Hollywood for Dallas. At a stop in New Mexico, the producer selected Kay Gater, a "blonde cashier at the Pay Less Drug Store," as his "Real Indian Princess." In the photograph, taken on the tarmac of the TWA terminal, two cowboys on horseback are seen twirling lariats overhead to "rope some of the beauties."[4] Once again, Granlund's uncanny ability to draw press coverage landed his efforts on the front page of the newspaper, complete with an oversized photograph with scantily clad women.

Granlund had only recently signed a contract for two shows that he would stage during the run of the World's Fair, the "Congress of Beauty" and the "Aztec-Sun Worshipers." Granlund's proposed shows, along with another announced attraction, the luridly titled "Amazons in No-Man's Land," were among the presentations *Variety* editors deemed part of a "major trend expected to be prevalent at the fair, the exhibition of girl shows."[5]

For his Aztec segment, Granlund planned an Indian girl ballet and other outdoor activities "à la nude ranch," with World's Fair visitors watching from behind glass. The planned glass enclosure became something akin to a livestock enclosure. Granlund's second show was scheduled to be in a small theater that would seat some 1,500 paying customers, who hoped to glimpse the skimpy-costumed revue members representing all parts of the country, the results of Granlund's talent search, and aided — as Variety pointed out — by Busby Berkeley and Earl Carroll.

No longer able to access the deep pockets of gangland backers, Granlund enlisted Charles Hertzig of the Metropolitan News Company to provide the financing. Hertzig, who in 1900 pooled his money with that of Myer Rosen, Louis Weinstock, Joe Kalmanoff and Morris Eisenman to begin the newspaper enterprise, surely intended to profit from the venture. He and his delivery partners had taken their early cash investment and rented a basement at 172 Henry Street, where the young immigrants bundled the four Yiddish daily papers they carried. The horse and wagon delivery business carried copies of the papers to far-flung uptown trade locations. In their first year, the five grossed $150,000[6] — a figure that rose to nine million dollars annually by 1950. Later, the five businessmen provided papers at their cost to a youngster named Dave Sarnoff, who sold copies to street-vending newsboys at a ten cent profit. Sarnoff later became chairman of Radio Corporation of America, or RCA. The Metropolitan News Co. survives as a philanthropic foundation.

Hertzig might not have realized what sort of program he was backing.

When Faith Bacon signed with NTG, her "fawn dance" routine was described without hesitation as being part of "the Fair's nudity sweepstakes." Della Carroll, whose "Streets of Paris" act fell through, signed on with the Granlund stages as a "featured N. T. G. nude." Music would be provided by two bands contracted by Meyer Davis, a bandleader and recording artist who originally led his own orchestra, but found it more profitable to hire musicians whom he contracted out as society-circuit performers. Several versions of the Meyer Davis Orchestra might perform on any given evening at various weddings, balls, and political galas.

The Aztec-Congress of Beauty exhibits found a comfortable location within the "amusement zone" of the World's Fair, a section allowed to remain open after the rest of the exposition shut down at ten P.M. and to maintain business operations until three in the morning. Exterior and interior lighting throughout the amusement zone allowed around-the-clock shows, if the organizers would have allowed it. Estimates placed the occupancy of the quadrant of the fair at nearly a quarter-million at any given time.

It would be a peep-show paradise.

Alongside the Granlund exhibits would be Jack Sheridan's "Living Magazine Covers," a voyeuristic second-floor window through which robe-draped models could be viewed powdering their long legs; the "Artist's Colony," a walk-through exhibit that would feature actual painters in addition to the nude—or nearly-so—models; and the "Arctic Girl's Temple of Ice," which would feature a model supposedly frozen in a block of ice.

Viewed from the tram, the panorama on the opposite side of Fountain Lake would have appeared to arriving fair-goers as an alien city of the future, with dramatic spires and buildings of experimental shape and color, viewed over the tops of open-air tour boats jammed with sightseers crisscrossing the small body of water.

It was everything that the promoters had promised, even when seen from afar: windmills from Holland, lighthouses from the rocky shoals, flags and tents, castles with parapets, Victorian London storefronts, giant garish paintings, and teeming crowds drinking it all in. Dignified barkers in suits and ties tempted the constant crowds with the wonders that lay just beyond the ticket-seller's counter. Guily-Guily, the King of Magic—clad in his red fez and the glittering drapery of his silver costume—and his lovely assistant produced seemingly unending lengths of silken kerchiefs from his mouth and caused rubber balls to disappear into the very air.

For the weary: a ten cent foot massage. For the inquisitive: a copy of the *New York Post*. There were tawdry shows and scientific wonders, zoological exhibits and a bathysphere, all side by side under the umbrella of Amusements, through which passersby walked and tractor-driven trams carrying loads of human cargo maneuvered. Exuberant nude statues posed atop curving spires with chromium wings appeared ready to carry the entire structure skyward. What might have been a preview of Disney's "Tomorrowland" occupied a huge theater building labeled "Time-Space," painted with swirling planets and a fiery sun. Beyond the wandering clowns and Keystone Cops were long-legged promoters of the Enchanted Forest and tiny, bikini-clad dancers offering exotic moves that could only be seen through the wrong end of a telescope.

Granlund would have appreciated Morris Gest's "Little Miracle Town," the Jewish-American theatrical producer's final show business venture, in which he showcased the "World's Greatest Midget Artists." The "little people" could be seen at play and at leisure, dressed in military costume, natty shirts and ties, and floral print dresses of the pre-war era, in proportionally correct but tiny houses constructed to accommodate their size.

Johnny Weissmuller, Hollywood's Tarzan of the Apes, appeared at Aquaworld, if not in person, then at least in the larger-than-life smiling mural, while bands performed nearby for the dance moves of the spirited Rosebuds presented by Billy Rose.

Beyond the merry-go-rounds and dancing monkeys of Children's World, past Eskimo World and the Arizona Cliff-Dwellers, fair-goers could be exposed — quite literally — to the world of Granlund and his Amazonian Aztec showgirls. In his corner of the World's Fair, those who had never before glimpsed a daring Broadway show would encounter — all in the name of art — topless women in exotic headwear, posing in the briefest of G-strings, with or without an accompanying Charles Atlas–type bodybuilder. In their sometimes-awkward poses, the models strained to moderate their breathing to enhance the illusion of a living photograph, holding stock-still within the large painted frame that served as the magazine until the lights finally dimmed and they could relax. At times, reacting to the whispered comments, the models broke into smiles or laughter before recovering and resuming their mannequin-like stances.

Robert Coleman offered an even-handed assessment: "This is a revue combining the best and worst features of the nightclub, vaudeville, and burlesque," he wrote in May, describing emcee Gladys Clark as a "brassy blonde" who introduced a startling collection of women trained in the art of undressing, although he noted that "most of the featured girls don't have much undressing to do." Among them were Della Carroll, who came dressed in a bouquet of roses which were plucked and tossed to audience members; Yvette Dare, who enlisted the aid of a parrot in removing her costume; and Faith Bacon, whom Coleman described as having "no protection from the Spring breezes" as she conducted her interpretive dance.[7] Two of the dancers were arrested on June 22 for indecent exposure, and photographed wearing overcoats as they were escorted away by police.

As a fair patron, Coleman liked best the singers and dancers who maintained their modesty in giving their performances, and joined the audience in giving the comedians "the good old razoo. N. T. G. would do well to sweep them out right away."

The "Congress of Beauty" show that was intended for a small indoor theater was instead presented in a large tent. It offered a miniature forest through which "students of human anatomy may stroll along pastoral pathways and witness some 75 scantily clad and easy-on-the-eyes damsels at play."[8] Coleman, before leaving the exhibit to file his story, overheard "one first-nighter" say to his companion upon leaving: "Remind me not to take my wife to this."

Variety turned in similar sentiments, if perhaps slightly more forgiving. "The authentic Aztec ballet is a robust dance production piece, having to do first with the femme (Chiquita), then her sweetheart (Galvan) and finally the blonde goddess (Jean Carmen) being thrown into the sacrificial flames by a giant ape (Emil Van Horn). A fantastic idea, well staged."[9] Giving credit to stage manager Dave Gould, *Variety* called the staging and dance numbers "top flight" while noting that the "opening night mechanical difficulties were surprisingly few."

The Aztec Sun Worshipers, having little beyond nudity to offer, gave critics little to work with. The May 31, 1939, review called it the longest walkthrough at the Fair, complete with an artistically landscaped garden around the main tent, inside of which "nudity is stressed," with no attempt at a revue or performance, but merely "a chance for the strolling visitors, at 25 cents per, to inspect feminine charm at close range. Compared to other shows displaying undraped femininity in marching formations, etc., NTG's outdoor exposition promises to become a prerequisite on the out-of-towner's list of midway stops."[10]

Granlund expressed satisfaction at the Congress of Beauty, although his participation was kept to a minimum. While the World's Fair continued its run, he busied himself at the Midnight Sun and his regular rounds of touring revues through the theaters of New York City. He told columnist Robert Coleman that he planned to talk to Lee Shubert about bringing the exposition to a Broadway stage, at which time he would add another fifty minutes to the show and a couple of vaudeville-style comedians. (Granlund continued to find comics in favor, even if his audiences found them increasingly tiresome.)

His revue at the Shubert Theatre in Brooklyn in April 1939 was crushed by the *Variety* critic, who began with the fact that the show started late and played to an audience filling only the first three rows of seats: "The N. T. G. revue [is] dirty and lacking in talent. In presentation and content, in work and action, it's burlesque. But burlesque makes no pretense of hiding under another name, whereas N. T. G. is presumably playing to family audiences in a residential [neighborhood]. A couple of N. T. G.'s cracks during the show are 'He turned pansy' and 'You look like a broken-down fairy.' Though a gentleman farmer, Granlund isn't referring to horticulture or elves. Nor does he walk behind Collins to prompt him; nor does that cause Collins to rise on his toes merely for the purpose of stretching."[11]

There was no respite in the assault. Calling out the fact that the dancers were on loan from the Midnight Sun, the critic derided Granlund for failing to introduce the women by name, but only calling attention to Eve Arden and her veil dance. That dancer was the same Eve Arden who would be nominated for an Academy Award for Best Supporting Actress for *Mildred Pierce* (1945) and gave an Emmy Award–winning performance on *Our Miss Brooks* in 1953. She had appeared in the *Follies* as a dancer in 1934.

The *Variety* reviewer, perhaps bent on panning Granlund, saw none of Arden's potential in her Brooklyn performance. "Her talent lies strictly in her sparsely clad chassis. The 'dancing' is merely a monotonous manipulation of the veil to give the audience an occasional peek."[12] Watching from those front three rows was a small audience, almost entirely men. Their up-close appreciation for the performing arts might have been greater than that of the *Variety* critic who called Marion Wilkins' Moorish dance routine "very poor," the singing of Dorothy James as nowhere near "her looks," and the dancing of the White Sisters as mere "contortion work." For the comedians, Granlund's reliable team of Collins and Peterson, the writer reserved his harshest criticism. "They are strictly in the burley idiom. Usually funny, they are laughless in this spotting."

Just beyond the psychological blow came a physical one. In the early morning hours of August 11, 1939, Granlund was driving from his World's Fair exhibit, traveling west on the dark pavement of Sixty-ninth Road. In his car was 28-year-old Tex Walker, Thompson Hill, 26-year-old Paul Winkler, his 25-year-old wife Ruth, and one other. Unbeknownst to Granlund, another car packed full of Fair patrons was heading south on West Drive. The intersection of Sixty-ninth Road at the Grand Central Park Extension was cluttered with a high, overgrown wire fence, set near the roadway in an area of dense trees and shrubs. At fifteen minutes before four o'clock Friday morning, the two cars collided at that intersection.[13]

Behind the wheel of the second car was light-heavyweight boxer Gus Lesnevich,[14] a New Jersey native who turned pro in 1934. The Lesnevich automobile was also filled to capacity at the time of the accident; three of his six young passengers suffered injuries, including 18-year-old Frances Dobson, 23-year-old Dorothy Garrity, and 21-year-old Joseph Lombardi. Beatrice Augenti was eighteen when she climbed in the Lesnevich car in the early hours of that Friday morning. She died at twelve-thirty that afternoon.

Police investigating the crash made no arrests, and gave offered no explanations as to the probable cause. Ten days later, they changed their minds.[15] Detective Edward Hattrick of the Newtown police department charged Granlund with criminal negligence in the death of Augenti, and the Broadway Swede was taken into custody at his Congress of Beauty exhibit. He was driven to the Newtown station in Queens and booked on the charges.

Hattrick told Magistrate Anthony P. Savarese that the arrest of Lesnevich was imminent, and that between the testimonies of the two parties, the court, "upon hearing all the evidence, might decide whether which, if either, of the drivers should be held responsible for the death."

Granlund was released into his own custody, and in Queens Felony Court on August 21, Magistrate Savarese determined that "there may be some civil responsibility here on the part of one or both drivers, but that is a matter for another court. There is nothing in the evidence in this case to indicate any criminal negligence on the part of either driver. Both are discharged."[16]

Following their fateful meeting, and the subsequent court ruling, the lives of the drivers involved in the accident took dramatically different directions. Gustav George Lesnevich continued to box out of Cliffside Park, New Jersey, and in 1940 took on Billy Conn, the National Boxing Association light-heavy-weight champion. Lesnevich lost by decision. A year later, in a bout against Anton Christoforidis, then the title-holder, Lesnevich punched his way into ownership of the champion's belt by decision, and held it until 1948 when he lost by decision to Freddie Mills. Lesnevich was named "Fighter of the Year" by *Ring* magazine in 1948, and served — while he was the reigning light-heavy-weight champion — in the United States Coast Guard from 1943 to 1945.

Six days after the court decision involving the fatal car accident, Granlund shut down both his New York World's Fair exhibits. Three months after the court's ruling, he would face a civil lawsuit filed by relatives of the young woman who died in the crash.

Claiming that the Fair operators were charging "exorbitant" rates, Granlund ended both his Congress of Beauty and Aztec exhibits, letting go all 120 of the affiliated employees.[17] A *New York Times* article of August 27, 1939, called the Congress of Beauty "one of the largest amusement concessions at the World's Fair"[18] and an attraction that had paid some $30,000 in rent and percentages since opening on May 27. Granlund was quoted as claiming the Fair officials had given back only enough money to meet payroll and an insufficient amount to pay creditors.

Granlund asserted that the presentation by the Fair of a bill to the Congress of Beauty in the amount of $1,487 for electric installation had been preceded by the continual issuing of bills for smaller amounts. "We are perfectly willing," Granlund said, "to carry on and pay the World's Fair their ten percent of our admission charges, but they insisted that we pay other charges so absurd and unjust it is impossible to continue."[19] Among the other fees to which Granlund objected were a $50 per week assessment for water, $35 for garbage, and $22 for ticket stubs.

To add further injury to insult, Granlund was punched in the face in a dispute over his publicity photo bill. The newspapers made light of the former boxer's inability to hold his own with the "little man" presenting the bill.[20] "The cabaret producer, known also as N. T. G., today caused the arrest of Herman Marcus, 38, sales manager for a photographic firm at 13 W. 36th St., on a charge of disorderly conduct. In West Side Court before Magistrate Masterson,

Granlund, 6 feet, two, and towering above the 5 feet, six defendant, said Marcus had struck him several times."

According to the report, Granlund showed the magistrate his discolored right cheek as evidence of the attack, which he said occurred in his own office in the RKO Building on Sixth Avenue. For his side, Marcus told the magistrate that he had come to collect a $500 debt from Granlund, owed for some photographic portraits delivered by the studio, and that he "had only pushed Granlund."

The father of the late Beatrice Augenti pushed Granlund as well. A week after Gus Lesnevich successfully defended his title against Tami Mauriello, the boxer appeared in court in Hackensack, New Jersey, wearing dark glasses to conceal a deep bruise over his right eye. He was to testify in a civil suit that claimed both he and Nils Granlund were negligent in the August 11 accident.

The jury ruled on November 19, 1941, that Granlund was at fault in the crash, and ordered that he pay $5,000 in damages[21] to Henry Augenti of Fort Cobb, New Jersey. Augenti had sought $50,000 of both drivers, but the jury held Lesnevich blameless in the crash.

The beginning of Granlund's New York downfall predated the World's Fair fiasco.

Unknown to many of Granlund's friends and supporters, his venture into the dangerous waters of proprietorship had crashed into the myriad rocks and invisible dangers so near the surface in the case of celebrity restaurant owners. Granlund was no chef, no saucier, no kitchen manager. Gauging from his free-spending habits and his lack of concern over the prevailing pay scales for performers, Granlund was lacking in accounting proficiency as well. His shoot-from-the-hip ideas had been largely targeted at the front of the house, dealing with tables and chairs, the size of the dance floor, the stage location, the type of entertainers, and the determination of which orchestra to engage in filling the room with music.

The press, he could handle. He was a publicity-savvy entertainer who had invested all of his money in an enterprise that was, in effect, being run by others spending his money for supplies and payroll, while his own contribution was more and more often being viewed as old school.

A week after his gala Midnight Sun debut, when Theodore Strauss of the *Times* was just getting around to mentioning that Broadway socialite Prince Mike Romanoff was seen there on opening night, the writer could not resist a couple of quick jabs at Granlund and his dancers, whom he said should be "seen and not heard."

"When it comes to anything much more than parading," he said of the supply of chorus dancers, "they tend to confirm N. T. G.'s pretty tiring remarks as to what dopes, as he puts it, they all are."[22]

Even the "prince" was better seen than heard. One of the most overt of the world's impersonators, Mike Romanoff claimed to have been born Prince Michael Dimitri Alexandrovich Obolensky-Romanoff, a nephew of Russian Tsar Nicholas II. Most of his later associates in Hollywood knew better. He was, in actuality, Hershel Geguzin, a Lithuanian immigrant who worked as a pants presser in Brooklyn before taking up the more profitable trade of impersonation. He first changed his name to Harry F. Gerguson and then discovered that his dreams of a better life could become reality just by claiming to have one. Russian royalty was not so far removed, by his estimation, from Lithuanian peasantry, and — passing himself off as a member of the Russian royal house — he gained admission to elite society company to which most would be excluded. Through his observations, he learned enough to be called upon by Hollywood moviemakers to serve as a viable consultant for films with European settings, and was well-paid for his work. Later, he opened the popular Romanoff's Restaurant in Hollywood, where he regularly entertained the film crowd.

Whether Strauss was aware of the charade is unknown, but his remarks in observing "the kid himself was on exhibition at the opening last Tuesday of Nils Thor Granlund's new spot" indicate the sort of respect and pedestal-press held in reserve for true royalty.

The Midnight Sun, within weeks, was a royal Swedish mess. While Granlund continued to pay the same rates for his chorus girls as the Shuberts and Earl Carroll, he was earning the payroll money through appearances at other venues. On December 5, 1938, scarcely more than two months after his opening, the business enterprise Swedegran Restaurant, Inc., operating the Midnight Sun with Granlund as president of the corporation, filed for voluntary bankruptcy,[23] proceeding under the recently created Chapter XI of the Chandler act.

In June 1938, just six months previous to Granlund's filing, Congress amended the codes dealing with bankruptcy, allowing for the reorganization of public and privately held companies as a means of survival.

Granlund, facing liabilities of $38,720 in addition to contracted debts for advertising, leases, and publicity totaling $68,608, proposed a monthly installment plan that could commence the following February. The $100,000+ liability figure in 1939 is comparable to $1.46 million in 2007, when adjusted for inflation.

In the course of six months, Granlund had taken a lesson in business economics at the hard school, where diplomas are called experience.

Taking his revue on the road once again,[24] Granlund continued to beat about the circuit for audiences that would respond to the burlesque show that he called vaudeville. It was in the face of waning public sentiment for such shows, particularly when tickets sold for the revue went to families and children.

Billy Rose, the New York City entertainer and club owner, in a piece written for the *American Weekly* news syndicate, declared "the Nudity Bubble has burst, and today many of the dancers who juggled it are looking for barrels."[25] (The "barrels" of his reference were the often-presented vaudeville stage answers for a lack of clothing, a large wooden keg hung by suspenders from the shoulders.) Demonstrating his flair for alliteration, Rose continued: "Burlesque, bulwark of bawdry, is badly bludgeoned," and cited a time when posting a "For Men Only" sign guaranteed audiences to the point of posting a secondary sign noting SRO — Standing Room Only.

"The peepshows of both World's Fairs have also made a discovery," said Rose in the August 5, 1940 article. "The public no longer pays a quarter to see a naked girl. Don't you believe it? Neither do a lot of so-called showmen — and they're tottering a few steps further Over the Hill to the Poorhouse every day."

Rose, who was forty years of age at the time of his observations, recalled having seen the great names of the Burlesque Era, and those performers who made their way to the legitimate stages of Broadway and Hollywood. "From time to time," he continued, "the producers tried to cleanse their stables, but the moronic herd they had wooed (and which had driven out the respectable middle-class element) wouldn't put up with it." According to Rose, the lowbrow audiences forced producers to compete for the "bluest" gags, the most outrageous and suggestive skits, and the barest of costumes. He cited 1928 as the year the true strip-tease was introduced and "Naked Nature, as raw as a bowl of chopped onions, became burlesque's big selling-point."

"A Night at the Moulin Rouge," which Rose called a "nude and lush revue," exemplified to the showman the inability to profit with nudity on the legitimate stage, losing $50,000 in eleven weeks, and playing to an audience of 118 on opening night in Davenport, Iowa. "The public has been doing a lot of wholesome, serious thinking," Rose observed. "You can't make much headway in show business trying to lead public taste — you've got to follow it."

His comments very nearly mirrored those of Granlund of not-so-many months previous, reflecting on the changing face of entertainment. Granlund, however — as noted by several reviewers—continued to produce the same burlesque tradition of old, while simply calling the shows by more acceptable names.

"In spite of the loud protests of the strip-tease press agents that strip-tease is an art," said Rose, "to me it is just plain baloney. I could teach any girl in 30 minutes to do the act. All she has to know is to strut back and forth on the stage and pull a few zippers." Rose included the World's Fair trade in his observations. "Things have drastically changed since 1939," he wrote, eight months into 1940. "The Congress of Beauty, run by [Granlund], closed in the middle of last season despite the charms of fifty nude beauties." He also noted the absence of skin-shows like the Crystal Palace and its nude entertainers Rose Royce and her dove dance, the Amazons, Frozen Alive, the peepshow Crystal Lassies by Bel Geddes, and Salvador Dalí's conception, the Dream of Venus— all of which shuttered after the turn of the year.

According to Rose, more than a half-million dollars was lost on the Fair's amusement zone due to the failure of the strip-shows. Newspaper column-inches and magazine pages that were once devoted to the "art" disappeared; he attributed this to changing American values and more conservative tastes among theatergoers.

Variety did devote a column to Granlund's early 1940 show at the State Theatre in New York City, perhaps due to its annual nature and the tenure of its run. It showed no particular kindness for the sake of tradition. "The routines are poor," wrote the critic, "and the revue starts like a turkey, but before it's over the audience, rather than the production, is doing the gobbling. Granlund this outing leans more on talent than on flesh-display, and that's the chief reason for the show's click."[26] The reviewer believed Granlund was merely lending his name and experience to the six-showgirl revue, repeating his Broadway cabaret routine of tossing noise-making clappers into the orchestra area seats to lend a nightclub feel to the afternoon performance.

By the time his cross-country revue reached the West Coast in March, Granlund found ample room on a stage near Hollywood and Vine. As late as August 1939, a restaurant in the vicinity of one of the best-known Hollywood intersections was hosting private dinner parties. They were not gala, blow-out events that featured glitzy stars and cigar-smoking movie producers, nor were they boisterous, cake-erupting, bachelor parties. The Florentine Gardens might rent out for the evening to allow (say) a doctor and his wife to stage a family-and-friends get-together for their son's birthday.

Owner Frank Bruni booked Granlund and his revue for a series of shows in hopes of increasing the night trade,[27] and his first outing received a salute from *Variety*: "Granlund's first Hollywood nitery pitch should click nicely if the present pace is continued,"[28] the critic wrote on March 20, 1940. "Show is breezy and smart, rolling up a neat score on the entertainment side. Specialties are first rate and the line of 20 girls perform with dash and aplomb." The writer noted that Granlund was "all over the place, bobbing around the tables" as he worked the audience.

Still, Granlund relied on the voyeuristic qualities of his acts to sell the show. In his first outing at the Florentine Gardens, it came in the guise of a basketball game played between chorus girls outfitted in short shorts and sweaters. "Audience participation is given a heavy play," the *Variety* critic continued, "probably engendered by its success in radio. Males are drawn from the tables for conga lessons with the girls, and, as a laugh-provoker, several oldsters are run on with baby bonnets covering their conks for a round with the cuties."

The show described by the opening night critic is virtually identical to that reviewed years before in New York City, in which patrons donned "baby bibs" and crawled about the stage. If nothing else, the Granlund formula was strong in its consistency.

Other writers, viewing the West Coast act for the first time, tended to be generous, apparently for the sake of nostalgia. The Florentine Gardens, described in a 1940 magazine article as "off the beaten path of clubs frequented by the movie set," had hosted the Granlund revue for two months at the time of the writer's visit. "Hollywood is becoming more like Broadway," wrote the author, "the Broadway I left about seven years ago. This section of Hollywood Blvd. hasn't the class and distinction that it once boasted, and the tip-off is that Grauman's Chinese Theatre, once an ace two-a-day movie house, has gone grind."

The writer cited the impending demise of the Florentine Gardens, rescued from its fate by Granlund and his "bevy of beauties," who in eight weeks time had turned the establishment around and was drawing the interest of the movie crowd. Having witnessed the Granlund Broadway revues, the writer found himself in familiar territory: "When I entered the Florentine Gardens, N. T. G. was on the floor doing his stuff. I might have been back at the Hollywood Restaurant on Broadway, for Granny was giving out the same stuff. He looked a little older and his face was a little fuller, but N. T. G. still has the same line of chatter and the same enthusiasm, and all the girls looked exactly the same to me — although later I learned that it was a whole new crop. But they did look the same: blonde, scanty costumes, their bodies covered with white powder and a black and blue mark on a thigh."[29] While the writer demonstrates a clear fondness for the revue he recalled from his days covering the nightclub scene in New York City, his nostalgic turn notes the same routine that East Coast writers covering Granlund's routines on a regular basis had come to regard as tired or stale.

"When I entered," he continued, "N. T. G. was giving out with a line of chatter about the girls, the orchestra was blazing away, and the girls were singing a ditty that went on like this: 'Your wife's at her mother's, so have a good time. Hello, stranger, hello.' The chorines would rush to the ringside tables and shake hands with a stranger.

"I knew what was coming."[30]

Anyone who had ever seen a Granlund revue would have known what was coming. His reliance on audience participation and his poking fun in the direction of the elderly or the overweight served as the basis for his show closer, a spinning, dizzy patron, or public display of group buffoonery. "There would be one sucker in the crowd," explained the writer in his May 15, 1940, piece. "One old man who would like a chorine and start holding her hand and talking to her. There's always an 'Uncle Henry' in the audience. Sure enough, Granny spotted one old man...."

"Go ahead, Uncle Henry," Granny shouted to him. "Get up there and dance and have a good time."

As was his custom, Granlund would incorporate his "Uncle Henrys" into the remainder of the evening's entertainment, reminding him to have his good

Presenting NTG's dancing beauties

Featured dancers at the Hollywood Florentine Gardens as depicted in the nightclub program for "Gayeties of 1942" from "America's Premier Cabaret Impresario," Nils Granlund (courtesy McHuston Archives).

time while he could, and face the music from his spouse later. The chorus girls knew the routine as well, and throughout the show took time to direct attention, along with dramatic embraces and kisses, to the showman's patsy. "Uncle Henry" could enjoy the attention even at the expense of the embarrassment of guests at the table. Before the evening's end, at least one of the showgirls would plant an obvious lipstick-enhanced kiss on the forehead or bald spot of the guest, as a souvenir of the evening.

There was enough positive response to his act that the Granlund revue was extended at the Florentine Gardens. By the fourth month, Granlund was looking for long-term living quarters.

Harry Carey, one of the giants of the silent film era (who later won an Academy Award for his performance in *Mr. Smith Goes to Washington*), was among the movie crowd set that found Granlund's revue at the Florentine Gardens early on. He was on his way to New York for an extended performance and worked a deal with Granlund, offering to swap residency at his Los Angeles ranch for quarters at Granlund's New Jersey home.[31]

A review in *Variety* from a writer seated in the very same audience of

May 15, carried a completely different reaction from that of the magazine writer. "Second edition of what NTG must laughingly call a revue is about as hodgy-podgy a conglomeration of misdirected effort as has cavorted in any of the better grottos in some time. And Granlund can take the full rap, net."[32] The writer laid blame for the failure of the acts and dancers solidly at Granlund's feet, citing his "constant interruptions and bellowings from uninvited tables." It was "chaos and disorder," as Granlund slapped the derrieres of his showgirls and kept up his line of patter, eliciting reactions such as "ain't he a card?"—which the writer believed to be an act hardly suitable for the suave Hollywood clientele.

"Such crudities belong in the joints with long bars or deep in the alfalfa belt, but it's no go with the home guard. It's much too corny and as dated as burlesque,"[33] wrote the critic, who advised Granlund to take a walk over to the establishment of Earl Carroll, a two-year veteran of the Hollywood scene, that he witness the proper manner to present a nightclub revue.

"Taylor and Allen are ballroom dancers who offer nothing that hasn't been done before and better," he continued. "Lorraine de Wood doesn't live up to Granny's billing as a terrific chanteuse. Sugar Geise, a shapely, cuddly blonde, is billed as a 'Hollywood Institution.' Information, please. She sings and dances so-so, but her stock in trade is to look and act cute."

Not only did the Dave Gould–choreographed production numbers lack precision and demonstrate "careless rehearsal," the chorus girls were spotted between numbers in street dress, sipping drinks and dancing with the customers, something that Granlund vowed never occurred among his troupe. The *Variety* critic took exception to the practice as well, noting "that biz was ruled out of the cheap joints along Skid Row by the police commish."

Still, there were others who had never been exposed to that wacky, zany Swedish showman, and could write with honesty that Granlund "brought with him a new idea in nightclub entertainment, the keynote of which is informality. The audience joins with the chorus to perform some of the dance numbers, the cast kids the customers and N. T. G. kids both the cast and the customers. Every night is party night at the Florentine Gardens."[34]

In the accompanying photographs, Granlund is shown at the microphone among the dining patrons, with a caption stating

A 1942 portrait of Granlund accompanying a biographical sketch in *The Playgoer*, the program of the Florentine Gardens revue (courtesy McHuston Archives).

"Granlund is famous for his heckling remarks to the customers." Other photographs show customers taking part in the "baby" number and the "Be a Farmer" number, in which men don oversized cowboy hats and end up in someone else's dinner jacket.

Heckling, the sort of humor managed with glamourous good-nature by Texas Guinan in her emceeing days and after World War II by New York comedian Don Rickles, became Granlund's signature style as he brought himself front and center in headlining the revues. Guinan managed to inject her femininity into the jabbing remarks, taking off any cutting edge, while Rickles learned his trade by responding to hecklers in his own audience, in the manner that comedian Jack E. Leonard had done earlier. Rickles may have owed his caustic-flavored success to the support of singer Frank Sinatra, a powerful figure in entertainment circles, who loved Rickles' act and promoted him among his show business acquaintances.

Granlund, perhaps no longer considering himself simply the emcee, favored the "beautiful but dumb" insults that he scattered among his chorus girls, tossing them such lines as "Will you go to my dressing room and see if I'm there?" at which point the dancer would quickly skip offstage, as though carrying out his nonsensical request. His insults among the customers included the older "Uncle Henry" types, bald heads, and oddities. "Granlund figured out his most recent insult last week," wrote Frederick Othman, "when Mrs. Robert Montgomery appeared at his nightclub in weird-looking hat."[35]

"All evening I kept looking at that hat," he said. "I'd just go over and stare at it and not say a word. Pretty soon the people began to snicker whenever I'd look her way. When she was about ready to leave, I walked over to her with a bottle of champagne and I said, 'Lady, here is your prize for the screwiest-looking hat ever seen in this joint.'"

So long as the girls and the audience played along, Granlund's method of humor worked fine. It was not the sort of routine based on jokes, witty repartee, or snappy comebacks. He had a series of lines that he relied on — no matter how many times he brought them out and dusted them off — to elicit what he hoped would be a positive response among his patrons. They were lines that worked best the first time an audience heard them.

The insults worked well enough for the Hollywood crowd that the film producers asked to use the Florentine Gardens revue as the basis for a musical comedy entitled *Rhythm Parade*. There was little to the wartime movie beyond the NTG stage and his dancing revue, but it brought additional attention to the nightclub. He claimed to be disappointed that he couldn't heckle the movie audience like he did at the Florentine.[36] "People like to laugh," said Granlund. "They'll laugh at an actor, but they'd rather laugh at somebody sitting in the next seat."

According to the Broadway Swede, Monogram Pictures declined to call its ticket-buyers "saps," and as a result *Rhythm Parade* would be a "musical movie, sans insults."

Frederick C. Othman wrote in his September 24, 1942, piece that Granlund "had shows in six different clubs run by six different gangsters. NTG insulted everybody, gangsters included. Nobody's shot him yet."

To his credit, Granlund had brought the Florentine Gardens out of the doldrums. He still managed to attract positive press alongside his original dismal revues, largely on the attraction of his chorus girls, who were more than willing to pose for cameras in whatever clothing Granlund required. His longtime friend Lee Mortimer continued to do his part, flying out to visit Granlund in February 1942 and bringing back pictures and stories for the New York *Sunday Mirror* in which a laughing and casually dressed Granlund is seen in the company of several chorus girls, looking comfortable and fit. Those stories were picked up by wire service syndicates to be carried nationwide.[37]

Others, like Louella O. Parsons, a Hollywood gossip writer for the International News Service, was among his earliest supporters[38] and in a column marking his one-year anniversary in Tinseltown, described him as "the dynamic Nils Granlund."

The year included a rocky start and some unkind words, but enough first-time customers could be found at Hollywood and Vine that the revue was always fresh — to *some*body. Events in the near future would provide an almost-endless supply of new "stooges" who had time to kill, money to spend, and an active interest in long-legged chorus girls.

Eleven

Boom and Bust
at the Gardens

Without promotion something terrible happens: nothing!
— P.T. Barnum

The bombing of Pearl Harbor came on December 7, 1941. Much of Southern California experienced an immediate transformation of machining and manpower — and not just men. The "Rosie the Riveter" campaign brought women into the workforce in record numbers to fill jobs formerly held by men. Los Angeles and surrounding areas experienced an unprecedented growth, not only in population, but in manufacturing and service industries as well.

Some of it began before the bombing of the American ships, the event that would draw the United States into World War II. Howard Hughes, the Texas oil millionaire now better known for his moviemaking and aviation interests, set up his Hughes Aircraft Company in Playa Vista, California. Douglas Aircraft had already established a plant at Santa Monica, and before the U.S. entered the war had opened another facility at El Segundo. A former employee of Douglas, Jack Northrop used the same locale for the opening of his own company, Northrop Aircraft, near Mines Airfield at what would later become Los Angeles International Airport. Long Beach increased its manufacturing base with an expansion by Douglas Aircraft in that city in 1941, and before the war's end, had 160,000 employees scattered among their three major plants in Southern California.

The ports of Long Beach housed the U.S. Naval Shipyard, and ports at that city attracted the men and women who would become shipbuilders. Los Angeles experienced a 35 percent increase in population in certain demographics during that same time, as workers — many of whom had been out of work since the height of the Great Depression — moved to California to fill the booming employment rolls.

Many of those who relocated did so on a temporary basis, leaving families behind to mind the children or the farm, while living in Southern California as economically as possible in an effort to send money home. They came from all parts of the country, but many were those from the hard-hit heartland, struggling farmers and ranchers for whom the Depression had been especially devastating. Among the relocated Midwesterners were a large percentage for whom it represented the first opportunity to visit the part of the country they had seen in the movies and read about in the gossip columns.

Just about everyone had heard of Hollywood and Vine.

When the opportunity presented itself, it was not so far to travel for the chance to see a movie star, or just to visit Hollywood in collecting memories to take back to the Heartland. Some had paychecks, substantial and regular, for the first time in years. Some had not had the opportunity to experience any significant manner of entertainment, recreation, or vacation, since the onset of the depression.

For Granlund, the World War II years would be an economic boom of unprecedented opportunity. Not only did the doors of the Florentine Gardens swing regularly in welcoming the nightly trade, those who passed into the nightclub were — for the most part — people who had never experienced the type of show that Granlund had been offering for decades. They were "green" and the exact sort of patron that could best enjoy the riotous version of burlesque that Granlund had honed into personal routine.

It was an opportunity to which Granlund could devote his full attention, and without distraction. In August, Jimmie Fidler asked in his syndicated gossip column "Fidler in Hollywood," "[H]ave nightclub star NTG (Nils Granlund) and his missus reached an understanding?"[1] The gossip item was in reference to Granlund's appearances without his wife and in the company of others. The couple, having survived the difficulties of double careers, could not do the same for double coasts. Rose remained in New York with her sister Eileen after the Los Angeles experiment for Nils extended beyond a year. "I agreed to go into the Florentine Gardens for six weeks just to see what could be done,"[2] said Granlund. "The six weeks stretched into six months to five years before I finally left."

True to form, he immediately upped the pay scale for the chorus girls at the Florentine Gardens in an attempt to draw higher caliber employees than the ones he found when he arrived. The girls of his touring company, for the most part, all returned to New York, requiring Granlund to fill his production with an entirely new set of dancers.

The Broadway Swede later wrote to his old friend Lee Mortimer in his continuing search for beautiful and talented showgirls. "Expected to be in New York by now," Granlund wrote to Mortimer, which the columnist reported in the *Daily Mirror*, "but am working on a new show with Paul Whiteman to open here December 3. Business still terrific and approaching colossal. (I now talk Hollywoodese.) I was going East to find showgirls and possibly dancing girls.

There isn't a showgirl in Hollywood as pretty as Adele Jergens. Adele would knock 'em dead here. Practically every kid in my show is doubling in films and making plenty. Least they earn is $16.50 a day extra, mostly more."[3] The daily pay quoted by Granlund would equate to $244 in adjusted 2007 dollars.

Among his recent Hollywood acquaintances was Sam Ledner, who headed the dance department at Paramount Studios for fifteen years; Ledner, a New York native, had recently wrapped up work on 1942's *Holiday Inn*. Granlund told Mortimer that the "big shot at Paramount is great to my girls and gives them plenty of work. Any accepted New Yorker who comes out here will do great in pictures."

Always one to drop names, Granlund wrote to his friend that many of his former dancers had been by to visit, some asking for contacts in London to hire on with revues entertaining troops in Europe. With his background in publicity, Granlund knew that there was little more appealing that the chance to be seen with movie stars, or to be in a place where the stars themselves went to be entertained. "Rudy Vallee," Granlund continued, "now in the agency business, comes in regularly with John Barrymore. Great Profile's ad libbing from the ringside is sensational, but largely unprintable."

Barrymore had recently starred as Evans Garrick, an actor of renown with a penchant for drinking, in the 1940 release *The Great Profile*. As Granlund continued his brief correspondence with Mortimer, he was able to name-drop an additional half-dozen Hollywood stars and notables who had visited the Florentine Gardens: Errol Flynn, Rex St. Cyr, Lady Furness, Gloria Vanderbilt, and Jimmy Stewart, who came in wearing his Army uniform. At nightspot Slapsie Maxie's for a celebrity birthday

Granlund in a portrait commemorating his 96th consecutive week as producer at Hollywood's Florentine Gardens (photograph by Maurice Seymour, courtesy Ronald Seymour).

celebration, Granlund claimed "everyone in Hollywood nightlife was there," including comedian Milton Berle.

It was not all perfect among the Hollywood nightspots. "Copacabana closed," Granlund reported. "Sorry to see Mario fail here. You know the Silver Screen closed some time ago, but the Wilshire Bowl opened up again with a low-priced policy and show seems to be doing very well."[4]

The closing of the Silver Screen might have hit a little close to home for Granlund. The nightspot, owned by John Murray Anderson, had a cabaret atmosphere that exploited the movie industry. Anderson, like Granlund, presented such novelties as sirens, slapstick, bathing beauties, Keystone Cops and glamour gals in a production primarily intended for tourists. It was much in the same fashion as the borderline-burlesque being presented by Granlund at the Florentine. Still, he continued pushing his brand of showmanship, claiming yet another producer was trying to convince him to take another vaudeville show on the road. Granlund felt there was a new and increasing demand for live shows such as his, and believed that Charlie Koerner of RKO Pictures was moving his studio in a similar direction.[5]

Ever the planner, but confined to his tried-and-true itinerary, Granlund regretted his lack of opportunity to return to New York City. "Above all," he wrote to Mortimer, "would love to get back to the Big Street a few days—and nights—and browse around and see my old friends. Two years since I've been back. Believe Broadway is ripe for big, colorful girl-shows and fun. Lack of laughs and party-spirit killed most of the big places on Broadway. Laughs and gals—that's a surefire formula."

It was pure NTG.

Leading up to the wartime economic boom, Granlund and his New York Broadway acquaintance Earl Carroll had the two cabaret-type shows making the biggest marks in Hollywood, before the short-lived venture of Anderson at the Silver Screen. It was a circumstance that columnist Paul Harrison found to be puzzling. Apparently, Harrison had not been privy to the conclusions presented by Billy Rose and others regarding the burlesque-renamed-cabaret-shows.

"I don't know why some such entertainment hasn't been presented before,"[6] Harrison wondered. "[Carroll and Granlund] both are conducting large, glittering dens of skin in Movie-town, but their offerings are the sort you'd find anywhere from Chicago to Miami. Granlund goes in for the bareness and bantering, while Carroll still favors the type of show in which lush Amazons strut around carrying stuffed pheasants." Ironically, the primary focus of Harrison's article was Anderson's Silver Screen nightclub, which was using Hollywood names as part of his filmthemed scheme, and failed long before troubles began for Granlund or Carroll.

Plenty of comparisons between the shows of Granlund and Carroll offered the accurate — if simplistic — view that Harrison concluded. Still, both nightspots experienced a previously unmatched level of success during the early war years, and observers have a tendency to equate financial and popular success with genius. A 1942 gossip column from Mark Hellinger praised Granlund, who "has kiddingly introduced his beautiful girls on café floors ... and when we caught him at Hollywood's huge Florentine Gardens the other night, he was just as hilariously successful as he had ever been back in the hey-hey day of prohibition.

"There's a great movie in Granlund, if the boys ever get around to writing it."[7]

In late spring 1942, Granlund sent Lee Mortimer a telegram sounding as though the New York columnist operated an employment service or had a personal hotline to each unemployed chorus girl seeking work on a stage. "Need about six girls new show opening May 15," Granlund wired, in abbreviated telegram fashion. "Must be here May 1. Have girls contact me. Will pay $35 a week, free meals, transportation. Sixteen week contract."[8]

"There are about 2,000 chorus girls in New York," Mortimer lamented at the particulars, while passing along in his column the specifics of Granlund's offer. "Most of them are out of work. But they all want to go to Hollywood. So this should solve the problem for six."

The film industry saw the war years as a time to lift the spirits of the nation, and films such as 1942's *Rhythm Parade* could offer singing and dancing and pretty girls, along with a simple story and a happy ending. Granlund had appeared briefly in the musical *Mr. Broadway* (1933), scripted by then-newspaper writer Ed Sullivan, and in a 1934 turn as himself in *The Girl from Paradise*, an E.W. Hammons production set in Granlund's Paradise Restaurant. *Rhythm Parade* from Monogram Pictures marked his Hollywood screen debut.

Like *The Girl from Paradise*, the film was set in Granlund's nightclub, and featured the Florentine Gardens' Ted Fio Rito Orchestra along with the Mills Brothers, whom NTG had originally engaged to play the lounge, but later moved to the main stage.

Granlund had an association with African American performers dating to his live microphone nights on WHN and part of his appreciation for the sort of jazz music offered with regularity at the Cotton Club and other New York clubs. His radio shows broadcast shows live nightly, and he had no qualms about presenting African American singers and performers before his white audiences, although most stages were color-segregated. The Mills Brothers, an act that began in Ohio in the late 1920s, achieved a place in the Vocal Group Hall of Fame in 1998, and were featured on CBS radio in the early 1930s on Rudy Vallee's hour-long show. The Mills Brothers were touring Europe at the outbreak of World War II, and when they returned to the United States in 1941, they found their place among popular vocal groups largely usurped by newcomers called the Ink Spots.

By 1942, Granlund could afford headliners who might have been out of his league previously, but he stuck with the familiar names with whom he had a history. Harry Richman, his longtime radio associate at WHN, Ozzie Nelson, Sophie Tucker, and Paul Whiteman all took the stage at the Florentine Gardens. The Mills Brothers had worked for Granlund before, and took up his offer for long-term work.

"They had long since passed their peak of popularity," said Granlund. "One of the brothers had died ... but I figured they still had some of the old magic and I put them in the cabaret lounge, off the main dining room. I had no feeling of discrimination in doing this. I simply felt it would be better business to prove their popularity with a small group before trying them on the main floor which seated 600 people."[9]

In booking the Mills Brothers into the Florentine Gardens, Granlund was the first to place an African-American entertainment act on a major Hollywood nightclub stage. He went on to see that the Mills Brothers were included in *Rhythm Parade*. When the film played at New York's Brooklyn Majestic, the reviewer offered his concise assessment: "The band is Ted Fio Rito's. The girl who is to be the star is Gale Storm. Her brain-storming publicity agent is Chick Chandler, and the producer is the double-talk specialist Cliff Nazarro. Nils T. Granlund is used as an M.C. A baby, perhaps Gale's, almost causes the show to be called off. That's the excitement, what there is of it."[10]

The *New York Post* "Movie Meter" rated it as Fair, on a scale from Poor to Excellent. Publicity shots used for the film around the country included captions that called the Florentine Gardens a "famous" Hollywood nightspot.

Later in the year, Granlund was asked by director Leslie Goodwins to produce a chorus line and nightclub setting for his Lum and Abner project, *Goin to Town* (1944).[11] He claimed to have had difficulty finding the right showgirls. "The girls used to seek me out," said Granlund. "Now I go scouring the town without results."[12] The producer solicited dancers on two separate occasions and claimed to receive only sixty-three

Granlund (right) and orchestra leader Ted Fio Rito in 1942's *Rhythm Parade*, a wartime film set at the Florentine Gardens featuring NTG as himself (courtesy McHuston Archives).

responses. "It would have been five times that number on other days," Granlund was quoted as saying.

Part of his difficulty was facing the contract system of the film studios in locking in actors and performers to short-term contracts at $100 a week. He was offering $25 a day, but it was short-term work with no promise of follow-up film work.

Granlund was asked if the potential showgirls were instead working in wartime defense department plants or had simply taken to heart all the admonitions about staying away from Hollywood. "Probably both," he answered.

It was just before the war boom that a young Canadian and her mother took $25 of the girl's second-place beauty contest winnings and purchased a showy outfit in which she could audition before Hollywood showman Earl Carroll. The daughter was underage, but pretty beyond her years. The man working the door at Carroll's theater asked the girl to lift her blouse as a preliminary audition, explaining that it was Carroll's policy.

"I won't do it,"[13] the girl told her mother.

Marie explained to her daughter that she had already missed a day's work in shuttling her to the audition, and that she intended to make the most of the outfit and the time by seeking out another audition. All her life, Marie had hoped for a chance at stardom, but having missed her own opportunity, she had taken up an apartment in Hollywood in hopes that her daughter could find success where she had not.

Crossing the street and heading north on El Centro to Hollywood Boulevard, Marie pointed to the expansive building across the street, the one with a large sign identifying it as the Florentine Gardens. Marie again reminded her daughter of the money already invested in achieving an audition, and the two let themselves in through an unlocked door.

The interior was dark and silent. The two walked through the bar to the cavernous dining room, at the end of which was the stage accommodating Paul Whiteman's orchestra set-up. They found a man seated near the stage. "My name is Marie Middleton," said the mother, "and this is my daughter, Yvonne."[14]

Marie asked for the person in charge. Yvonne, unprompted, remarked that she liked the appearance of the nightclub and might consider working at the Florentine Gardens. The heavyset man leaned back and looked out over his glasses, before replying, "So, you'd really consider it, would you? I guess we're pretty lucky, huh?"[15]

The man in the glasses was Dave Gould, the choreographer for all of Granlund's revues at the Florentine Gardens. The girl was later known as Yvonne De Carlo, an actress who starred on stage and in films, but is perhaps best remembered at the end of her career when she played Herman Munster's garishly painted vampire wife on the television comedy series *The Munsters*.

It was early in the afternoon, and Granlund was not in. Gould advised the two that he could be caught before the show, if they returned around seven. He told Yvonne that he would let Granlund know to expect someone and counseled her to wear a bathing suit under her dress, adding that Granlund preferred the color red.

Yvonne Middleton had taken the second place beauty contest money while wearing a red bathing suit, and when she returned that evening, she was wearing it under her dress. The dreary atmosphere of the darkened house had been replaced with glittering lights and an electric atmosphere. The backstage area buzzed with activity as showgirls darted back and forth in preparing for the first performance of the evening.

She found the operator of the Florentine, whom she later recalled as a "tall, thin, middle-aged" man, who took her hands in his own as he asked if she could dance. Granlund remembered that — at his introduction to De Carlo — she had a "doll-like face, with childish full lips and glistening brunette tresses."[16]

Moving to a dressing room, Granlund asked to see her legs and Yvonne lifted her skirt to the edge of the red bathing suit. He nodded his approval and ran through a series of questions about where she was from and what she hoped to do with herself. During the questioning, he discovered that Yvonne had been raised in the home of her Sicilian grandfather, a man Yvonne called Papa De Carlo. He did not ask Yvonne's age.

Granlund asked her to make herself ready in her bathing suit and be prepared to perform, just in case. Presently, Yvonne and her mother stood at the edge of the stage, and when Granlund looked over, anticipating the orchestra send-up, he winked.[17] After a drum roll and musical crescendo, the show took flight, shoes of the dancing girls clattering on the stage to the music of Paul Whiteman's orchestra. They were absorbed in watching the routine when Granlund walked by and whispered, "Be ready...." As the number wound down, Granlund stepped forward, microphone in hand. The showman told the audience that he had a young performer offstage who wanted to join the show, but he knew nothing about her, not even whether she could sing or dance. Introducing her as "Miss Yvonne De Carlo," he beckoned her onto the stage.

Yvonne, perhaps surprised at his renaming of her for the introduction, hustled across the stage to join Granlund at the microphone. The Swede put an arm around her shoulder and telling De Carlo to "show us what you can do." Granlund pointed to the orchestra, gave his customary "Let 'er go!" and stepped into the darkness, leaving young Yvonne center stage, trembling on the knees she had confidently displayed such a short time before. The orchestra struck up an accompaniment to the pianist solo-beginning of "Tea for Two," the sheet music provided Granlund by Yvonne's mother.

The familiarity of the song, the music to which she had hoped to audition, made it a little easier. Yvonne De Carlo went to work, smiling and dancing, her shoes tapping to the rhythm as she moved back and forth in front of the crowd. De Carlo recalled later that the time on stage for the audition seemed like forever, and imagined that she had exhausted every dance move in her repertoire. Eventually the orchestra stopped, the piano ended, and the dancer stood alone, smiling to the polite applause.

Granlund returned to the stage and asked the audience to vote by applause whether he should include Yvonne in his troupe, to which the crowd responded with whistles and cheers. "Okay, little girl," he remembered saying. "You've got the job."[18]

Granlund's take on what he described as De Carlo's "timid tap routine" that evening was that the "dancing was not spectacular, but her presentation was so charming that she won the hearts of all who saw her." He hired her on at $35 a week, an amount De Carlo remembered as being more than most men received for five ten-hours days laboring in a factory.

On that Monday in August, 1940, the person who would later be called the most beautiful girl in the world began her long Hollywood career.

De Carlo remembered the Florentine Gardens as being a rung or two down the ladder from Earl Carroll's nightclub, where the costumes were filmy and lacy "in the Paris mode." Granlund preferred bangles and sparkles.

"It was the caviar crowd at Carroll's," explained De Carlo, "meat and potatoes at the Florentine."[19]

De Carlo remembered Granlund as one who could communicate with regular Joes, with a repertoire of raunchy jokes and double entendres that were more obvious than esoteric. Her impression of the man was that he was "rough cut, but gentle" with an interactive onstage style in the manner of Don Rickles, but with a playful tone. As she recalled after his death, Granlund was always one to pick up the dinner tab and give support —financial or otherwise — to anyone who asked.

As part of his kidding humor, Granlund had a blonde "special friend" named Sylvia McKay, an onstage sidekick who suffered the brunt of his "beautiful but dumb" routine. McKay had come west from New York City, and had danced in the Follies. She appeared in 1943 with former *Vanities* star Beryl Wallace in the movie *The Kansan*. Yvonne De Carlo recalled that "beautiful but dumb" was all an act and that McKay "was no dummy."

Granny's nickname for her was Miss Unconscious, and he used it on and off the stage. In the film *Rhythm Parade* he introduces her as such to a group of guests seated at a table in the nightclub, which served as the set for the movie.

As for De Carlo, she was dubbed "Dingbat" by Granlund, and while it was not a particularly flattering reference, the actress was pleased that he considered her a part of his inner circle, whom he always called by nickname. As De Carlo remembered it, to be addressed by a given name by Granlund was an indication of his reserve regarding the person.

While Granlund saw that Miss Unconscious received a part in *Rhythm Parade*, he made sure that she was listed in the credits under her real name.

Although by the time of the filming De Carlo had a movie studio contract, Granlund wrangled a spot in the film for her, a dancing role which went uncredited.

As Granlund remembered it, he arranged early on for choreographer Gould to give De Carlo some private lessons to ready her for feature dancing, and later she remembered working in the back chorus line position, asking for help from Gould. Her continual practice eventually caught Granlund's attention. "Never lose that hunger, kid," the showman told her. "That's the way to get places in this town. I've seen plenty of girls come and go, and I know what I'm talking about."[20]

Granlund eventually moved her to the front line chorus, and months later, he offered her a feature routine. To "feature" was to dance a solo while the chorus worked routines in the edges of the stage, or stopped altogether to allow a full appreciation of the center stage routine. De Carlo, a traditionally trained dancer, practiced the ballet "toe" position until her feet bled.

Granlund's feature for her? A gorilla act.

She was outfitted in a revealing chiffon-veiled costume in which she danced gracefully until a man in a huge gorilla costume bounded out, "killed" the onstage sultan watching the performance, and carried her off — indelicately slung over his hairy shoulder. On one occasion the audience was exposed to a "wardrobe malfunction" when the lower part of her skimpy costume broke a strand and she was forced to struggle not only against the ape, but to maintain a semblance of modesty as well.[21]

Within months of her employment at the Florentine Gardens, she was singled out backstage and whisked from the establishment by two policemen who took her into custody on behalf of the U.S. Department of Immigration. She was an undocumented alien, having overstayed her visa. De Carlo suspected that a jealous coworker likely provided a tip in an effort to get her off the Hollywood stage.

Deported on the next train to her home-

Granlund and his long-time "special friend" Sylvia McKay, who danced at the Florentine Gardens and hosted parties at Granlund's home, in a scene from *Rhythm Parade* (courtesy McHuston Archives).

Yvonne De Carlo with Granlund's horse Kickapoo, on which she made rodeo appearances and took frequent equestrian outings with her boss (courtesy McHuston Archives).

town of Vancouver, Canada, she immediately wrote to Granlund, who had no idea she was not only underage, but a Canadian citizen. "She disclosed for the first time that she was in the United States on a visitor's visa," he remembered.[22]

De Carlo continued her dancing on Canadian stages while Granlund worked to convince U.S. officials that she would have employment, at the time one of the requirements for admission to the United States. A telegram Granlund sent on her behalf was among the sentimental mementoes kept by De Carlo for the remainder of her life. In it, the showman described her as a "unique and splendid performer" who would be in Granlund's employ for a long time with every chance for a splendid career. A later letter set a salary at forty dollars a week, a figure considered low by the Canadian officials, as De Carlo recalled.

Yvonne returned to Granlund and the Florentine Gardens, and within two years applied for citizenship. Granlund remembered her working hard for her paperwork, studying dance in between performances at the Orpheum Theatre in Los Angeles and the Florentine Gardens.

Granlund often described Yvonne as one of his "kids," and the actress recalled that the impresario treated her as a daughter when she showed up for rehearsals at the Florentine. The two established a long-term relationship which may have been strictly paternal, but she quickly became one of Granlund's favorites. He gave her freedom to experiment with routines at the Florentine, and she invented a number of dances that Granlund allowed her to perform.

It was offset, to some extent, by the part of Granlund's show that she found particularly demeaning, the portion in which men from the audience would be invited onstage to dance with the chorus girls. That segment not only demeaned the showgirls, but audience members as well, as they were outfitted with baby bibs or encouraged to dance in rolled-up pants and silly hats.

Regardless of the lack of taste in aspects of his nightclub act, Granlund did care for his showgirl family. He went out of his way to find additional work for the dancers outside the Florentine Gardens that would allow them to supplement their income. It was somewhat self-serving, of course, since the dancers would be identified as coming from the Florentine Gardens. He was, first and foremost, a publicity agent.

One of the frequent activities was appearing in parades or rodeos on horseback. This was restricted to the showgirls with equestrian skills or, lacking that, an ability to balance on the back of a horse in costume. Granlund, now living as a bachelor, discovered that De Carlo could ride horses and the two frequently spent days together along the trails that edged Los Angeles.

De Carlo remembered that Granlund owned three horses of his own, and the fact that she had learned to ride as a child in Canada endeared her to the showman. Granlund rode a horse called Chief, while De Carlo sat atop Kickapoo, a "spirited chestnut stallion."

As a result of the success at the Florentine, Granlund set himself up in a spacious house above Franklin Avenue near the Greek Theatre. De Carlo, a frequent visitor in the years in which she danced at the Florentine, remembered the home as elaborately decorated, with a party room filled with expensive prints of hunting scenes. He hosted expansive parties with a guest list that included high society from Los Angeles to New York, down-to-earth vaudevillians and chorus girls, and everything in between.

De Carlo attended one of Granlund's parties when she was first starting out, when she and her mother Marie were still pressed for money. She claimed later that she was only joking when she asked for a pound of butter to take home to her mother, but Granlund saw to it from that point on, that she left with a plate of butter for Marie — no matter who was present at the party — a gesture of goodwill that the showman never considered a possible source of embarrassment for De Carlo.

Even at the height of its wartime popularity, the Florentine Gardens had an appeal only to a certain segment of the nighttime crowd. Artie Shaw, one of the top bandleaders of the time, encouraged De Carlo to leave Granlund's lowbrow act to pursue a more serious career. His offer to pay her a month's salary while she looked for other work convinced her to leave the Florentine Gardens without notice.

Typically — as De Carlo recalled — Granlund did not hold a grudge, but instead, upon later running into his former employee, made her promise to continue attending the parties at his house and to maintain their horseback riding occasions.

De Carlo found an agent and a B-movie part, but then nothing followed. Rather than "admitting defeat to Granny," she auditioned for Earl Carroll, this time taking off the blouse to become part of the formal troupe that danced for the one-time New York showman.

Where Granlund encouraged his dancers to take outside work, Carroll forbade it. De Carlo had scarcely learned the routines when she was offered a part in Paramount's *This Gun for Hire*, which she took despite Carroll's policy. When she appeared later at Carroll's theater, still in the film company makeup, she was fired on the spot.

If that were not enough, her mother Marie — living vicariously through her daughter — immediately approached Carroll and threatened to expose the fact that he had hired an underage dancer, unless he put De Carlo back in his troupe. Carroll not only refused, he called other nightclubs and suggested they pass on any underage dancer named De Carlo who might approach them seeking work.

She went back to Granlund, who hired her without reservation.

By 1943, Granlund was being touted by his New York agent as the "Nation's Top Grosser,"[23] with three consecutive years at the Florentine Gardens in association with owner Frank Bruni. The Season's Greetings card claimed, in addition to wishes for the holidays, that "the Florentine Gardens, with N. T. G. and His Show, plays to more people than any Cabaret Restaurant in the World."

Where Hollywood Boulevard had previously been vacant at mid-afternoon, the bustling activity of a major U.S. city during wartime was apparent at every turn. Granlund sent his revue to entertain the troops at the Hollywood USO on Cahuenga Boulevard, and later allowed his girls to dance with the soldiers at the Hollywood Canteen. The area between Hollywood Boulevard and Sunset teemed with military personnel, arriving and departing, heading for leave or leaving for war. All manner of attractions sprang up almost overnight, giving the area the feel of a carnival midway.

Some of the regular forms of entertainment shut down, but others popped up just as quickly. One of the steady venues was the rodeo, and for the girls in the Florentine revue, it represented a continuing stage outside the Gardens. Granlund continued to support his dancers in their efforts, and applauded De Carlo when she was hired on for bit parts in a couple of movies for Paramount. When on August 19, 1942, she signed a six-month contract with Paramount, he wished her nothing but the best.

She immediately went to work on a film, but not for Paramount. The studio loaned her to Monogram Studios for the filming of *Rhythm Parade*, the movie being shot at the Florentine Gardens. Granlund had requested a role for De Carlo.

Before the war had ended in Europe and the Pacific, another battle began on Hollywood Boulevard. Jimmie Fidler reported in his gossip column on February 10, 1944, of a rift between Florentine owner Frank Bruni and his stage show impresario.[24] "Look for legal fireworks," said Fidler, "between NTG (Nils Granlund) and the Florentine Gardens, Hollywood nitery where he's been producing revues; the café's management has omitted his name in recent advertising."

Ironically, Fidler continued in his column with the news that *Incendiary Blonde*— the life story of Granlund's old friend Texas Guinan — would have its world premiere at a warehouse in New York City, very near where she held court in her Larry Fay — Nils Granlund days.

Granlund claimed that his departure from the Florentine Gardens came as a result of his nostalgia for New York's Broadway scene. But his chronology that would indicate a move from the Florentine Gardens directly to the stages of New York must be attributed to pride or lapsed memory. The initials NTG were dropped from the Florentine Gardens in late 1944 or early 1945, but he remained front and center stage there for at least another year. The Fidler-hinted legal fireworks, if they occurred at all, did not keep Granlund from using the Florentine Gardens as his "stage" when he returned to the microphone and studio in 1946 to host an ABC radio show.

In 1944, Granlund was hired by director Frank McDonald to play himself in the feature film *Take It Big*, which was released on June 9. That same year, he was contracted by Leslie Goodwins to provide a nightclub scene for the Lum and Abner project, *Goin' to Town*.[25] Co-stars Chester Lauck and Norris Goff portrayed Lum Edwards and Abner Peabody, co-owners of a general mercantile shop called the "Jot 'em Down Store." The radio play upon which it was based ran from 1932 until 1954, and was set in the then-fictional town of Pine Ridge, Arkansas, where Lum and Abner spent their time conjuring money making ideas, only to see them fall flat. For *Goin' to Town*, Granlund put together a cabaret setting complete with dance floor, tables, orchestra, and chorus girls, and — although his onscreen time was extremely limited — he introduced a couple of his signature routines including the Bumps-a-Daisy, in while Lum and Abner play the Granlund audience "stooges" who are brought on stage, suffer the high-water cuff-rolling of their slacks, and spin and bump into the assorted dancing chorines.

Lee Mortimer of the *Mirror*, perhaps — by this time — Granlund's oldest friend, managed to produce another near-full-page spread on the Broadway Swede in 1945. Mortimer, in highlighting the many "discoveries" of Granlund, made no mention of the showman's current situation.[26]

Don Allen, writing in March 1946,[27] featured Granlund—complete with candid photograph—heckling from the stage at the Florentine Gardens. In a rundown of the nightlife attributed to Hollywood, "not a town for stay-up-lates," Allen's photographer Bob Wallace captured Granlund holding the hand of one of his showgirls, ready to "heckle a baldheaded customer at the Florentine Gardens, one of Hollywood's biggest clubs."

So many years after he first brought the slapdash routine to the West Coast, he continued to ply it as his formula to please an audience.

TWELVE

The Brink of a Return

Every crowd has a silver lining.
— P.T. Barnum

When the complete break finally came between Granlund and Frank Bruni, owner of Hollywood's Florentine Gardens, Granlund had already begun looking outside the nightspot for other employment opportunities. During his prominent years in New York, traveling with his revues was a part of his daily life. In California, Granlund largely confined himself to the local stage work required of the emcee at the Florentine. In late 1945, he began contemplating a return to New York City.

Granlund noted in his memoirs that he "opened a club in the Greenwich Village," inferring that he was an owner or operator of the establishment, when in fact, his chorus line was simply booked to provide a long-weekend's dancing revue. His return to a New York stage drew several notes in the New York City newspaper columns, most pointing out the lengthy amount of time that had elapsed since the one-time "king" had appeared in Manhattan. Despite a big opening night, Granlund later called his return a mistake, saying the performance was both a "thrill and a heartbreak," and an attempt to revive the past that he should never have attempted.

His regret was long after the fact. Even after mediocre reviews of his Greenwich Village Inn engagement, Granlund stayed in New York City for a time, booking his chorus girl routine into several marginal nightspots. He was a paid performer — in some cases, well paid, but he had expenses as well. His use of the phrase "opened a nightclub" in reference to his New York City return was more in line with "opening night" at a newly remodeled club or "opening act" at a more established venue.

He did spend some time in Los Angeles between his break with the Florentine Gardens and the wave of "nostalgia" that drew him back to the East Coast. During that period, he took up the radio microphone again, this time on KHJ, running a half-hour network broadcast carried across the country,

187

including New York City, where it aired on WABC each weekday afternoon from three to three-thirty.

"Broadway's fabulous Nils T. Granlund," wrote Lee Mortimer of the *New York World*, "inventor of the cabaret minimum charge and innovator of practically every nightclub fashion now in use, has returned to an early love — radio."[1]

By the time of Mortimer's 1945 column, most of the men who had shared the offices of Marcus Loew's corporate headquarters in New York City were on the West Coast, comfortably enthroned at various Hollywood film corporations, reigning over millions of dollars worth of sets, payrolls, and productions. Granlund, whose flair for publicity had few equals, could easily have found himself within the inner circle of any of several major U.S. film corporations, if only by maintaining his early ties with the Loew's hierarchy.

But he simply could not leave behind his harem of attractive young showgirls.

The Broadway Swede, who ran speakeasies during prohibition, but did not smoke or drink, who operated cabarets for gangsters, but had nothing to do with gambling or bootlegging, who made money by the fistful but gave it away nearly as quickly — had but a single vice.

"The glamour gals got him,"[2] wrote Mortimer, summing up Granlund's Achilles heel as succinctly and accurately as might be expected of a long-time friend. The columnist recalled in his column the clubs and cabarets Granlund haunted, like "Frivolities, Silver Slipper, Guinan's, etc." as well as "the old Hollywood Restaurant, the Paradise, the Midnight Sun, after which Granny went native under Southern California's palms, extending a six-week booking at Hollywood's Florentine Gardens into a run of seven years...."

His post–Florentine radio show, entitled *You're in the Act*, was another stylistic fallback for Granlund. It featured amateur performances that were broadcast from the stages of the Florentine Gardens, part of his final association with that nightspot. Granlund's midday radio show had him taking the stage at a time the cabaret would normally have been dark and empty anyway. Mortimer pointed out that audience members with a "suppressed desire to sing, dance, play an instrument, or otherwise entertain" could find a creative outlet under Granlund's onstage guidance. Mortimer, always supportive of Granlund's creative efforts, wrote that the radio show would contend for a majority of daytime audiences "addicted to such impromptu entertainment."

Apparently, those addicts were in insufficient numbers. *You're in the Act* did not remain on ABC's schedule for long. By 1946, Granlund had successfully shopped the show to CBS[3] where it fared no better.

With the severing of his connection to the Florentine Gardens, and his amateur hour program having drawn the vaudeville hook, Granlund began making calls to his gossip column friends to promote his plan for a return to the stages of Broadway.

N. T. G.

Listen to N. T. G. starring in
"YOU'RE IN THE ACT," sparkling new audience participation show presented by Columbia Broadcasting System, Mon.
through Fri. at 11 A.M.

These famous initials stand for Nils Thor Granlund, famous cabaret master of ceremonies and showman, who has had his greatest success at Frank R. Bruni's Florentine
Gardens, where he made his West Coast debut in March, 1940. Since then nearly two
million persons have enjoyed the many revues in which N. T. G. has appeared.

Celebrated on Broadway as the originator of informal night club entertainment,
N. T. G. contributed his part to the fast tempo of the post-war "Roaring Twenties." His
Paradise Club and Hollywood Restaurant offered bored New Yorkers something that
made them sit up and rub their eyes.

Radio, in turn, offered a field for Granlund's talents: as a pioneer radio announcer
and program builder, he originated the first amateur shows on the air, as well as bringing
Harry Richman, Eddie Cantor and many others to the microphone for the first time.

N. T. G.'s trademark is a combination of gorgeous girls, humorous banter and the
informality he promotes by his fun-provoking audience participation numbers.

A 1946 CBS announcement for an audience participation show featuring Granlund,
"You're in the Act" (courtesy McHuston Archives).

Jack O'Brian reported in his syndicated column on December 9, 1945, that Tony Pastor's Uptown Café in New York City would change its name to the Frivolity Club,[4] borrowing a moniker from a previously successful spot that — coincidentally — hosted Granlund's first onstage outing. O'Brian, perhaps aware of the possibility that his readers' memories of Granlund may have faded during his long absence, reminded them of the collection of stars discovered by the showman, mentioning "Barbara Stanwyck, who then was just plain Ruby Stevens, Joan Leslie, Joan Crawford, Paulette Goddard, Frances Neal (Mrs. Van Heflin), and a lot more." Granlund's run at the Frivolity Club would begin December 21.

Other writers remembered all too well Granlund's penchant for heckling-style comedy and scantily-clad showgirls. "N. T. G., of course, still follows this formula,"[5] wrote Jack Gaver, who pointed out that Granlund's engagement at the Greenwich Village Inn was his first NYC appearance since 1939. He surmised that Granlund would be "glad to get back to his Hollywood home" after the eight-week run.

"I like the way I can live out there," Granlund told Gaver just a short time after his New York return, although describing Hollywood as "cold, hard, and tough" while recalling Broadway as a "warm pals-y place. You can be down on Broadway but your friends will still talk to you."

Granlund was only just discovering how tough it could become, but did not make it any easier on himself by repeating his old stories, and name-dropping his "discoveries," talking about the Prohibition era when he had opened nightclubs for the "boys who were on the shady side of the Volstead act."[6] Gaver spared his readers the reminder that the Prohibition act was a bit of history from a quarter-century previous.

Opening night at the Greenwich Village Inn brought out a lot of Granlund's old buddies and former employees, and the reactions to his revue seemed to be gradated by how familiar Granlund was to the particular writer. *Variety* in its coverage of Granlund's long career rarely offered any glowing terms. The 1946 item may have been the best he ever received from that publication. "Many of the hipsters are to be found in the Village these nights,"[7] wrote the critic, "because of the first N.Y. nitery turn of Nils T. Granlund (NTG) in seven years." The review noted that Granlund still retained a New York City following that made him worth the "reported $3,500 that's being shelled out for him." The Greenwich Village Inn performance was a revival of the "insulting type of show where the payees, talent, and the spots are on the receiving end," and the critic offered that "some of the uptown cafés could profit with the NTG appliqué."

The Greenwich Village Inn stage offered a change from Granlund's cabaret custom, which involved tables in close proximity to the stage, allowing a maximum amount of stage-crowd interaction. The *Variety* critic noted that arrangements for the stage show had been made hurriedly, and that the establishment was so concerned about the possibility of bad press that critics had been barred from rehearsals and the soft-opening performances before the debut. The Inn's management, he wrote, was "fearful that the muggs aren't hep enough" to understand the situation, but added later, "the Inn was right to some extent."

The Granlund heckling found its way into print with *Variety's* quote of his remark, "If I ever find any talent in my shows, I'll throw it out." What came later may have read harshly, but it could have been written by Granlund himself, regarding his preference for working with females with "looks and little else. If she ever learns to think," he said of one of his chorus girls, "it'll ruin her." To be expected, the review ended in summarizing Granlund's standard show closer, the audience participation gimmick with "customers terping with the line gals."[8]

In an edition of his "Broadway" column years after Granlund's big night, Jack O'Brian made casual mention of his own outing to the Greenwich Village Inn, noting the company in which he sat and the fact that the occasion was the opening of Granlund's new show.

Granlund remembered the table as well. Seated with O'Brian were New York Yankee baseball star Joe DiMaggio, Manhattan restaurateur Toots Shor, and Hollywood mogul Mike Todd, along with newspaper columnists Walter

Academy of
Theatre Arts

The New
Rainbow Studios

THOR GRANLUND, GENERAL MANAGER

WILL & GLADYS AHERN, GENERAL MANAGERS

1627 CAHUENGA BLVD. • HOLLYWOOD 28, CALIFORNIA • HOLLYWOOD 3-5633

Dec. 3, 1956.

My Dear Amanda:

        Thanks for your nice note. I'm osrry you don't
like Florida. It seems to me to be much better than cold New England.

        Book will be off the press Dec. 10, and will be
officially on sale Jan. 8. I hope this means a turning point in
my fortune. Bob Hope is dickering to buy it for a big price, and
play me in picture.

        I haven't much money, but this $2 might buy
something for the kids. I'll try to do better later.

        Love to all,

              Nils.

On his Academy letterhead, Granlund sent news to his granddaughter Amanda of the sale of his memoir (courtesy Amanda Howard).

Winchell and Damon Runyon, whom Granlund described as "two of my oldest friends, Broadway pals of thirty-five years or more."[9]

Runyon, suffering from advanced stages of throat cancer, still enjoyed the late night company of his friend and fellow writer Winchell. Granlund recalled that, by then, Runyon had lost his ability to speak and was forced to communicate by writing notes on a small pad that he carried. A note from Runyon that made its way backstage during a break in the entertainment read, "Great show, welcome back."

It was after Runyon's death and the subsequent publication of Jack Weiner's biography *The Damon Runyon Story*, that Jack O'Brian revisited that night at the Greenwich Village Inn. "It was during dinner at Toots Shor's," wrote O'Brian, "and my party was seated next to Damon, who was dining alone."[10] O'Brian noted that Runyon had been cornered by a "bore" who had seated himself at Runyon's table and — without the possibility of vocal interruption — was pontificating on the troubles of the newspaper business. Runyon passed a note to O'Brian asking to be bailed out of the situation.

O'Brian stood and informed Runyon that his party was off to see Granlund's comeback performance at the Greenwich Village Inn, to which Runyon scribbled a note to his companion that he would have to be excused for the sake of a potential story. When the man offered to come along, Runyon "pretended that deafness suddenly was an added affliction."[11]

As for Winchell, his look-back on Granlund's revue came from the perspective of early 1947 and the appearance of fan dancer Sally Rand, who had been engaged after Granlund's departure as an attempt to reviving flagging audiences. According to Winchell, the Greenwich Village Inn was "40 Gs in the pink for the season. In two weeks Sally cut that deficit in half."[12]

Most of the expenses paid out by the Greenwich Village Inn during the current season had gone to Granlund and his troupe. Even Rand was not enough. Earl Wilson reported in May that the Greenwich Village Inn was closing for the summer, but hoped to renew its lease.

Meanwhile, Granlund moved the revue to the Rio Cabana, which the week before had been called the La Conga Club.[13] Granlund knew the layout of the building. It was the same place in which he had opened an act twenty years before at the then-new establishment makeover called the Frivolity Club. *Variety* remembered the association between the Frivolity and Granlund, who "was called in to rescue the club from financial woes, and had a run of 66 weeks."[14]

Having covered the Granlund act for twenty years, *Variety* was as familiar with Granlund as the impresario was with the Frivolity Club, and called his "basic theory of giving the mob a galaxy of undraped femmes" something that had not changed in the twenty years since he had first appeared at the venue. Granlund's opinion that he could simply continue to produce the same brand of show year after year was not shared by the *Variety* critic who believe that "a little more is needed." Where Granlund believed his act was — as *Variety* called it — "conducive to repeat trade," many aspects of the show only worked for first-time audiences. His patter was the same heckling routine that he repeated night after night. The critic noted that the success of the club would "hinge on whether NTG's basic premise is correct."

Working with Granlund at the Frivolity was comedian Billy Vine, who marginally impressed the critic, and overall the NTG revue received a passing grade. The premise, as it turned out, no longer kept its promises. The repeat business that Granlund had hoped for just wasn't there. The etched-in-stone style of entertainment the Swede relied upon required plenty of first-time "stooges" in the audience. There weren't enough of those finding their way into the Rio Cabana.

Regarding his New York City return, Granlund lamented that things had changed, and that the chorus and showgirls of the majority of current Broadway revues had "neither the talent nor personality"[15] of those he had employed in his day. He laid the blame on producers who, he said, failed to work at getting the "real beauties," but instead only issued chorus calls and expected the "right girls to drop in." Producers in the Ziegfeld era had to "dig for their beauties," Granlund told Jack Gaver. The one-time Broadway fixture could only recall the way things used to be, remembering how he had "started Texas Guinan as a club entertainer,"[16] and how his Prohibition-era replacement of women "on the make" with "clean-cut kids from the Broadway shows" had altered forever the entire cabaret business.

"Broadway had changed so much I hardly knew it,"[17] Granlund later wrote of his New York City return, citing a blindness caused by nostalgia as the reason for his impressions of the current state of affairs. The "glittering, scintillating Era of Wonderful Nonsense" that he remembered from his days on the part of Manhattan once called the "Main Stem" had been replaced, he believed, by hot-dog stands and the type of clubs he considered honky tonks.

Even in reminiscing about the Broadway of old, Granlund attached no blame to his own current product, but instead charged that his diminished drawing power was caused by a changed atmosphere in New York City nightlife. Believing that he still held the magic formula for success, he stated with stubborn confidence that he could have "fought through and made a success in the Village,"[18] but claimed that his heart was no longer in it, and he beat a retreat to California.

His return to Hollywood coincided with a break in the filming schedule of Yvonne De Carlo. Universal Studios had released *Black Bart*, in which De Carlo had top billing along with Dan Duryea, on March 3, 1948, the same day Louella O. Parsons reported in her column that Granlund and De Carlo had been seen together at the Fox and Hounds.[19] Her description of the "strange twosome" hints that Parsons may not have known that De Carlo, by now a veteran of twenty-six films had received her first show business paychecks from Granlund, and that the two had been frequent horseback riding companions

Academy of
Theatre Arts

The New
Rainbow Studios

NILS THOR GRANLUND, GENERAL MANAGER   WILL & GLADYS AHERN, GENERAL MANAGERS

1627 CAHUENGA BLVD. • HOLLYWOOD 28, CALIFORNIA • HOLLYWOOD 3-5633

My Dear Amanda#

      I promised your mother I would send you a watch for
graduation, but then told her I could not send it right away. I will
make it up to you, and will send you a little money every week, when
I can. I have sold my life story, called " Blonds, Brunettes and
Bullets, " and will be able to do better for you later. Right now
it isn't easy.

          Love, to you and everyone.

          Nils.

In this 1956 note to his granddaughter Amanda, Granlund hints at his difficult financial times (courtesy Amanda Howard).

over the years. Parsons wondered if Granlund was "trying to sign Yvonne " for a show.

Many of the archaeological remnants of Granlund's past fell victim to time and change. WHN radio in New York, the station which Granlund literally moved into New York City and ran single-handedly for a time, became a historical footnote in August, when the former Loew's enterprise began promoting the initials of its corporate successor, Metro-Goldwyn-Mayer.

The airwaves that gave New York the NTG of nightly jazz, interviews, and entertainment would be identified as WMGM, although the station — along with the film studios— were still under the ownership of Loew's Inc. Jack Gaver reported for United Press that "New York City's second oldest standard radio station will change September 15 when it moves to new quarters at 711 Fifth Avenue."[20]

Gone was the stack of equipment in Granlund's former offices in the Loew's State Building. The new address had formerly been the first home of the National Broadcasting Company. Gaver did recall Granlund's contributions, noting that WHN was operating back in the days when "radio was a novelty and long before it was a profitable outlet for talent," in an era when Broadway stars considered it a lesser form of entertainment. Even so many years after the fact, Gaver remembered that Granlund had given many of those same stars their "first baptism of radio" on his WHN show, and was responsible for creating the live "remote" broadcast when he took his microphones to the boxing arenas, nightclubs, and political events.

As he searched for a new direction, Granlund fell back on old contacts. His financial backer at the Paradise Club, Charles "The Chinaman" Sherman, had an assortment of friends and enemies, among them members of the New York syndicate who had been invited to step into the organizing gambling operations in Havana, Cuba, in 1938.

In that year, crime boss Meyer Lansky sent in operators who quickly turned Havana into a tourist mecca, drawing society crowds, stars, and high rollers into the glitzy casinos. One of the men heading up a facet of the Havana gambling was named Wilbur Clark.

Las Vegas at that time had none of its current glitz. It was a desert community with a pre-war "strip" consisting of a single hotel, a modest traveler's stop opened in 1941 that was advertised in 1948 as the Hotel El Rancho Vegas. John Lochhead of San Mateo's Benjamin Franklin Hotel was brought in at that time as the new manager of the inn "at the sign of the windmill"[21] on Highway 91. Owner Tommy Hull had added a few gas pumps to increase the allure of his 62-room "resort." Las Vegas also had a nightclub called Pair O' Dice. Gambling was legal, but it was mostly found in Reno, and primarily consisted of card games dealt among ranch hands.

Wilbur Clark, from his experience in Havana, knew how to operate a casino, and acquired the lease to the El Rancho. (Granlund remembered the date as 1943, although others recall Clark arriving in Las Vegas in 1944.) Soon after taking over the El Rancho, Clark hired Granlund to stage a show there. While Tommy Hull had a chorus line at his Golden Club at Reno in 1943, the NTG revue became the first glittering chorus line act on the Las Vegas strip.[22] Granlund received a note from Clark after the fact, crediting the NTG revue with putting "the El Rancho over to a big success."

Clark did succeed in the venture, and in 1947 began construction on his desert palace, which he would call Wilbur Clark's Desert Inn. In 1950 he revealed that he ran out of money during construction and was forced to hand off 74 percent of the hotel ownership to a Cleveland, Ohio, gambling syndicate consisting of Sam Tucker, Moe Dalitz, Maurice Klineman, and Tom McGinty in exchange for $1.5 million.[23] After its eventual completion, Clark operated the Desert Inn with his "silent partners."

The success of Granlund's earlier Vegas show cemented his Nevada reputation, and a Sherman associate named Moey Sedway contacted him to bring in another revue, this time at the brand-new Flamingo, which opened the day after Christmas in 1946, when the hotel construction was not entirely complete.

Moey Sedway had a background similar to that of "The Chinaman." As a teenager, he was already fleecing street vendors as part of a "protection" racket he ran with his best friend Ben Siegel, a mobster who became the first to land in Las Vegas, by then trying to live down the nickname Bugsy.

Granlund liked Sedway, but was nervous about Siegel's involvement at the Flamingo, the first mob-owned hotel on the strip.[24] When Los Angeles nightclub owner Billy Wilkerson ran out of money on his lavish Flamingo project, he had turned to New York money from Harry Rothberg, Meyer Lansky, Gus Greenbaum, and Moe Sedway. Siegel had been charged by Lansky with the running of the Flamingo, but Siegel almost immediately left for Hollywood, turning over much of the oversight of the hotel operations to Sedway.

The Flamingo received nationwide press coverage at the time of its opening. Almost all of it claimed that the resort was more impressive than what Hollywood could have produced. Granlund wanted to take his revue to the Flamingo stage, but the "fly in the soup" was Bugsy.[25]

Siegel maintained an opulent home in Beverly Hills for his girlfriend Virginia Hill. He was seated inside her house reading a newspaper on June 20, 1947, when a gunman slipped into the backyard and began firing through the window. Siegel was hit numerous times; his killer was never captured.

Sedway repeated his offer to Granlund after Siegel's death and Granlund moved into the Flamingo.

Granlund set out in 1947 (although he incorrectly recalled the date as 1949) to produce a show for the resort. The revue lasted long enough for Granlund to "discover" actress Sheree North who was later featured on the cover of Life magazine and starred in numerous films and television shows, at one point in 1954 taking a role which the wildly popular Marilyn Monroe was to have played.

Leaving Las Vegas, he landed a spot with the Wilshire Club in Los Angeles. It was no nightclub, though. Wilshire Club was a beverage.

The schtick remained unchanged, the media used in delivery had changed. Before hawking soda pop, Granlund found an opening in television. It was still a relatively new medium and stations were open to experimentation with the programming. KTLA in Los Angeles took a chance, and by the summer of 1948 columnist Jack Lait (Lee Mortimer's co-author for the 1955 book *New York Confidential*) was reporting that Granlund "is pioneering again,"[26] presenting youngsters on television in the manner he had done on radio in New York. The Broadway gossip columnist noted that the Swede was "the first New York air star" with his radio program on WHN. According to Lait, Granlund had "the top television show of California," although from the East Coast, Lait's claim may have been nothing more than Granlund's boast. Within the year, Granlund was no longer getting his paycheck from KTLA.

By August of 1949, Granlund had convinced the Globe Bottling Company of Los Angeles to sign on as a sponsor of *Hollywood Road to Fame*, the showman's new incarnation of his amateur hour, which KTSL Channel 2 agreed to carry on Friday nights at 6:30.[27] KTSL was the first television station to be licensed in Los Angeles and later was renamed as the network-owned KCBS-TV.

Wilshire Club was a soft drink sold in 12-ounce cone-topped cans that had every appearance of antique screw-top motor oil containers. The drink did not last long, but afforded Granlund a chance to continue on the air doing something he believed suited him — and his act — perfectly. Television allowed him to combine all his experience in show business: sound from radio, sight from cabaret shows, and talent scouting from vaudeville. Plus, he believed that as a "hunting ground" for new talent,[28] it was unbeatable.

There was enough interest in what Granlund was doing that he landed a second KTSL program, a move that surprised critic Terry Vernon, who wrote in 1950 that KTSL was considered "Old Reliable, because they so very seldom change their program schedule."[29]

With their newly expanded operation, KTSL required additional programming, and as Vernon put it, "NTG starts a new show," an hour-long affair called *Backstage with NTG* that was billed as an informal, behind-the-scenes amateur variety show. His weekly program would bring together the winners of the daily contests to determine the final amateur winners. Vernon profiled Granlund in May of 1951 in a short article complete with a photograph. The NTG biography was headlined "Laplander in Fame's Lap" and Vernon wrote that Granlund arrived in the United States as a child-sailor, that he introduced in 1915 the gaily lighted premieres of Broadway shows, conducted world tours, and retained an ability to speak seven languages.[30]

In 1951, Granlund was passing out ice tongs at a food market on Van Nuys Boulevard,[31] as part of a celebrity appearance for his soft drink sponsor. The other "celebrities" making an appearance with him were accordionist Donna Koach and vocalist Elain Zazuetta. The two youngsters earned their celebrity status as multiple winners on the NTG–Wilshire Club amateur show and, as amateurs go, had achieved a local celebrity status, of sorts. The ice tongs they

The Royalton

44 WEST 44th STREET, NEW YORK 36, N. Y.

Jan. 24, 1957.

Amanda Dear:

 Just received your note. Have sent some money for your Mom, but thought you might need a few dollars to spend.

  Will be on show again to try to win $10,000. Hope you see it.

  Love,

   Dad.

After making a successful appearance on the game show *The Big Surprise*, Nils T. Granlund wrote his granddaughter with the news (courtesy Amanda Howard).

were handing out to the public alongside Granlund were "absolutely free from Wilshire Club," and made of hammered chrome.

The *Van Nuys News* chronicled Granlund's recent visits with his winners and his complete "talent troupe" as they entertained at the Pacific Coast Army and Navy stations, and noted his celebration of two years on KTSL with the *Hollywood Road to Fame*.

The Albuquerque *Tribune* lauded the accomplishments of another young amateur, 14-year-old Sue Rae Claussen, who planned to audition for a local radio show in October 1951. She was a veteran of the Granlund amateur show, and listed the experience as part of her brief entertainment résumé. On August 24, 1952, an Iowa newspaper was carrying the big news of their hometown contestant, nine-year-old Jerilyn Oliver, who with her brother Denny had won first prize on the Granlund program the previous winter.[32] Young Jerilyn and her mother were back in Hollywood for a second shot at the brass ring on the *Hollywood Road to Fame*.

Granlund was hosting yet another program by the time KTSL changed their call letters to KNXT. His programming time slot was 11:15,[33] the final presentation before signoff (in a time when television stations were turned off at night). His show was *Treasure Chest of Talent*. The guest on April 24 for that day's fifteen-minute program was Los Angeles Superior Court Judge A.A. Scott.[34]

It may be a testament to his public relations ability that he was able to turn the late, late show vehicle into something a little closer to prime time, but Granlund's opportunities remained in decline. Part of the problem had to have been his insistence on the potential of his long-tried formula. But part of the success was his familiarity with the same. By May 1953, Granlund had been sifting the haves and the have-nots of Southern California long enough that the Long Beach *Press Telegram*, in mentioning a programming change, credited him with giving a start to many local youngsters. Granlund's discoveries were no longer the long-legged chorus girls, jazz musicians, top-flight comedians, or singers. They were the violin-playing, tap-dancing, horn-honking, card-tricking children of proud and opportunistic parents.

His "New Talent Showcase" heralded in the *Looking and Listening* column of May 22, 1953,[35] must have been a reference to the inexperience of the talent. The showcase certainly was not new. How long Granlund had been off the air is not clear, but the headline notes that "NTG Returns to Television." KNXT put Granlund back in prime time with Wilshire Club again as his sponsor. "Same format," the writer noted in describing Granlund's program, in that "he tries to give a boost to aspiring talent, some good, some pretty bad." The show was akin to NBC's *The Gong Show* of the late 1970s or the Fox Network's *American Idol* program's early contestant auditions in the 2000s. Granlund ousted Gene Autry, the Singing Cowboy, from the time slot.[36] NTG was shot out of the saddle before September.

As that month got underway, Granlund took his act to KHJ-TV, Channel 9,[37] where the program was called *Stars and Models with NTG*. The television writer for the *Long Beach Independent* noted that the program's name would quickly be shortened by newspaper listing editors[38]; in fact, the *Press-Independent* was already listing the show simply as *Stars and Models*. The 7:15 P.M. panel-type show featured professional entertainers and a group of experts who—like the *American Idol* panelists—gave critiques to the would-be stars. The entertainers, naturally, were all female. The media writer made note that Granlund's program duplicated a show being carried by a competitor.

Granlund was convinced his amateur program would work. It didn't. KHJ-TV agreed to give him another shot, resuscitating the NTG vehicle *Hollywood Road to Fame*, but running only a single program per week, a one-hour edition airing at noon on Sundays.[39]

In any broadcasting scenario, the star is only up—until knocked down. Media positions, in many ways, are no different than the Wild West gunslinger who, after having dispatched enough challengers to gain a reputation as a fast draw, must spend the rest of his life defending it against young pistoleers who hope to achieve their own infamy. For every program on the air, every actor in a part, every producer with an idea, there are unending lines of would-be replacements waiting for a stumble, a showdown, or a death.

Granlund's quick-draw was not so quick any more. His arms were heavy and the gun in his hand—the silver microphone—had upon it the tarnish of reminiscence with bullets cast in the leaden molds of days long past.

Of all of his acquaintances over the decades on Broadway and in Hollywood, no one remembered Granlund like *New York Mirror* columnist Lee Mortimer. He never gave up on the Swedish showman who had hosted so many late night—early morning sessions at the farm in New Jersey. It was Mortimer who first heard of Granlund's troubles.

His several television programs having gotten the axe, Granlund moved his amateur talent hunt from the TV screen to a small rehearsal hall, made available by a financial backer who supported the showman's plan to create a show business academy. Unfortunately, Granlund himself was no longer in a financial position to bring the plan to fruition.

Mortimer tried a low-key appeal for support in August 1955, under the sub-heading "Gratitude Is in the Dictionary."[40] Pointing out that Granlund "held out a helping hand to any youngster who found it tough sledding," Mortimer inferred that Granlund was now in a position to need a helping hand himself: "Recently, he took over a talent school and studio in Hollywood," noting that the academy promised to deliver the stars of the future, but only with assistance from "the stars of the present who got there because NTG helped them."[41] The appeal for financial aid was repeated in the *New York Daily Mirror* less than a year later.

Within two weeks of the original Mortimer column calling for those stars

who had been given a boost by Granlund to come to his aid, the *Mirror* columnist had some good news, reporting in August 1955 that Granlund — "who
invented the modern cabaret"[42] — was penning his memoirs. Granlund, having
read a Mortimer item that mentioned a former NTG showgirl, wrote the columnist to ask for help in recalling some of the "Dumb Dora" showgirl stories that
might be memoir material.

The stories were the focus of much of his onstage presentations and
Granlund intended to mine the same material for his manuscript. Mortimer
was only happy to oblige, attaching to the memoir announcement one of
Granlund's often repeated anecdotes about showgirl Helen Gray. The "innocent, unsuspecting, wide-eyed, small town gal" had made a promise to her
mother that she would not take up drinking or smoking upon her arrival in
New York City. After her first appearance in Granlund's Paradise revue, she
was offered a celebratory cocktail. She declined. A few minutes later, the host
repeated the offer, which was again declined. The third visit brought an offer
of caviar, to which the thoroughly exasperated Helen shouted, "Didn't I tell
you I never drink?"[43]

Mortimer reported that, from then on, Helen Gray was simply known as
Caviar.

He closed the column recalling that he had only recently retold the story
to another Broadway showgirl, who listened intently and then inquired, "Yes,
but what kind of drink *is* caviar?"

They were the "Dumb Dora" stories that Granlund and Mortimer loved
to share.

The talent academy never met with real success, and Granlund's money
woes continued. In late August of 1956, the always faithful Mortimer commented on Granlund's Broadway recollections, which by then were in the publisher's proof stage. In "New York Confidential," the columnist awarded his
"Mortimer Medallion" to the "inventor of modern nightlife"[44] and discoverer
of Joan Crawford, Ruby Keeler, and Yvonne De Carlo, who was "still in there
kicking at Hollywood's Academy of Theatre Arts."

Twelve days after Mortimer's initial NTG note, columnist Walter Winchell
weighed in, wording it as a tip-of-the-hat to Mortimer and his "Mortimer
Medallion" in repeating news of Granlund's current affairs. Both writers mentioned the title of the forthcoming book (which Mortimer promised would be
a "sizzler") from the man who "knows more about show business and the
underworld than anyone alive."[45] Granlund, wrote Mortimer, had fallen out of
sight and "many of his friends have been wondering what happened to him."
He included in his column a portion of a recent letter from Granlund that
explained his plan to "help kids become successful." Although Granlund's
intentions may be have pure, his wording had a mercenary ring in noting he
had "never received a dime" for his past efforts, and that "now, we intend to
make some money from people we help."

As Mortimer reported it, Granlund's letter included news of the talent academy located at the Rainbow rehearsal halls in Los Angeles, "a big school, with top teachers in every branch of show business."

Yvonne De Carlo remembered the fifties for Granlund as "some very lean years,"[46] in which the showman had dropped from sight, relegated to a time in history that Walter Winchell's column called "the NTG days."[47]

In January 1957, advance copies of his book were being made available to reviewers. Frank Morrisey wrote for the *Oakland Tribune* that it was a "fantastic story." In 2005, Clifford J. Doerksen described it as a "boffo memoir [...] assuming it is reliable."[48]

Granlund traveled to New York in January on a joint mission of publicizing his soon-to-be-released book and raising money for his talent school project. *The $64,000 Question* was a popular CBS quiz show that spawned an NBC knockoff called *The Big Surprise*, hosted by TV stalwart Mike Wallace in the days before his journalistic turn. Granlund landed a spot on the latter[49] and answered enough questions on his first appearance to earn the right to return in succeeding weeks in pursuit of the $100,000 top prize. On January 22, 1957, Terry Vernon of the *Long Beach Press-Telegram* noted that the showman was shooting for a $3,000 prize on that evening's *Big Surprise* broadcast.[50]

On the February 4, 1957, episode, appearing after Mrs. Margaux Rehman of New York City and Hollywood legend Errol Flynn, Granlund was introduced as the "expert on the Roaring Twenties."[51] Just before the beginning of his segment, Wallace related to the now-aging showman that "mail has poured in for you from all over the country, famous people — old friends of yours— the great ones of yesterday." The letter-writers all wished Granlund to know how pleasing it was to see him, Wallace noted, and Granlund replied that he was even getting letters from some of his former showgirls saying "my daughter is now eighteen, and I want her in your chorus."[52]

When asked by Wallace if he would risk his winnings for a larger prize, Granlund responded by noting that he had come to New York for four days, as "a guest of the David McKay Company," the publisher of his memoir. "Here it is, four weeks later," Granlund told Wallace, "and I'm still here with one suitcase and one shirt."[53] Opting to leave the show with his $10,000 winnings, Granlund stated that he could delay no longer a show he was producing at the Hacienda Hotel in Las Vegas. It was a "great big, beautiful, new hotel," as Granlund described it, built by Warren Bayley at the far south end of Las Vegas Boulevard, at that time an isolated area about a mile from the Flamingo. "I'm going to put on the biggest show in the history of Las Vegas," Granlund bragged, "in the finest hotel, on the biggest stage."

It was Nils Thor Granlund the promoter in action.

In truth, the Hacienda was constructed with "economy-minded travelers"[54] in mind, along with those who brought their children on vacation. Using billboards and coupons to promote the lower-cost hotel, the establishment

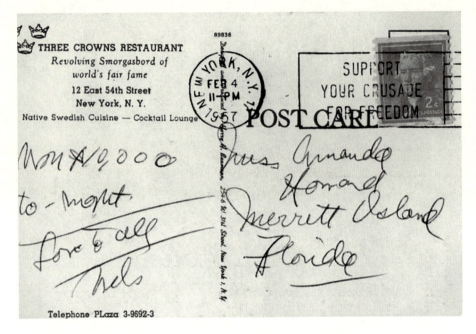

After a celebratory dinner, Nils Granlund penned this postcard announcing his winnings on the game show *The Big Surprise* (courtesy Amanda Howard).

became known to locals as "Hayseed Heaven." The hotel was imploded in 1996 to make room for the Mandalay Bay Resort.

Wallace presented Granlund with a passbook from Chase Bank that indicated the winnings had been placed in an account on his behalf. While the showman might have been secretly bursting at the prospect of the money, he gave an appreciative smile for the applauding audience and made a gracious exit.

To celebrate, Granlund dined on "native Swedish cuisine" at the Three Crowns Restaurant at 12 East 54th Street,55 and penned a note to his granddaughter in Florida: "Won $10,000 to-night, Love to All, Nils." He mailed the restaurant postcard at eleven o'clock that same evening.

Time magazine later printed a story — in an ironically timed April 22, 1957, article — that included Granlund's episode in a recap of the scandalous, rigged nature of the question-based television shows. The item claimed that Granlund's winnings came on "extremely easy" questions, and that the showman "admits that some of the questions he answered during his screening interview may have turned up on the show itself."

The money would have been a godsend to the financially embattled Granlund, but as Yvonne De Carlo recalled, "[T]he IRS snatched that for back taxes."56

April Fool's Day of 1957 brought for Granlund the sort of tricks that might be expected of the date, promises of a great kick ending with the football pulled away, the magic tablecloth improperly snatched from under the best china, or the good-faith handshake ending in a shock from the hidden buzzer.

George Freedley, writing in his "Of Books and Men" column for the April 1 *New York Morning Telegram*, gave notice that Granlund's "lively book"[57] just released by David McKay publishers will be "frank and amusing" to readers. Marie Blizard, of the Bridgeport, Connecticut, *Post*, liked the man but not the memoir, believing that "telling a life story and writing it, alas, are two quite different things."[58]

The *Saturday Review* said Granlund's recollections "are a must for anyone partial to the Roaring Twenties." Yvonne De Carlo believed the publication "gave him a new flash of recognition"[59] that might assist him in getting back on track.

The book did bring his name back into focus for many who had forgotten Granlund over the years,[60] and he intended to make the most of it. Earl Wilson reported in his Broadway gossip column on March 10, 1957, that Granlund intended to co-author a biography of Danish silent film star Carl Brisson,[61] who was in failing health in Copenhagen. The biography, Granlund claimed, would be filmed by the actor's son Fred Brisson, the Danish-American producer who was married to award-winning actress Rosalind Russell.

Granlund, in April 1957, was able to wrangle an interview in Las Vegas for the possibility of staging a revue at the Riviera. As Yvonne De Carlo remembered, all that remained was the signing of the paperwork at an attorney's office to complete the deal.[62]

For the Easter weekend of April 20, he was in Las Vegas where Gene Littler was to defend his Tournament of Champions golf title at the Desert Inn Golf and Country Club. Granlund intended to catch the golf professionals in action[63] as part of a business-pleasure trip that he hoped would conclude with the landing of a revue contract at one of the Strip's major hotels.

It was raining early Monday morning and the roads were slick.[64] Shortly after ten in the morning, Granlund climbed into a taxicab outside the front doors at the Riviera, spoke briefly to the driver, fifty-six-year-old Donald Mann, and sat back with satisfaction. He had every belief that his hard luck of the past few years had ended, and that the NTG initials could again adorn a glittering showplace filled with appreciative audiences. Mann paused before pulling out onto the Las Vegas Strip, described then as Highway 91, waiting for a break in traffic that was noted for its excessive speeds as drivers migrated from one end of the resort area to the other. Mann eased the cab forward and out of the parking lot.

Granlund had only time to shout, "Where'd he come from?"[65] before the screeching impact.

The taxicab buckled like cardboard when it was slammed broadside by a

Publisher David McKay underwrote a trip to Florida for the promotion of Granlund's memoirs. Granlund hoped to meet with his ex-wife Mabel during his stay but she declined to see him (courtesy Amanda Howard).

car that police estimated was traveling at 70 miles an hour. Granlund was catapulted from the crushed taxi and his head slammed against the wet Las Vegas pavement, where he lay until he could be scooped into an ambulance and rushed to Southern Nevada Memorial Hospital. Mann suffered minor back and rib injuries. He would recover after receiving a traction splint for a broken arm.

The driver of the speeding car, 32-year-old William McAdams, a Las Vegas bartender, refused to take a blood test for possible alcohol content. He was treated at a Las Vegas hospital.

Racing to the hospital after receiving word of the accident was Harold Belfer, a producer and movie choreographer who was working in Las Vegas as a show packager. Yvonne De Carlo recalled that it was Belfer who telephoned her regarding Granlund's accident. "The hospital was trying to locate Granny's family,"[66] she said, recalling that Belfer knew nothing of Granlund's next of kin and believed that De Carlo could provide information. She knew little of the showman's family, and realized that he had "been abandoned by just about everyone." When the hospital finally reached De Carlo with news of Granlund's death, she told the caller that she would take care of the final arrangements. Granlund had died three hours after the accident.[67]

Word of the tragedy spread quickly. Eddie Cantor, whom Granlund had introduced to radio for the first time, was stunned. "I just can hardly believe it," he said. "He was a wonderful guy and discovered many people who are now stars."[68]

Newspapers across the country, in which his name in recent years had merited only the briefest sentences in gossip column notes, all carried the news of his demise—many of them printing the report on the front page. Several papers repeated an early wire report that indicated Granlund left no survivors, while others ended their death notices with similar incorrect assessments, including mentions that Granlund left no relatives "except for his widow Rose, from whom he was separated years ago."[69]

Granlund did not speak much of his estranged wife Rose, even to his close friend Yvonne De Carlo. A reporter finally contacted Bertha C. Klausner, who had negotiated the book contract for Granlund's memoirs, and she pointed out that that the showman was married early in his career and that Rose, his second wife and widow, lived in New York.

The *New York Times* reflected more of the facts. "Mr. Granlund's first marriage ended in divorce. He married Rose Wenzel, the dancer, in 1926."[70] Of all the papers covering his death, none devoted more space to it than the *Times*.

"With the assurance of his Norse ancestors sailing uncharted seas," the writer exclaimed in the next edition in print after the showman's death, "Mr. Granlund won early success as a motion picture press agent, radio personality, and nightclub showman." The death notice pointed out that that the initials NTG were as well known in the Roaring Twenties as those of F.D.R. were to become in politics a decade later.

Calling his productions "girlie shows," the *Times* recalled how the revues brought money rolling into the nightclubs, and that while broadcasting from Billy Gallagher's Monte Carlo club, Granlund had been asked by the owner for suggestions toward improving business, down badly due to Prohibition. Granlund, the writer noted, advised Gallagher to stage a competition among show girls. As a friend and adviser to Texas Guinan, Granlund suggested that she drop the café designation and call her establishment a "nightclub."

The death notice in its entirety covered nearly a quarter-page.

Yvonne De Carlo had a longtime friend named Patricia Starling who had appeared in several films and also rode in the Granlund-produced rodeo shows. Many times she accompanied De Carlo in visiting Granlund, and the three often spent full days riding his horses along the bridle paths not far from his home. "Pat Starling and I saw that Granny had a decent funeral and burial,"[71] said De Carlo, who selected Forest Lawn Cemetery as Granlund's final resting place, not for its prestige, but because it was the spot where he and the showgirls rode horseback. She contacted as many of the Swede's former dancers as she could and bought a floral arrangement for the casket that read, "To Granny from the Girls."[72] She recalled that the memorial service was sparsely attended.

Following the service, the former Florentine Gardens dancers retired for a "wake of sorts," and it was generally determined that there were a multitude of people who owed Granlund for past favors who failed to appear for his memorial. De Carlo lamented that several of the showman's buddies who "accepted his hospitality and food and drink for years" simply ignored their friend's death.

Newspapers carried photographs of the "Granlund Girls," veiled former showgirls clad in black, emerging from the service. The INS syndicate reported on the funeral arranged by "an actress he helped lift from the chorus line to screen stardom." He was buried on April 25 near a bridle path he often rode along when the cemetery was open "ranch country" years before.

Writer Sid Feder, who worked with Granlund in penning his memoirs, wrote in his newspaper column "Longhorns & Short Tales" that it was hard to imagine anyone as full of life as Granlund being dead, but even Feder had been kept out of the more sordid details of Granlund's history. In pointing out the presumed irony of Granlund's death in a car accident, Feder noted that "anything over 30 miles an hour is strictly a dirty word with Granny."[73] According to the columnist, Granlund had never had an accident and was "probably the most careful driver you ever saw." Feder overlooked or was uninformed about the New York fatality for which Granlund was judged responsible and liable for damages. No mention of that accident was included in the memoir.

Feder remembered Granlund as the sort of person who—if he had two dollars—would "push one of his two into your pocket." Before Granlund's fatal crash, when it was Feder in a Los Angeles hospital, he was discharged after treatment but ordered to remain in bed for an additional six weeks. According to Feder, Granlund made the 26-mile drive from Hollywood and Vine to Tujunga daily, for what extended into an eight-week convalescence.

"Granny makes this run at his steady 30 miles an hour," wrote Feder, who added that Granlund invariably stopped on his way to pick up a filet mignon or a sweet Hawaiian pineapple to bring to the recovering patient. Realizing that his friend was "lonesome more than anything else," Granlund would bring along a "pretty or two from among all the bevy of pretties he is talent-scouting" to keep Feder company for a time.

Feder told his readers that, a few days before the fatal accident, he had received a letter from Granlund in which the showman pledged to make reservations in Feder's name for the soon-to-be-opened Granlund revue in Las Vegas. Granlund had gone to Miami for what he termed a "fling," but told Feder he was "back home ... and still broke. But it was worth it."[74]

Granlund's dear friend Lee Mortimer was badly shaken by the news. "The Granny of thousands of show-beauties who worked for him and loved him, is gone," he wrote,[75] calling it both "sad and ironic" that the showman died only weeks after starting on the road to a comeback.

After Granlund's death, Mortimer no longer minced his words, noting that the showman had been "washed up" for years and was "struggling in Hollywood, all but forgotten by many of the headliners" whom he had given a boost on their respective roads to stardom.

Like Yvonne De Carlo, Mortimer believed that the publication of Granlund's memoirs would catapult him back into the limelight and create a demand for his services. The Granlund memoirs had only just hit the stores; with no author to publicize the release, it scarcely rated a mention just months after its publication, and quickly disappeared—just as Granlund had done. Before the tragic accident, Mortimer felt certain that the tide had turned for his friend, since Granlund was signed to go to Miami to get girls for a new show and hotel in Las Vegas. "Almost anyone you can think of," claimed Mortimer, "got a first boost from Granny and when he couldn't give a kid a job, he was always there with a hand-out for eating money and room rent. That's why he was broke in his later years."[76]

Mortimer had experienced a tragic loss of his own in the death of his wife Ann Mortimer, and Granlund had written to his friend earlier in the month offering condolences and advice: "You should make a big effort to look at it this way, you have had a great happiness, a peace of mind and soul in know-ing and having this wonderful girl as your constant companion. Instead of thinking of the loss, think of the wonderful experiences of your life with her, brief as it was. Loving her as you did, this great love you had for her should make you happy instead of sad. Try to forget the loss and remember only the happy times you had together."

"And now my old friend Granny is dead, too," concluded Mortimer. "We had many happy times together."[77]

Rose Wenzel Granlund, the estranged wife back in New York, had her own tough times in recent years. The experience of her sister Eileen, who went to court to recover damages from the auto accident that disfigured her, may have inspired Rose to seek financial damages as a result of the fatal crash. On May 19, 1957, Rose, "the attractive blonde widow," filed a $125,000 damage suit[78] against C.F. Shaw, the owner of Blue Cab Company, Donald Mann, the driver, and William McAdams, the driver of the other vehicle. The suit charged reck-lessness or negligence and was filed on behalf of herself and "other heirs." The "others" were never specified, although Granlund did have heirs from his first marriage.

A coroner's jury investigation conducted immediately after the accident had deliberated two hours and fifteen minutes before returning a finding of "no negligence" on the part of the cab driver, who had been interviewed while confined to a wheelchair at Southern Nevada Memorial Hospital. The coroner's report indicated Granlund died of "a basal skull fracture caused by the accident."[79]

It was October 1958 before Rose's civil lawsuit went to a jury comprised of three women and nine men.[80] The week-long trial recessed for the evening, and the following day, the jury — after six hours of discussion — awarded damages in the severely reduced amount of $8,500 to be paid by the Blue Cab Company.

Incidentally, on the same street in Las Vegas, on the same date, a second accident would be included in a number of the printed reports: Popular singer Eddie Fisher had stopped to make a left-hand turn "when his car was struck from the rear by one driven by Miss Lu Altman of Las Vegas."

The 28-year-old Fisher was the current headliner at the Tropicana and his car was knocked head-on into a third car, driven by Robert J. Kerr of Durante, California. The singer was shaken up but uninjured. Fisher had just ended a four-year variety show on NBC and would find himself in the public eye for decades to come with his Hollywood marriages and divorces.

As a popular singer not attached to any particular orchestra or band, Fisher represented a new form of vocal entertainment, and the irony of his escaping the April 22 accident unscathed, while Granlund's death — and his association with a form of entertainment considered well past its time — cannot be overlooked. It was almost sardonically cruel that Granlund died while contracting for a stage show in Las Vegas, where the term "Vegas-style revues" could just as easily have been "Granlund-style revues." He was set to bring the glittering, long-legged chorus girls in revealing costumes to the one city in which that form of entertainment would still work, a city of bright lights, loud music, glitzy showgirls, and plenty of first-time stooges to bring up on stage.

Greater still is the irony that the man who had brought countless hopefuls to fame, more than a few to fortune, and created the foundation on which so much of the entertainment media have been built — was almost completely forgotten by the time of his death. There is no mention on the Hollywood Walk of Fame for the man who invented the movie trailer, no honorary Academy Award in technical achievement for the man who first filmed a commercial to show in movie theaters. Radio historians cannot recall the man who first took the microphone out of the studio and brought live music into the homes of radio listeners. There is no ESPN statuette for the first electronic sports reporter, the man who put his microphone into the faces of the boxers before and after the bouts. Television archivists have no special folder for the man who introduced a live show from an airplane circling over the New York skyline, and who stood onstage among the first to unveil this experimental new entertainment medium to the public. There is no plaque in Las Vegas for the man who was the first to bring a chorus troupe onto stages later famous for line-kicking showgirls in glittering costumes.

His native country has no memorial to the Broadway Swede, and without doubt there are no legends of the showman among the descendants of the reindeer-herding Laplanders of the Arctic Circle.

Like a single glittering burst of light over Times Square, he dazzled those whose faces basked in the glow of his energy, and then disappeared.

Signature of Nils Theodore Granlund, having dropped the middle name that honored his father in favor of Thor, the hammer-wielding Norse god of thunder (courtesy McHuston Archives).

Perhaps the ultimate irony was the lonely burial arranged by his special friend Yvonne De Carlo, one of the very few who never forgot the Swedish showman and his influence on her life. "No man has ever been kinder to me,"[81] she said. "As I look back over the years, I wonder if my search for a substitute father didn't end that August evening of 1940 when I walked into the Florentine Gardens.

"May God rest your sweet soul, Granny."

Chapter Notes

Prologue

1. Larry Harnisch, "Interview with Bob Rains," *Los Angeles Times*, Blogs: *The Daily Mirror*, April 22, 2007.
2. Yvonne De Carlo, *Yvonne* (New York: St. Martin's, 1987), page 50.
3. Ibid.
4. Harnisch, *Los Angeles Times*.
5. Refer, for example, to dialogue in the Monogram movie *Rhythm Parade* (1942).
6. Harnisch, *Los Angeles Times*.
7. De Carlo, *Yvonne*, page 201.

Chapter One

1. Ulla-Maija Kulonen, Irja Seurujarvi-Kari, and Risto Pulkkinen (editors), "The Saami: A Cultural Encyclopedia," (U.K.: Cambridge University Press), *Polar Record*, 42, Number 4 (2006).
2. "Samis Don't Want to Be Lapps," *Aftenposten*, aftenposten.no, February 8, 2008.
3. Nils T. Granlund, with Sid Feder and Ralph Hancock, *Blondes, Brunettes, and Bullets* (New York: David McKay, 1957), page 7.
4. Avery Amanda Howard, interview, January 11, 2009.
5. Granlund, *Blondes*, page 7.
6. "Rhode Island Deaths, 1630–1930," (Internet database), Provo, UT, The Generations Network, 2000.
7. Granlund, *Blondes*, page 7.
8. Robert C. Ostergren, *A Community Transplanted* (Madison: University of Wisconsin Press, 1988), page 112.
9. 12th Census of the United States, Providence, Rhode Island, Enumeration District 46, Sheet 13.
10. Draft Registration Card 1918: Registration Location, New York County, New York, Roll 1786807, Draft Board 148.
11. Granlund, *Blondes*, page 8.
12. Ostergren, *A Community Transplanted*, page 111.

13. Ellis Island [Online Database], ellisisland.org, May 6, 2008.
14. Ostergren, *A Community Transplanted*, page 124.
15. Ellis Island [Online Database].
16. "Fast Atlantic Passages; Records Made Between NY and Southampton," *New York Times*, April 12, 1891, page 20, reprinted from the *Liverpool Journal of Commerce*.
17. Ibid.
18. "Strongest Women in the World," *New York Times*, March 16, 1894.
19. Ibid.
20. Philip Scranton, *Endless Novelty: Specialty Production and American Industrialization* (Princeton, New Jersey: Princeton University Press, 1998), page 109.
21. Allen Kastrup, *The Swedish Heritage in America* (Swedish Council of America, 1975), page 522.
22. "History," State of Rhode Island General Assembly, Rhode Island History, Chapter 6, rilin.state.ri.us, October 27, 2008.
23. 12th Census, Providence.
24. Granlund, *Blondes*, page 9.
25. Ibid., page 11.
26. "John B. Herreshoff, Yacht Builder, Dies," *New York Times*, July 21, 1915.
27. Richard V. Simpson, *Herreshoff Yachts; Seven Generations of Industrialists, Investors, and Ingenuity in Bristol* (Charleston, SC: History Press, 2007), page 33.
28. Granlund, *Blondes*, page 12.
29. Ibid.
30. 12th Census of the United States, Providence, Rhode Island, Enumeration District 46, Sheet 13.
31. "Rhode Island Yacht Club," entry, *1919 City Directory*, Providence, Rhode Island.
32. Granlund, *Blondes*, page 14.
33. "John R. Rathom" [Obituary], *New York Times*, December 24, 1923.
34. 13th Census of the United States, Providence, Rhode Island, Enumeration District 205, Sheet 10B, [Employment] "Sporting Editor."

35. S.T. Joshi, *A Dreamer and a Visionary: H.P. Lovecraft in His Time* (Liverpool: Liverpool University Press, 2001), page 58.

36. Granlund, *Blondes*, page 20.

37. "Jamestown Honors Prince; Warships Salute Wilhelm of Sweden and Thousands Welcome Him," *New York Times*, August 20, 1907, page 1.

38. Granlund, *Blondes*, page 16.

39. "Newport in a War Over Prince's Visit," Special to the *New York Times*, August 6, 1907, page 1.

40. "Jamestown Honors Prince; Warships Salute Wilhelm of Sweden and Thousands Welcome Him," *New York Times*, August 20, 1907, page 1.

41. Ibid.

42. Granlund, *Blondes*, page 17.

43. John N. Dobson, *Bulls, Bears, Boom, and Bust*, "Nelson Wilmarth Aldrich" [Entry], (Santa Barbara, CA: ABC-CLIO, 2006), page 307.

44. Granlund, *Blondes*, page 17.

45. "Prince to Go to Sahara; Wilhelm of Sweden Plans Book on His Experiences," Wireless to the *New York Times*, January 16, 1933, page 17.

46. Granlund, *Blondes*, page 19.

Chapter Two

1. Frank Cullen, Florence Hackman, and Donald McNeilly, *Vaudeville, Old and New* (New York: Routledge, 2006), page 27.

2. Mel Gussow, *Edward Albee: A Singular Journey* (New York: Applause, 2000), page 23.

3. David Bakish, *Jimmy Durante: His Show Business Career* (Jefferson, NC: McFarland, 1995), page 32.

4. William A. Everett and Paul R. Laird, *The Cambridge Companion to the Musical* (Cambridge: Cambridge University Press, 2002), page 26.

5. *Programme*, Albee Theatre, Providence, Rhode Island, September 9, 1895.

6. Ibid.

7. Granlund, *Blondes*, page 20.

8. Ibid.

9. "Loew's Spooner," Cinema Treasures, cinematreasures.org, October 31, 2008.

10. "Arrest of Actress Stops a Vice Play; Cecil Spooner Rides to Night Court in Patrol Wagon," *New York Times*, December 10, 1913, page 1.

11. Granlund, *Blondes*, page 20.

12. Mark Knowles, *Tap Roots* (Jefferson, NC: McFarland, 2002), page 142.

13. "Thespians Wed in Boston; Miss Marion Bent Becomes the Bride of Patrick Rooney," *New York Times*, April 11, 1904, page 9.

14. Granlund, *Blondes*, page 20.

15. Leroy Ashby, *With Amusement for All* (Lexington: University Press of Kentucky, 2000), page 120.

16. "People: People," *Time* magazine, July 27, 1942.

17. Ashby, *Amusement*, page 120.

18. Avery Amanda Howard, interview, January 11, 2009.

19. 13th Census of the United States, Providence, Rhode Island, Enumeration District 205, Sheet 10B.

20. *Rhode Island Marriages, 1636–1930* [Online Database], Provo, UT, The Generations Network, Inc., 2000.

21. "Record of Marriage," Certificate 250, Division of Vital Statistics, Rhode Island State Department of Health, November 21, 1983.

22. Barry Witham, "Newspaper Article on Colonel Felix Wendelschaefer," *Theater in the United States 1750–1915* (Cambridge: Cambridge University Press, 1996), page 196.

23. "Providence Opera House," Cinema Treasures, citing *The Board of Trade Journal*, *April 1915*, cinematreasures.org, October 31, 2008.

24. Granlund, *Blondes*, page 21.

25. Patricia Erens, *The Jew in American Cinema* (Bloomington: Indiana University Press, 1984), page 77.

26. Andrew R. Heinze, *Adapting to Abundance* (New York: Columbia University Press, 1990), page 208.

27. Frank Rose, *The Agency: William Morris and the Hidden History of Show Business* (New York: HarperBusiness, 1995), page 33.

28. Granlund, *Blondes*, page 24.

29. "Rhode Island Deaths, 1630–1930" [Online Database], Provo, UT, The Generations Network, Inc., 2000.

30. "Rhode Island Marriages, 1636–1930" [Online Database], Provo, UT, The Generations Network, Inc., 2000.

31. "Rhode Island Deaths, 1630–1930" [Online Database], Provo, UT, The Generations Network, Inc., 2000.

32. Warren G. Harris, Theater Historian, "Loew's Avenue B," *Cinema Treasures*, cinematreasures.org, posted October 13, 2005.

33. Granlund, *Blondes*, page 49.

34. "Mason Opera House Brilliantly Opened," *Los Angeles Herald*, June 19, 1903.

35. Granlund, *Blondes*, page 28.

36. Emily Gibson and Barbara Firth, *The Original Million Dollar Mermaid: The Annette Kellerman Story* (Crow's Nest, N.S.W., Allen and Unwin, 2000), page 118.

37. Granlund, *Blondes*, page 29.

38. "The Stage," *Oakland Tribune*, Oakland California, June 15, 1913, page 9.

39. "Mayor Will Parade in Model Bathing Suit," *Oakland Tribune*, Oakland California, July 4, 1912, page 5.

40. "Lew Fields Surprises Loew: 'Hanky Panky' Company appears in Vaudeville in Bronx," *New York Times*, September 19, 1912, page 11.

41. "M'Goorty Is Best: Eastern Expert Sizes Oshkosh Battle," *Daily Northwestern*, Oshkosh, WI, March 19, 1913.

42. Ibid.

43. Yvonne De Carlo, *Yvonne* (New York: St. Martin's Press, 1987), page 10.

44. "Free Press Show for Charity Today: Jolly 'Hanky Panky' Folk to Put on Entertainment at River Park," *Winnipeg Free Press*, Winnipeg, Manitoba, Canada, July 29, 1913, page 9.

45. Ibid.

Chapter Three

1. Frank Rose, *The Agency: William Morris and the Hidden History of Show Business* (New York: HarperBusiness, 1996), page 33.

2. William Morris Agency, LLC, "Agency Overview and History 2008," wma.com, July 3, 2008.

3. Rose, *Agency*, page 33.

4. "Vaudeville War Ends," *Atlanta Constitution*, Dateline: New York, March 4, 1911, page 10.

5. "Has Been a Gold Mine: Marcus Loew, Vaudeville King, Made a Big Killing When He Became Owner of Hanky Panky," *Cedar Rapids Republican*, Cedar Rapids, IA, November 29, 1914, page 18.

6. Clarence J. Bulleit, "Vaudeville War Is Ended After Fifteen Years of Hard Fighting," *Indianapolis Star*, Indianapolis, IN, March 19, 1911, page 52.

7. "Loew and Morris End Vaudeville War," *New York Times*, March 4, 1911

8. Ibid.

9. Granlund, *Blondes*, page 41.

10. "Death of T. Henry French," *New York Times*, December 2, 1902, page 9.

11. "Palisades Park Is Sold"; *New York Times*; special to the *New York Times*, Dateline: Hackensack, NJ, May 1, 1935, page 19.

12. Granlund, *Blondes*, page 43.

13. "Nicholas M. Schenck, 87, Dead," *New York Times*; March 5, 1969, page 47.

14. Granlund, *Blondes*, page 44.

15. Garnet Warren, "Confessions of the Queen of Press Agents, *Fort Wayne Sentinel*, Fort Wayne, IN, August 5, 1911, page 21, copyright 1911 by the *New York Herald*.

16. Thirteenth Census of the United States 1910, Washington, D.C., National Archives and Records Administration, T624, 1,178 rolls, Manhattan Ward 20, New York, NY; Enumeration District 1200.

17. Warren, *Confessions*, August 5, 1911.

18. "Publicist Is Dead: Reporter on Old World and Press Agent for Al Jolson Was Radio Personality"; *New York Times*; August 14, 1958, page 29.

19. Ibid.

20. "Nellie Revell Sees Broadway at Last: Is Guest at Great Dinner of Friars," *New York Times*; May 26, 1924, page Sports 17.

21. Granlund, *Blondes*, page 45.

22. Ibid.

23. Ibid.

24. Robert Grau, "Fortunes Built on Nickels and Dimes," *Elyria Evening Telegram*, Elyria, OH, November 12, 1912, page 5.

25. N.T. Granlund, "The Story of Marcus Loew," *Anaconda Standard*, Anaconda, MT, March 26, 1914, page 12.

26. *"Pleasure Seekers* a Spectacle Only," *New York Times*; November 4, 1913, page 9.

27. "Sigmund Lubin Dies; Pioneer in Movies; Philadelphia Optician, Once a Producer, Succumbs to Heart Disease at 72," *New York Times*; September 11, 1923, page 15.

28. "Marcus Loew Buys Metro Pictures," *New York Times*, January 6, 1920, page 1.

29. "A Producer at Harvard: Marcus Loew Tells Business School of Some Experiences in Motion Pictures," *New York Times*; April 17, 1927, page X5.

30. Granlund, *Blondes*, page 46.

31. "Film Company Gets Criterion Theatre," *New York Times*; November 3, 1913, page 9.

32. "New Theatre Opens in Times Square: Detailed Plans of the Winter Garden Announced," *New York Times*; page 11.

33. Granlund, *Blondes*, page 46.

34. "Movies Score on Legit in New York," *Lincoln Daily Star*, Lincoln, NE, November 9, 1913, page 25.

35. Granlund, *Blondes*, page 48.

36. "Movies Score on Legit in New York," *Lincoln Daily Star*, Lincoln, NE, November 9, 1913, page 25.

37. Ibid.

38. Granlund, *Blondes*, page 249.

39. Lee Mortimer, "NTG on Radio—and Still Walking on Air," Nightlife, *New York Daily Mirror*, March 14, 1946, page 26.

40. May Mann, "Going Hollywood," *Ogden Standard-Examiner*, Ogden, UT, January 10, 1941, page 9.

41. "Marcus Loew May Build Chain of Theatres in West," *Manitoba Free Press*; Manitoba, Canada, April 21, 1914, page 8.

42. "Joseph Schenck in Jail: Loew's Booking Agent Arrested on a Nixon — Nirdlinger Warrant," *New York Times*; September 27, 1913, page 13.

43. Ibid.

44. "Vaudeville Strife Ends: Loew Gives Up Philadelphia Theatres on an Agreement with

Keith," *New York Times*, December 12, 1913, page 13.

45. Ibid.

46. "Blow by Car Door Kills," *New York Times*, April 9, 1921, page 7.

47. "Buys Big Corner in Yorkville Area," *New York Times*, March 2, 1921, page 27.

48. William G. Harris, "Loew's Eighty-sixth Street Theatre," *Cinema Treasures*, cinematreasures.org, November 12, 2005.

49. "The Real Estate Field," *New York Times*, April 4, 1916, page 22.

50. William G. Harris, "Loew's Orpheum," *Cinema Treasures*, cinematreasures.org, July 12, 2005.

51. "Theatrical Notes," *New York Times*, October 18, 1913, page 13.

52. "Thieves Rob Theatre Safe," *New York Times*, December 27, 1913, page 5.

53. Granlund, *Blondes*, page 50.

54. "Fein Faces Another Trial," *New York Times*, January 22, 1914, page 12.

55. "Lawyer's Drew Up Gangs' Contracts," *New York Times*, May 14, 1915, page 22.

56. "Had Fixed Rates for Gang Raids," *New York Times*, May 13, 1915, page 24.

57. "Dopey Benny Convicted," *New York Times*, January 21, 1914, page 1.

58. "Gangs Wiped Out," *New York Times*, July 12, 1915, page 14.

59. Granlund, *Blondes*, page 50.

60. Arnold Shaw, *The Jazz Age: Popular Music in the 1920s* (New York: Oxford University Press, 1987), page 13.

61. Granlund, *Blondes*, page 51.

62. Ibid.

63. "Lottie Mayer," *Ogden Examiner*, Ogden, UT, October 8, 1913, page 8.

64. "Diving Girl Killed Behind the Curtain: Comedian Merry in Front, and Even Girl's Partners Didn't Know of Her Death," *New York Times*, October 22, 1913, page 1.

65. "Loew in $4,000,000 Vaudeville Deal," *New York Times*, Dateline Kansas City, MO, March 27, 1914, page 11.

66. Ibid.

67. "To Bring German Actors," *New York Times*, October 18, 1915, page 9.

68. "Loew Blow," *Time* magazine, November 12, 1956.

69. "MGM Reshuffles," *Daily Intelligencer*, Doylestown, PA, Dateline UPI New York, January 10, 1963, page 1.

70. Allen J. Scott, *On Hollywood: The Place, The Industry* (Princeton, NJ: Princeton University Press, 2004), page 12.

71. Granlund, *Blondes*, page 52.

72. Ibid.

73. Ibid.

74. Karen E. Goulekas, *Visual Effects in a Digital World: A Comprehensive Glossary of Over 7000 Visual Effects Terms* (San Francisco: Morgan Kauffman, 2001), page 517.

75. Arthur Frank Wertheim, *Vaudeville Wars: How the Keith-Albee and Orpheum Circuits Controlled the Big Time and Its Performers* (New York: Palgrave Macmillan, 2006).

76. Geoffrey Nowell-Smith, *The Oxford History of World Cinema* (New York: Oxford University Press, 1999), page 25.

77. Simon Louvish, *Cecil B. DeMille: A Life in Art* (New York: Thomas Dunne Books, 2007), page 60.

78. Cecil B. DeMille, "An Address Before the Commonwealth Club, San Francisco California, November 7, 1947.

79. Granlund, *Blondes*, page 54.

80. "The Squaw Man," *La Crosse Tribune*, La Crosse, WI, Spotlights, March 12, 1914, page 8.

81. "The Squaw Man Shown at the American Theatre," *Anaconda Standard*, Anaconda, MT, March 19, 1914.

82. Gary Wayne, "Seeing Stars: Hollywood Museums," The Hollywood Heritage Museum, seeing-stars.com, July 9, 2008. Note: Samuel Goldwyn's ghostwritten *Behind the Screen* (New York: George H. Doran, 1923), page 21, notes the production cost of *The Squaw Man* as $47,000.

83. "Alfred Zukor," *Silent Ladies and Gents*, silentgents.com, July 9, 2008, originally published in *Blue Book of the Screen* by Ruth Wing (Hollywood, CA: Blue Book of the Screen, 1923).

84. Granlund, *Blondes*, page 57.

Chapter Four

1. New York City Directories [Online Database], Provo, UT, The Generations Network, Inc. 2005. Original data: Marine Z, 1917, Section G, page 729.

2. Granlund, *Blondes*, page 58.

3. Avery Amanda Howard, interview, January 11, 2009.

4. 1910 United States Census: Year: *1910, Providence Ward 6, Providence, Rhode Island*, Roll: *T624_1443*, Page: *8B*, Enumeration District: *213*, Image: *1024*.

5. Declaration of Intention of Marriage, Rhode Island State Registrar of Vital Statistics, certified copy March 14, 1984.

6. Draft Registration Card, New York County, New York, Roll 1786807, Draft Board 148.

7. *World War I Draft Registration Cards, 1917–1918* [Online Database], Provo, UT: The Generations Network, Inc., 2005. Original data: United States, Selective Service System. *World War I Selective Service System Draft Registration Cards, 1917–1918*.

8. Cranston Directory, 1938–1939.

9. Avery Amanda Howard, interview, January 11, 2009.

10. Portland, ME, *Press Herald*, March 30, 1947.

11. Avery Amanda Howard, interview, January 11, 2009.

12. Social Security Death Index [Online Database], Provo, UT, The Generations Network, Inc., 2000. Issuing State, Maine, Issue Date: Before 1951.

13. *The Playgoer*, Florentine Gardens, Hollywood, California, "Who Is NTG?," John F. Huber, Publisher, 1942, page 5.

14. "Caruso Aids Tank Corps, *New York Times*, September 16, 1918, page 9.

15. Ibid.

16. Granlund, *Blondes*, page 76.

17. "Caruso Aids Tank Corps, *New York Times*, September 16, 1918, page 9.

18. Granlund, *Blondes*, page 77.

19. William E. Geist, "George Jessel, Comedian, Dead; Known as 'Toastmaster General,'" *New York Times*, May 26, 1981, page 12.

20. *New York Times*; *Caruso Aids Tank Corps*; Sept. 16, 1918, page 9.

21. Granlund, *Blondes*, page 87.

22. Ibid.

23. Clifford J. Doerksen, *American Babel* (Philadelphia: University of Pennsylvania Press, 2005), page 23.

24. Ibid.

25. Granlund, *Blondes*, page 87.

26. François Weil and Jody Gladding (translators), *A History of New York* (New York: Columbia University Press, 2004), page 231.

27. Granlund, *Blondes*, page 87.

28. Ibid., page 89.

29. Clifford J. Doerksen, *American Babel*, page 25.

30. "The History of WHN," *Times Newsweekly*, timesnewsweekly.com.

31. "Radio New Autumn Season Stirs Interest," *New York Times*, September 2, 1923, page X10.

32. Granlund, *Blondes*, page 90.

33. "Radio New Autumn Season Stirs Interest," *New York Times*, September 2, 1923, page X10.

34. Granlund, *Blondes*, page 92.

35. "Radio Show in New York This Week," *New York Times*, September 21, 1924, page XX15.

36. Granlund, *Blondes*, page 93.

37. Nils T. Granlund, *Blondes, Brunettes, and Bullets* (New York: David McKay, 1957), dust jacket liner states "By Nils Thor Granlund."

38. Emily Wortis Leider, *Becoming Mae West* (Cambridge, MA: Da Capo Press, 2000), page 126.

39. Ibid., page 127.

40. Granlund, *Blondes*, page 93.

41. Emily Wortis Leider, *Becoming Mae West*, page 127.

42. Granlund, *Blondes*, page 91.

43. Harry Richman with Richard Gehman, *A Hell of a Life* (New York: Duel Sloan and Pearce, 1966), page 97.

44. Ibid., page 98.

45. Clifford J. Doerksen, *American Babel*, page 34.

46. Granlund, *Blondes*, page 102.

47. Ibid., page 91.

48. "Radio New Autumn Season Stirs Interest," *New York Times*, September 2, 1923, page X10.

49. Ibid.

50. Granlund, *Blondes*, page 101.

51. Note: Larry Fay's nightclub is referenced both as the "El Fay" and the "El Fey" in numerous articles and publications, by writers of Fay's time and historians. The spelling "El Fey" is that appearing in images of the nightclub entrance.

52. Granlund, *Blondes*, page 101.

Chapter Five

1. Peter McWilliams, *Ain't Nobody's Business if You Do* (Los Angeles: Prelude Press, 1998), page 473.

2. Ibid., page 475.

3. Christopher Gray, *New York Times*, "Streetscapes/230 West 42nd Street; from School to Residences, Flea Circus and Brother," June 16, 1996, Section 9, page 7.

4. Ibid.

5. Granlund, *Blondes*, page 119.

6. Sheila Weller, *Dancing at Ciro's* (New York: St. Martin's Press, 2004), page 44.

7. Ibid., page 48.

8. Ibid., page 44.

9. Granlund, *Blondes*, page 119.

10. "Fast Fokker Plane Makes Debut Here," *New York Times*, July 22, 1921, Section: Amusements, page 16.

11. Ibid.

12. Edgar A. Haine, *Disaster in the Air* (New York: Cornwall, 2000) page 347.

13. Granlund, *Blondes*, page 110.

14. "Crowd Up in Air at a Flying Meet: 50 Planes Exhibited at Curtiss Field and Spectators Are Taken on Flights. Latest Planes Are Shown: Interest of 5,000 Centres on Contest for Trophy for Maneuverability. Economy Tests Are Made: Trips with Passengers Cost Less Than Half of Railroad Fare—Parachute Leaps Thrill," *New York Times*, October 7, 1921, page 14.

15. "American Air Record Is Broken by Acosta," *The Washington Post*, November 23, 1921, page 1.

16. Granlund, *Blondes*, page 103.

17. Jonathan Van Meter, *The Last Good Time: Skinny D'Amato, the Notorious 500 Club & the Rise and Fall of Atlantic City* (New York: Crown, 2003), page 31.

18. Edward A. Taggert, *Bootlegger*, iUniverse (New York: Writer's Showcase, 2003), page 126.

19. Steve Angelucci, "All Mobbed Up," *Atlantic City Weekly*, January 20, 2005.

20. Granlund, *Blondes*, page 104.

21. "European Midgets at the Hippodrome," *New York Times*, November 29, 1914, Section: Society, page X8.

22. Robert Bogdan, *Freak Show: Presenting Human Oddities for Fun and Profit* (Chicago: University of Chicago Press, 1990), page 162.

23. "European Midgets at the Hippodrome," *New York Times*, November 29, 1914, Section: Society, page X8.

24. Granlund, *Blondes*, page 121.

25. Ibid.

26. "Dry Writs May Shut 300 Drinking Places," *New York Times*, December 17, 1922, page 14.

27. Ibid.

28. Leo Trachtenberg, "Texas Guinan: Queen of the Night," *City Journal*, Manhattan Institute, publisher (New York, 1998).

29. Ibid.

30. "Tex Guinan Goes on Trial," *Portsmouth Herald*, Portsmouth, NH, April 9, 1929, page 1.

31. Granlund, *Blondes*, page 122.

32. Ibid.

33. T.J. English, *Paddy Whacked: The Untold Story of the Irish American Gangster* (New York: William Morrow, 2005), page 121.

34. Ibid.

35. Granlund, *Blondes*, page 123.

36. Ibid., page 124.

37. Ibid., page 132.

38. Irving L. Allen, *The City in Slang* (New York: Oxford University Press, 1993), page 77.

39. Rusty E. Frank, *Tap: The Greatest Tap Stars 1900–1955* (New York: Perseus/Da Capo, 1990), page 33.

40. Ibid.

41. "Fifty Fight for Coats," *New York Times*, November 8, 1920, page 3.

42. "Night Life Figures Indicted," *New Castle News*, New Castle, PA, August 1, 1928, page 1.

43. "Broadway Dry War Jams Court Session," *New York Times*, August 7, 1928, page 23.

44. "Prohibition: Women and Wine," *Time* magazine, August 13, 1928.

45. "Broadway Dry War Jams Court Session," *New York Times*, August 7, 1928, page 23.

46. "108 Indicted in War on the Night Clubs," *New York Times*, July 31, 1928; page 1.

47. "Broadway Dry War Jams Court Session," *New York Times*, August 7, 1928, page 23.

48. "Gilbert Swan, "In New York," NEA Services, Inc., published in the *Fitchburg Sentinel*, Fitchburg, MA, January 27, 1929, page 16.

49. "Tex Guinan Goes on Trial," *Portsmouth Herald*, Portsmouth, NH, April 9, 1929, page 1.

50. "Texas Guinan Life of Party as Liquor Trial Starts," *Evening Tribune*, Albert Lea, MN, April 10, 1929, page 1.

51. "Drying Up New York—A Gigantic One-Woman Job," *Salt Lake Tribune*, Salt Lake City, UT, August 5, 1928, page 2.

52. Ibid.

53. "Night Club Is Philanthropic Institution, Says Hostess," *Montana Standard*, Butte, MT, April 11, 1929, page 20.

54. "Texas Guinan Life of Party as Liquor Trial Starts," *Evening Tribune*, Albert Lea, MN, April 10, 1929, page 1.

55. "Texas Guinan Enjoys Trial," *Daily News Promoter*, Havre, MT, April 10, 1929, page 8.

56. "Guinan Draws Crowd into Court," *Syracuse Herald*, Syracuse, NY, April 10, 1929, page 1.

57. "Texas Guinan's Hot 'Wise-Cracks' Disrupts Court," *Syracuse Herald*, Syracuse, NY, April 11, 1929, page 12 (continued from page 1).

58. "Crowd Laughs as Tex Replies to Questioning," *Sheboygan Journal*, Sheboygan, WI, April 11, 1929, page 1. Note: Conversations between Guinan and court performers quoted directly from Associated Press accounts appearing nationwide.

59. "Texas Guinan Wins Her Case, Gets Cheered," *Evening Tribune*, Albert Lea, MN, April 12, 1929, page 1.

60. "Queen of Night Clubs Acquitted," *Port Arthur News*, Port Arthur, TX, April 12, 1929, page 1.

61. "Only Fines Imposed in Night Club Cases," *New York Times*, April 16, 1929, page 19.

62. Ibid.

63. "Drying Up New York—A Gigantic One-Woman Job," *Salt Lake Tribune*, Salt Lake City, UT, August 5, 1928, page 2.

64. Ibid.

65. Granlund, *Blondes*, page 104.

Chapter Six

1. "New York Passenger Lists 1820–1957," [Online Database], Ancestry.com, Provo, UT, (The Generations Network, 2000).

2. Jeffrey D. Nichols, "The Fall of Skliris, Czar of the Greeks," *History Blazer Magazine*, December, 1996.

3. Chester B. Bahn, Cinema Critic, *Syracuse Herald*, Syracuse, NY, July 3, 1932, page 23.

4. World War I Draft Registration Card,

Location, St. Louis, Missouri, Roll: 2223, 24-131A, Draft Board 43.

5. "Ambassador Theatre Building," St. Louis Building Arts Foundation, buildingmuseum.org, published May 30, 2006.

6. Granlund, *Blondes*, page 180.

7. Ibid.

8. "New Theatre Planned," *New York Times*, April 1, 1921, Section: Real Estate, page 31.

9. "Dedicate Carroll Theatre; Lambs Provide Oratory and Owner's Wife Breaks a Bottle of Champagne," *New York Times*, February 18, 1922, page 17.

10. Alexander Woollcott, "The Play," *New York Times*, February 27, 1922, page 19.

11. Ibid.

12. "Irish Rout Police and Repel Fireman in a Broadway Riot; Women Claw Faces of West 47th Street Reserves; A DONNYBROOK DEVELOPS; Republicans Fill Earl Carroll Theatre," *New York Times*, November 27, 1922, page 1.

13. Ibid.

14. Granlund, *Blondes*, page 180.

15. Ibid.

16. "Equity Retaliates on Earl Carroll," *New York Times*, June 11, 1923, Section: Amusements, Hotels, and Restaurants, page 16.

17. Ibid.

18. "*Vanities of 1923*: A Gorgeous Revue," *New York Times*, July 6, 1923, Section: Amusements, Hotels, and Restaurants, page 8.

19. Ibid.

20. Granlund, *Blondes*, page 180.

21. Ibid., page 181.

22. Ibid., page 182.

23. Clark Kinnaird, "The Daybook of a New Yorker," *Evening Gazette*, Xenia, OH, May 9, 1928, page 4.

24. Ibid.

25. Granlund, *Blondes*, page 197.

26. Ibid.

27. "Swedish Royalty and Nobility to Have Large Company at Miss Manville's Bridal," *New York Times*, October 23, 1928, Section: Social News, page 34.

28. "Swedish Prince Has Big Night on Broadway," *Coshocton Tribune*, Coshocton, OH, page 3.

29. Ibid.

30. "Show Girls Taken In Raid," *The Daily Messenger*, Canandaigua, NY, July 16, 1930, page 1.

31. Ibid.

32. Raid Popularized Carroll's New York '*Vanities*' Exhibition," *Sheboygan Journal*, Sheboygan, WI, July 10, 1930, page 1.

33. Ibid.

34. Ibid.

35. "Don't Try to Be a Beach Beauty if Your Type Really Needs a Night-Club Setting;"

Syracuse Herald, Syracuse, NY, August 17, 1930; Magazine Section, page 2.

36. Ibid.

37. "Lovely Little Dancing Ladies Take to 'Stocks' and Even Essay Ducking School for Their 'Art,'" *Syracuse Herald*, Syracuse, NY, September 21, 1930; Magazine Section, page 6.

38. "Lost Hope," *Time* magazine, July 15, 1929.

39. Ibid.

40. "Show Girl Testifies Crash Cost Beauty," *New York Times*, May 21, 1935, page 1.

41. "Actress Cut on Face as Ehret Car Crashes," *New York Times*, June 20, 1932, page 1.

42. Ibid.

43. "NTG Clipping File," Billy Rose Theater Collection, New York Public Library, New York, NY.

44. "Tuesday Program Notes," *Syracuse Herald*, Syracuse, NY, July 23, 1935.

45. "NBC Programming Release, NTG Clipping File," Billy Rose Theater Collection, New York Public Library, New York, NY.

46. "Show Girl Testifies Crash Cost Beauty," *New York Times*, May 21, 1935, page 1.

47. Ibid.

48. Ibid.

49. "$250,000 Accident Suit Brought by Miss Wenzel Ends in Mistrial Today," *Kingston Daily Freeman*, Kingston, NY, May 21, 1935, page 1.

50. "Earl Carroll a Witness," *New York Times*, October 3, 1935, Section: Amusements, page 28.

51. "Wenzel Suit Nears Close," *New York Times*, October 4, 1935, Section: Financial, page 35.

52. "Eileen Wenzel Wins $90,000 Damage Suit," *The Tribune*, Albert Lea, MN, October 5, 1935, page 2.

53. "Weird Toll of Tragedy and Accident in the Wake of Young Leeds' Yacht," *Salt Lake Tribune*, Salt Lake City, UT, July 7, 1935, page 55.

54. "No Alibi Offered by Beaten Tommy," *Charleston Gazette*, Charleston, WV, August 31, 1937, page 9.

55. Ibid.

56. "Tom Farr to Wed New York Showgirl," *Daily Courier*, Waterloo, IA, March 21, 1938, page 10.

57. "Wonders of Wedlock Proclaimed by Farr," *The Lowell Sun*, Lowell, MA, March 22, 1938, page 10.

58. "Farr Unlucky at Love but Lucky at Flying," *Charleston Gazette*, Charleston, WV, April 22, 1938, page 21.

59. Social Security Death Index [Online Database], Ancestry.com, Provo, UT: The Generations Network, Inc., 2009. Original data: Social Security Administration. Social Security

Death Index, Master File. Social Security Administration, Issue State: New York, Issue Date: before 1951.

Chapter Seven

1. "Al Jolson to Make World Concert Tour; His First Appearance in El Paso Jan. 15; Said to Have 'Highest Guarantee Ever Paid an Artist,'" *New York Times*, November 27, 1929, Section: Amusements, page 34.

2. "Jolson Weds Young Dancer, Sails Abroad," *Syracuse Herald*, Syracuse, NY, September 22, 1928, page 2.

3. "Jolson Asserts Wedding Bells Are Premature," *Evening Independent*, Massillon, OH, September 13, 1928, page 14.

4. Granlund, *Blondes*, page 125.

5. Ibid., page 126.

6. "Al Jolson Sails with Bride, Who Was Ruby Keeler," *Sheboygan Journal*, Sheboygan, WI, October 22, 1928, page 4.

7. Ibid.

8. O.O. McIntyre, "Day by Day," *North Adams Transcript*, North Adams, MA, May 4, 1925, page 3.

9. "Night Club Owner Slain During Row," Associate Press, *San Antonio Express*, San Antonio, TX, January 2, 1933, page 2.

10. "Gunman Gangsters and Their State Beauty Friends," *San Antonio Light*, San Antonio, TX, February 12, 1933, page 41.

11. Ibid.

12. "Night Club Owner Slain During Row," Associate Press, *San Antonio Express*, San Antonio, TX, January 2, 1933, page 2.

13. Ibid.

14. "Larry Fay Is Slain in His Night Club," *New York Times*, January 2, 1933, Page 1.

15. Ibid.

16. "Gunman Gangsters and Their State Beauty Friends," *San Antonio Light*, San Antonio, TX, February 12, 1933, page 41.

17. "Joan Crawford Biography," joancraw fordbest.com/biography.htm, accessed May 29, 2008.

18. David Bret, *Joan Crawford: Hollywood Martyr* (New York: Da Capo Press, 2008), page 1.

19. Ibid., page 9.

20. Granlund, *Blondes*, page 133.

21. Ibid., page 134.

22. Bret, *Joan Crawford*, page 11.

23. Granlund, *Blondes*, page 134.

24. Bret, *Joan Crawford*, page 11.

25. Granlund, *Blondes*, page 135.

26. Charlotte Chandler, *Not the Girl Next Door: Joan Crawford, a Personal Biography* (New York: Applause, 2009), page 30.

27. Timeline, 1924, "Joan Crawford Biography," joancrawfordbest.com/biography.htm, accessed May 29, 2008.

28. Granlund, *Blondes*, page 135.

29. "What Is EAS?" Emergency Alert System, Office of Climate, Water, and Weather Services, United States Government, factsheet, June 23, 2004.

30. "Ship Is Afire 400 Miles Off Sandy Hook," *New York Times*, May 30, 1925, page 1.

31. Ibid.

32. Ibid.

33. "Burning Vessel Brought to Beach," *Oneonta Daily Star*, Oneonta, NY, June 2, 1925, page 1.

34. Mike Anderson, "The Great EBS Goof of 1971," ebstest.stlmedia.net, accessed July 24, 2009.

35. Granlund, *Blondes*, page 145.

36. Dawn Williams, *Me and My Father's Shadow: A Daughter's Quest and Biography of Ted Lewis, the Jazz King* (Seal Beach, CA: Sunrise House, 2005), page 197.

37. "'Ukulele Ikes' Body Claimed by Actors," *Charleston Gazette*, Charleston, WV, July 24, 1971, page 22.

38. Granlund, *Blondes*, page 145.

39. Earl Wilson, "It Happened Last Night," *The Morning Herald*, Uniontown, PA, June 7, 1957, page 4.

40. Granlund, *Blondes*, page 145.

41. "Prominent Boxing Manager Mysteriously Killed in New York; Death of Frank Marlow Blamed on Beer War—Victim Made Fortune in Boxing, Night Clubs, and Horses—Body Found in Bushes," *Lowell Sun*, Lowell, MA, June 25, 1929, page 16.

42. Ibid.

43. "Racketeers' Murders Attributed to Feuds," *New York Times*, December 27, 1929, page 1.

44. "Taken for Ride," *New York Times*, August 10, 1929, page 1.

45. "Racketeers' Murders Attributed to Feuds," *New York Times*, December 27, 1929, page 1.

46. "Friend of Rothstein Slain in Gang Feud," *New York Times*, June 25, 1929, page 1.

47. Granlund, *Blondes*, page 111.

48. "Slim Lindbergh Wants Plane in New York Right Away, Report," *Billings Gazette*, Billings, MT, June 15, 1927, page 1.

49. Ibid.

50. "Lindy Worries About 'St. Louis,' Companion Avers," *The Bridgeport Telegram*, Bridgeport, CT, June 15, 1927, page 1.

51. Ibid.

52. "Chaplin Shuns Radio 'Mike,'" *Wisconsin Rapids Daily Tribune*, Wisconsin Rapids, WI, December 24, 1926, page 28.

53. "Charlie Chaplin Shuns Microphone as Stars Perform," *Bridgeport Telegram*, Bridgeport, CT, January 14, 1927, page 6.

54. "Chaplin Shuns Radio 'Mike,'" *Wisconsin Rapids Daily Tribune*, Wisconsin Rapids, WI, December 24, 1926, page 28.

55. "How to Sell a One-Act Play," *New York Times*, July 14, 1915, page X2.

56. "Press Agent's Ashes Cast into Broadway," *Albert Lea Tribune*, Albert Lea, MN, March 2, 1929, page 4.

57. Ibid.

58. "Thrilling Sight, Sound Film of Graf Flight to Be Shown," *San Antonio Light*, San Antonio, TX, January 27, 1919, page 30.

59. Ibid.

60. "Suspect Sought for Quiz in NY Puzzle Shooting," *Fresno Bee*, Fresno, CA, November 5, 1928, page 14.

61. Granlund, *Blondes*, page 171.

62. Ibid.

63. "Tell How Rothstein Shielded Assassin," *New York Times*, December 3, 1929, page 1.

64. T.J. English, *Paddy Whacked; The Untold Story of the Irish-American Gangster* (New York: Harper, 2006), page 116.

65. Ibid.

66. "Link Killing to Acquittal; Detectives Investigate Connection," *New York Times*, January 9, 1922, page 17.

67. Granlund, *Blondes*, page 205.

68. Daniel R. Schwarz, *Broadway Boogie Woogie: Damon Runyon and the Making of New York City* (New York: Palgrave Macmillan, 2003), page 41.

69. Burton W. Peretti, *Nightclub City: Politics and Amusements in Manhattan* (Philadelphia: University of Pennsylvania Press, 2007), page 112.

70. "Night Club Agents Fined; Three Solicited Business in Front of Rival's Place," *New York Times*, November 20, 1927, page 9.

71. Lee Mortimer, "New York Confidential," *Mansfield News Journal*, Mansfield, OH, August 17, 1955, page 17.

72. "Thousands Attend Loew's Funeral," *New York Times*, September 9, 1927, page 1.

73. Ibid.

Chapter Eight

1. "Radio Talkies Put on Program Basis; Actors and Dancers Do Turns on City's First Broadcast on Regular Schedule," *New York Times*, April 27, 1931, Section: Radio, page 26.

2. Ibid.

3. Ibid.

4. "Television Stages a Talking Picture; Thousands at Radio Show See Screen Images Converse Over Loudspeaker Hook-up," *New York Times*, September 25, 1931, page 26.

5. Ibid.

6. Ibid.

7. Granlund, *Blondes*, page 97.

8. Ibid.

9. Granlund, *Blondes*, page 99.

10. Neil Gabler, *Winchell: Gossip, Power, and the Culture of Celebrity* (New York: Vintage, 1995), page 113.

11. Ibid., page 157.

12. T.J. English, *The Westies: Inside New York's Irish Mob* (New York: St. Martin's Griffin, 2006), page 26.

13. Walter Winchell, "On Broadway," *Daily Mirror*, Inc., reported in the *Wisconsin State Journal*, Madison, WI, page 3.

14. Granlund, *Blondes*, page 206.

15. Ibid.

16. Ibid.

17. "Seize 11 Hip Flask Patrons in Broadway Night Club," *New York Times*, April 26, 1930, page 1.

18. Hollywood Cabaret postcard, 1930.

19. James Aswell, "My New York," *Lowell Sun*, Lowell, ME, May 5, 1937.

20. James Aswell, "My New York," carried in the *Olean Herald*, Olean, NY, June 23, 1931.

21. Granlund, *Blondes*, page 226.

22. Leo Katcher, *The Big Bankroll: The Life and Times of Arnold Rothstein* (New York: Harper, 1959), page 243.

23. Burton B. Turkus and Sid Feder, *Murder, Inc.: The Story of the Syndicate* (New York: Da Capo Press, 1992), page 147.

24. Mark Hellinger, "Ziegfeld Beauty Weds Columnist," *New York Daily News*, Associated Press article carried by *The News-Palladium*, Benton Harbor, MI, July 12, 1929, page 3.

25. Granlund, *Blondes*, page 225.

26. James Aswell, "My New York," *Chester Times*, Chester, PA, March 17, 1934, page 14.

27. *New York Sun*, November 12, 1932, individual clipping from the Granlund clip file of the New York Public Library.

28. Granlund, *Blondes*, page 228.

29. Ibid., page 229.

30. E.J. Fleming, *Paul Bern: The Life and Famous Death of the MGM Director and Husband of Harlow* (Jefferson, NC: McFarland, 2009), page 191.

31. Granlund, *Blondes*, page 228.

32. *New York World Telegram*, December 10, 1932, Granlund clipping file, New York Public Library, New York City.

33. *New York Sun*, December 24, 1932, Granlund clipping file, New York Public Library, New York City.

34. Regina Crewe, *New York American*, December 18, 1932, reported in *San Antonio Light*, San Antonio, TX, page 10.

35. Nils T. Granlund clipping file, New York Public Library, New York City.

36. Paul Harrison, "In New York," *Syracuse Herald*, Syracuse, NY, September 27, 1933, page 14.

37. James Aswell, "My New York," distributed by Central Press, published in *The Ham-*

mond Times, Hammond, IN, March 16, 1933, page 4.

38. Ibid.

39. Ibid.

40. Granlund, *Blondes*, page 229.

41. Paul Harrison, "In New York," *Daily Globe*, October 23, 1934, page 3.

42. Lee Mortimer, *New York Daily Mirror*, Nils T. Granlund clipping file, New York Public Library, New York City.

43. Lee Mortimer, "Winchell on Broadway," carried in *The Nevada State Journal*, August 13, 1941, page 4.

44. Ibid.

45. "Florentine Gardens," *Life Magazine*, January 31, 1944, page 60.

46. Granlund, *Blondes*, page 231.

47. Paul Harrison, "In New York," *Dunkirk Evening Observer*, Dunkirk, NY, October 18, 1934, page 6.

48. Ibid.

49. "Latest Adventures of Doris and Babs," *Billings Gazette*, Billings, MT, June 27, 1937, page 29.

50. Ibid.

51. Granlund, *Blondes*, page 235.

52. *New York Sun*, New York City, December 18, 1933, Nils T. Granlund clipping file, New York Public Library.

53. Granlund, *Blondes*, page 237.

54. Bugs Baer, "Major Operations," "The Golden Girl," *San Antonio Light*, San Antonio, TX, November 28, 1937, page 55.

55. Ibid.

56. Granlund, *Blondes*, page 239.

57. "And No Wonder London Cabaret Girls Couldn't Take It," *Chillicothe Constitution-Tribune*, Chillicothe, MO, July 20, 1935, page 3.

58. Granlund, *Blondes*, page 239.

59. *Kokomo Tribune*, Kokomo, IN, May 27, 1930, page 4.

60. Lewis Lawes, *Twenty Thousand Years in Sing Sing* (New York: R. Long & R.R. Smith, 1932), page 83.

61. Granlund, *Blondes*, page 239.

62. Paul Harrison, "In New York," *Olean Times Herald*, Olean, NY, June 11, 1934.

63. "Young Folk Have All Grown Up, Broadway Directors Agree," *The Lowell Sun*, Lowell, MA, June 7, 1934, page 6.

64. Ibid.

65. Granlund, *Blondes*, page 222.

66. Ibid., page 223.

67. "NBC Personalities," NBC Program Service, NBC Press Department, Number 29, July 21, 1935.

68. Ibid.

69. "Boxing Bouts Slated During Present Week," *North Adams Transcript*, North Adams, MA, November 17, 1914, page 8.

70. "NBC Personalities," NBC Program Ser-

vice, NBC Press Department, Number 29, July 21, 1935.

71. Paul K. Damai, "Radio Short Circuits," *The Hammond Times*, Hammond, IN, June 26, 1935, page 21.

72. Ibid., page 17.

73. Granlund, *Blondes*, page 241.

74. "New Murder Hunt Started Up-State," *New York Times*, March 23, 1940, page 1

75. Clint Willis, *Wise Guys: Stories of Mobsters from New Jersey to Las Vegas* (New York: Thunder's Mouth Press/Avalon, 2003), page 156.

76. "Current Viewpoints: The Ravings of Dutch Shultz," *Syracuse Herald*, Syracuse, NY, November 4, 1935, page 12.

77. Granlund, *Blondes*, page 242.

78. "Quick Lime Grave Bares Ax Murder of Sherman," *New York Times*, November 5, 1935, page 1.

79. Ibid.

80. Ibid.

81. Granlund, *Blondes*, page 248.

Chapter Nine

1. "Loew's State," *Variety* magazine, November 24, 1937, Nils T. Granlund clipping file, Billy Rose Collection, New York Public Library, New York City.

2. K.L. Ecksan, "Radio News and Programs," *Oakland Tribune*, Oakland, CA, page 10.

3. News item, Nils T. Granlund clipping file, Billy Rose Collection, New York Public Library, New York City, September 10, 1935.

4. George Tucker, "Man About Manhattan," *Big Spring Daily Herald*, Big Spring, TX, October 22, 1935, page 4.

5. Ibid.

6. Dan Thomas, "Gave Up a Fortune," *Capital Times*, Madison, WI, January 23, 1930, page 16.

7. Granlund, *Blondes*, page 259.

8. Maurice Kann, "Sophistication Is Earmark of Harlow Picture; 'Red-Headed Woman' Carries Sex into the Open, Kann Finds," *Syracuse Herald*, Syracuse, NY, July 2, 1932, page 23.

9. Granlund, *Blondes*, page 261.

10. Ibid., page 265.

11. "Brother Seeks Facts," International News Service, New York, carried in the *Indiana Evening Gazette*, Indiana, PA, September 6, 1932, page 2.

12. Gilbert Swan, "See-Sawing on Broadway," *Appleton Post-Crescent*, Appleton, WI, April 29, 1927, page 6.

13. "Beautiful Delores' Multiple Heartbreak Ended in a Broadway Tragedy," *Port Arthur News*, Port Arthur, TX, February 16, 1936.

14. Ibid.

15. Lillian Campbell, "Three Picked as 'Queen of Radio,' *Evening Independent*, Massillon, OH, February 7, 1936.

16. *Variety* magazine, "Review: Hipp, Balto," August 3, 1938, Nils T. Granlund clipping file, Billy Rose Collection, New York Public Library, New York City.

17. Revue Advertisement, Nils T. Granlund clipping file, Billy Rose Collection, New York Public Library, New York City.

18. Grand Theatre advertisement, *Oshkosh Daily Northwestern*, Oshkosh, WI, April 3, 1937, page 11.

19. "Review: Palace," *Variety* magazine, Nils T. Granlund clipping file, Billy Rose Collection, New York Public Library, New York City.

20. "The Little Unknown Won the Plaudits and the Prize," *Port Arthur News*, Port Arthur, TX, June 7, 1936, page 52.

21. "Ohio Miss Wins Title; No. 2 Given More Attention," United Press, reported in *Circleville Herald*, Circleville, Ohio, page 1.

22. "Nils T. Granlund Heads Program at Loew's State," *New York Herald Tribune*, December 26, 1937, Billy Rose Collection, New York Public Library, New York City.

23. "Hollywood Cabaret Seeks to Reorganize; Broadway Restaurant Declares Season Has Been Worst in Night Club Business," *New York Times*, December 29, 1937, page 15.

24. Hollywood Cabaret advertisement, *Brooklyn Daily Eagle* , April 16, 1937, Nils T. Granlund clipping file, Billy Rose Collection, New York Public Library, New York City.

25. Ibid.

26. Item, *New York Evening Journal,* April 17, 1937, Nils T. Granlund clipping file, Billy Rose Collection, New York Public Library, New York City.

27. James Aswell, "My New York," *Hammond Times*, Hammond, IN, July 27, 1937, page 53.

28. Ibid.

29. "Hollywood Cabaret Seeks to Reorganize; Broadway Restaurant Declares Season Has Been Worst in Night Club Business," *New York Times*, December 29, 1937, page 15.

30. "Hollywood Cabaret Closes Its Doors; Moss Announces Inability to Operate Under Reorganization — 150 Persons Lose Jobs," *New York Times*, January 8, 1938, page 19.

31. Ibid.

32. "NTG," *New York Daily Mirror*, July 16, 1937, Nils T. Granlund clipping file, Billy Rose Collection, New York Public Library, New York City.

33. Robert Coleman, "Planning Chain of Palaces," *New York Daily Mirror*, July 11, 1937, Nils T. Granlund clipping file, Billy Rose Collection, New York Public Library, New York City.

34. Ibid.

35. Ibid.

36. NTG advertisement, Nils T. Granlund clipping file, Billy Rose Collection, New York Public Library, New York City.

37. "Lyric Theatre," Review, *Variety*, December 22, 1937, Nils T. Granlund clipping file, Billy Rose Collection, New York Public Library, New York City.

38. Review, *Variety*, Nils T. Granlund clipping file, Billy Rose Collection, New York Public Library, New York City.

39. "Liberty Stage Set Fri and Sat," *Zanesville Times Recorder,* Zanesville, OH, March 2, 1938.

40. Granlund, *Blondes*, page 254.

41. Milton Brackers, "Son to Take Place of Crown Prince in Delaware Fete; Gustaf Adolf, III, Will Stay on His Ship While Bertil Gives Monument to President," *New York Times*, June 27, 1938, page 1.

42. Elliott Arnold, "Skansen Inspires Granlund," *New York World Telegram*, August 6, 1938, Nils T. Granlund clipping file, Billy Rose Collection, New York Public Library, New York City.

43. Nils T. Granlund clipping file, Billy Rose Collection, New York Public Library, New York City.

44. "News of Night Clubs," *New York Times*, September 25, 1938, Nils T. Granlund clipping file, Billy Rose Collection, New York Public Library, New York City.

45. Danton Walker, "Broadway," *New York Daily News*, September 30, 1938, Nils T. Granlund clipping file, Billy Rose Collection, New York Public Library, New York City.

46. Item, *New York Journal American*, Nils T. Granlund clipping file, Billy Rose Collection, New York Public Library, New York City.

47. Dale Harrison, "My New York," *Reno Evening Gazette,* November 2, 1938.

48. Ibid.

49. Review, "State, NY," *Variety*, August 17, 1938, Nils T. Granlund clipping file, Billy Rose Collection, New York Public Library, New York City.

50. Review, "Strand, NY" *Variety*, Nils T. Granlund clipping file, Billy Rose Collection, New York Public Library, New York City.

51. "Letters to the Editor," *Variety*, Nils T. Granlund clipping file, Billy Rose Collection, New York Public Library, New York City.

52. Theodore Strauss, "Notes on Night Clubs," *New York Times*, March 26, 1939, Section: Arts and Leisure, page 134.

53. Ibid.

54. Lee Mortimer, "A Broadway Era on the Auction Block," *New York Sunday Mirror*,

Brown Agency Collection, New York Public Library, New York City.

Chapter Ten

1. George Ross, "In New York," *Dunkirk Daily Observer*, Dunkirk, NY, May 24, 1938, page 6.
2. Item, *Variety*, April 12, 1939, Nils T. Granlund clipping file, Billy Rose Collection, New York Public Library, New York City.
3. "People in the News," *Ogden News Standard*, Ogden, UT, April 13, 1939, page 1.
4. Photograph and Caption, *Albuquerque Journal*, Albuquerque, NM, April 15, 1939, page 1.
5. Review, "Aztec Sun Worshipper," *Variety*, May 31, 1939, Nils T. Granlund clipping file, Billy Rose Collection, New York Public Library, New York City.
6. "$9,000,000 Business Born in Pushcarts," *New York Times*, December 24, 1950, page 28.
7. Robert Coleman, Review, Nils T. Granlund clipping file, Billy Rose Collection, New York Public Library, New York City.
8. Ibid.
9. Review, "Aztec Sun Worshipper," May 31, 1939, Nils T. Granlund clipping file, Billy Rose Collection, New York Public Library, New York City.
10. Ibid.
11. Review, "Shubert Theatre," *Variety*, Nils T. Granlund clipping file, Billy Rose Collection, New York Public Library, New York City.
12. Ibid.
13. "Woman Killed, 6 Hurt," *New York Herald Tribune*, August 12, 1939, Nils T. Granlund clipping file, Billy Rose Collection, New York Public Library, New York City.
14. "1 Killed, 6 Hurt in Crash; Club Operator and Boxer are Drivers of Cars," *New York Times*, August 12, 1939, page 12.
15. "Granlund Held in Traffic Death; Fair Showman Denies Criminal Negligence in Crash That Injured Girl Fatally," *New York Times*, August 15, 1939, page 21.
16. "Granlund Freed in Death; Lesnovich, Boxer, Also Cleared in Fatal Automobile Crash," *New York Times*, August 22, 1939, Section: Amusements, page 15.
17. "Show Ends Labor Row; Dispute Settled by 'Congress of Beauty,'" *New York Times*, May 21, 1939, Page 41.
18. "NTG Show Closes; High Charges Blamed; Operators Contend 'Exorbitant' Fair Rates Forced Move," *New York Times*, August 27, 1939, Page 2.
19. Ibid.
20. "Little Man Beat Him, Says NTG," *New York American Journal*, December 14, 1939, Nils

T. Granlund clipping file, Billy Rose Collection, New York Public Library, New York City.
21. "Nils T. Granlund Loses Suit in Fatal Car Crash," *New York Herald Tribune*, November 19, 1941, Nils T. Granlund clipping file, Billy Rose Collection, New York Public Library, New York City.
22. Theodore Strauss, "News of the Night Clubs," *New York Times*, September 25, 1938, Page 156.
23. "Business Records; Bankruptcy Proceedings Assignments Judgments Satisfied Judgments Mechanics' Liens Satisfied Mechanics' Liens," *New York Times*, December 5, 1938, page 30.
24. Review, "State NY," *Variety*, January 17, 1940, Nils T. Granlund clipping file, Billy Rose Collection, New York Public Library, New York City.
25. Billy Rose, "No More Hicks So No More Tease in the Strip, *San Antonio Light*, San Antonio, TX, August 4, 1940, page 59.
26. Review, "State Theatre," *Variety*, Nils T. Granlund clipping file, Billy Rose Collection, New York Public Library, New York City.
27. "Odds and Ends in the Entertainment World, *San Antonio Light*, San Antonio, TX, December 6, 1942.
28. Review, "Florentine Gardens," *Variety*, March 20, 1940, Nils T. Granlund clipping file, Billy Rose Collection, New York Public Library, New York City.
29. Unidentified magazine article, clipfile-dated May 15, 1940, Nils T. Granlund clipping file, Billy Rose Collection, New York Public Library, New York City.
30. Ibid.
31. Harrison Carroll, "Behind the Scenes in Hollywood," *San Mateo Times*, San Mateo, CA, August 2, 1940, page 5.
32. Review, "Florentine Gardens," *Variety*, May 15, 1940, Nils T. Granlund clipping file, Billy Rose Collection, New York Public Library, New York City.
33. Ibid.
34. *Life* magazine, January 31, 1944, page 60.
35. Frederick Othman, "No Insults Allowed in Granlund's Debut," United Features Syndicate, *Winnipeg Free Press*, Ontario, Canada, September 24, 1942.
36. Ibid.
37. Lee Mortimer, "They Didn't Make the Movies," *New York Sunday Mirror*, February 2, 1941, Nils T. Granlund clipping file, Billy Rose Collection, New York Public Library, New York City.
38. Louella O. Parsons, Motion Picture Editor, INS, *Waterloo Daily Courier*, Waterloo, IA, March 7, 1940, page 18.

Chapter Eleven

1. Jimmie Fidler, "Hollywood Gossip," *Capital Times*, August 14, 1941, page 3.
2. Granlund, *Blondes*, page 287.
3. Lee Mortimer, *New York Daily Mirror*, clip item, Nils T. Granlund clipping file, Billy Rose Collection, New York Public Library, New York City.
4. Ibid.
5. Ibid.
6. Paul Harrison, NEA Service Staff Correspondent, "New Yorker Puts One Over on Hollywood," *Port Arthur News*, Port Arthur, TX, September 28, 1941, page 22.
7. Mark Hellinger, "Goin' to Town," "Best Bets of the Week," *San Antonio Light*, San Antonio, TX, December 6, 1942, page 59.
8. Lee Mortimer, *New York World*, 1942 clip item, Nils T. Granlund clipping file, Billy Rose Collection, New York Public Library, New York City.
9. Granlund, *Blondes*, page 279.
10. "Movie Review," *New York Post*, 1942 clip item, Nils T. Granlund clipping file, Billy Rose Collection, New York Public Library, New York City.
11. Harold Heffernan, North American Newspaper Alliance, syndicated column carried in *Valley Morning Star*, Harlingen, Texas, May 30, 1944.
12. Ibid.
13. Yvonne De Carlo, *Yvonne: An Autobiography* (New York: St. Martin's Press, 1987), page 5.
14. Ibid., page 6.
15. Ibid.
16. Granlund, *Blondes*, page 280.
17. Ibid.
18. Ibid., page 281.
19. De Carlo, *Yvonne*, pages 9–10.
20. Ibid., page 10.
21. Ibid.
22. Granlund, *Blondes*, page 281.
23. Season's Greetings card, Chamberlain and Lyman Brown Theatrical Agency, Nils T. Granlund clipping file, Billy Rose Theater Collection, New York Public Library, New York City.
24. Jimmie Fidler, "Fidler in Hollywood," *Nevada State Journal*, Reno, NV, February 10, 1944, page 4.
25. Harold Heffernan, North American Newspaper Alliance, syndicated column carried in *Valley Morning Star*, Harlingen, TX, May 30, 1944.
26. Lee Mortimer, clipped column dated 1944, Billy Rose Theater Collection, New York Public Library, New York City.
27. Paul Allen, clipped article, Billy Rose Theater Collection, New York Public Library, New York City.

Chapter Twelve

1. Lee Mortimer, "Nightlife," *New York Daily Mirror*, New York City, March 14, 1946, Nils T. Granlund clipping file, Billy Rose Theater Collection, New York Public Library, New York City.
2. Ibid.
3. Saul Pett, "Radio Ringside," International News Syndicate, *Hammond Times*, Hammond, IN, February 22, 1946, page 12.
4. Jack O'Brian, "Broadway," carried in the *Zanesville Signal*, Zanesville, OH, December 9, 1945, page 7.
5. Jack Gaver, "Broadway," carried in the *Dunkirk Evening Journal*, Dunkirk, NY, November 23, 1946, page 12.
6. Ibid.
7. Review, "Greenwich Village Inn," *Variety*, 1946, Nils T. Granlund clipping file, Billy Rose Theater Collection, New York Public Library, New York City.
8. Ibid.
9. Granlund, *Blondes*, page 287.
10. Jack O'Brian, "Broadway," *Oakland Tribune*, Oakland, CA, October 9, 1948, page 8.
11. Ibid.
12. Walter Winchell, "In New York," "Reviewing the Broadway Scene," *Brownsville Herald*, Brownsville, TX, April 4, 1947, page 4.
13. Danton Walker, "Broadway," *Evening Independent*, Massillon, OH, March 10, 1947, page 4.
14. Review, "Frivolity Club," *Variety*, 1947, Nils T. Granlund clipping file, Billy Rose Theater Collection, New York Public Library, New York City.
15. Jack Gaver, "Broadway," carried in the *Dunkirk Evening Journal*, Dunkirk, NY, November 23, 1946, page 12.
16. Ibid.
17. Granlund, *Blondes*, page 288.
18. Ibid.
19. Louella O. Parsons, INS Staff Correspondent, *Morning Avalanche*, Lubbock, TX, page 2.
20. Jack Gaver, "New York," *Delta Democrat-Times*, Greenville, MS, August 18, 1948.
21. Advertisement, *San Mateo Times*, San Mateo, CA, September 1, 1948, page 7.
22. Granlund, *Blondes*, page 290.
23. Associated Press, "Senators Outraged," *Mansfield News Journal*, Mansfield, OH, November 16, 1950, page 1.
24. Granlund, *Blondes*, page 290.
25. Ibid.
26. Jack Lait, "Broadway and Elsewhere," *Logansport Pharos Tribune*, Logansport, IN, August 31, 1948, page 4.
27. "NTG–Wilshire Club Show Due Saturday at Panorma Market," *The Van Nuys News*, Van Nuys, CA, July 5, 1951, page 4.
28. Granlund, *Blondes*, page 289.

29. Terry Vernon, "Tele-Vues," *Long Beach Independent*, Long Beach, California, May 1, 1950.

30. Terry Vernon, "Laplander in Fame's Lap," *Long Beach Independent*, Long Beach, California, May 6, 1951.

31. "NTG–Wilshire Club Show Due Saturday at Panorma Market," *The Van Nuys News*, Van Nuys, California, July 5, 1951, page 4.

32. "Williamsburg Girl in Hollywood TV," *Cedar Rapids Gazette*, Cedar Rapids, IA, August 24, 1952, page 26.

33. "Tele-Tips Tonight," *Long Beach Press-Telegram*, Long Beach, CA, April 24, 1952, page 33.

34. Ibid.

35. John Frederick, "Looking and Listening," "NTG Returns to Television with New Talent Showcase," *Long Beach Press-Telegram*, Long Beach, CA, May 22, 1953, page 19.

36. Ibid.

37. "More TV Tonight," *Long Beach Press-Telegram*, Long Beach, CA, September 2, 1953, page 24.

38. Terry Vernon, "Tele-Vues," *Long Beach Independent*, Long Beach, CA, September 2, 1953, page 22.

39. Terry Vernon, "Tele-Vues," *Long Beach Independent*, Long Beach, CA, May 9, 1954, page 28.

40. Lee Mortimer, "New York Confidential," carried in the *Logansport Pharos-Tribune*, Logansport, IN, August 4, 1955, page 4.

41. Lee Mortimer, "NTG Still in Show Biz, Runs Talent School," *New York Daily Mirror*, June 29, 1956, NTG, Nils T. Granlund clipping file, Billy Rose Theater Collection, New York Public Library, New York City.

42. Lee Mortimer, "New York Confidential," *Mansfield News Journal*, Mansfield, OH, August 17, 1955, page 17.

43. Ibid.

44. Lee Mortimer, "New York Confidential," *Kingsport News*, Kingsport, TN, August 21, 1956, page 4.

45. Ibid.

46. De Carlo, *Yvonne*, page 201.

47. Lee Mortimer, "Walter Winchell," *Charleston Daily Mail*, Charleston, WV, August 16, 1956, page 9.

48. Doerksen, *American*, page 33.

49. "Tuesday Television Programs, *Los Angeles Times*, January 29, 1957, page A6.

50. Terry Vernon, "Looking and Listening," *Long Beach Press-Telegram*, Long Beach, CA, January 22, 1957, page 28.

51. "The Big Surprise," quotes transcribed from a filmed copy of the television series hosted by Mike Wallace, January 29, 1957.

52. Ibid.

53. Ibid.

54. "Hacienda Hotel," Online Nevada Encyclopedia, onlinenevada.org., February 18, 2009.

55. Postcard, Three Crowns Restaurant, postmarked February 4, 1957, 11 P.M., Collection of Amanda Howard.

56. De Carlo, *Yvonne*, page 201.

57. George Freedley, "Of Books and Men," *New York Morning Telegram*, April 1, 1957.

58. Marie Blizard, Review, *Bridgeport Post*, Bridgeport, CT, January 27, 1957, page 30.

59. De Carlo, *Yvonne*, page 201.

60. "Nils T. Granlund Killed in Crash," *New York Times*, April 21, 1957, Nils T. Granlund clipping file, Billy Rose Theater Collection, New York Public Library, New York City.

61. Earl Wilson, "Ohioan on Broadway," *The Lima News*, Lima, OH, March 10, 1957, page 22.

62. De Carlo, *Yvonne*, page 209.

63. "Crash Ends Career of Impresario," *Chester Times*, Chester, PA, April 22, 1957, page 18.

64. "Strip Collision Kills Producer Nils Granlund," *Reno Evening Gazette*, Reno, NV, April 22, 1957, page 1.

65. "Blame Lacking in Auto Death Is Jury Verdict," *Nevada State Journal*, Reno, NV, April 27, 1957, page 18.

66. De Carlo, *Yvonne*, page 209.

67. "Crash Ends Career of Impresario," *Chester Times*, Chester, PA, April 22, 1957, page 18.

68. "Veteran Showman Nils T. Granlund Killed in Crash," *Daily Independent*, Monessen, PA, April 22, 1957, page 10.

69. "Rites Pend for Granlund," *Star News*, Pasadena, CA, April 23, 1957, page 5.

70. "Nils T. Granlund Killed in Crash," *New York Times*, April 21, 1957, page 22.

71. De Carlo, *Yvonne*, page 209.

72. "Show Beauties Bid Goodbye to Granlund with Ribbon," *Press-Telegram*, Long Beach, CA, April 26, 1957, page 26.

73. Sid Feder, "Longhorns and Short Tales," *Advocate*, Victoria, TX, April 25, 1957, page 7.

74. Ibid.

75. Lee Mortimer, "Special to the New York Daily Mirror," *New York Daily Mirror*, April 22, 1957, Nils T. Granlund clipping file, Billy Rose Theater Collection, New York Public Library, New York City.

76. Ibid.

77. Ibid.

78. "NTG's Widow Asks Damages," *New Mexican*, Santa Fe, NM, May 14, 1957, page 2.

79. "Jurors Selected," *Nevada State Journal*, Reno, NV, October 8, 1958, page 11.

80. "Blame Lacking in Auto Death Is Jury Verdict," *Nevada State Journal*, Reno, NV, April 27, 1957, page 18.

81. De Carlo, *Yvonne*, page 209.

Bibliography

Allen, Irving L. *The City in Slang*. New York: Oxford University Press, 1993

Ashby, Leroy. *With Amusement for All*. Lexington: University Press of Kentucky, 2000.

Bakish, David. *Jimmy Durante: His Show Business Career*. Jefferson, NC: McFarland, 1995.

Bogdan, Robert. *Freak Show: Presenting Human Oddities for Fun and Profit*. Chicago: University of Chicago Press, 1990.

Bret, David. *Joan Crawford: Hollywood Martyr*. New York: Da Capo, 2008.

Chandler, Charlotte. *Not the Girl Next Door: Joan Crawford, a Personal Biography*. New York: Applause, 2009.

Cullen, Frank, Florence Hackman and Donald McNeilly. *Vaudeville, Old and New*. New York: Routledge Press, 2006.

De Carlo, Yvonne. *Yvonne*. New York: St. Martin's, 1987.

Dobson, John N. *Bulls, Bears, Boom, and Bust*. "Nelson Wilmarth Aldrich" (entry), Santa Barbara, CA: ABC-CLIO, 2006.

Doerksen, Clifford J. *American Babel*. Philadelphia: University of Pennsylvania Press, 2005.

English, T.J. *Paddy Whacked: The Untold Story of the Irish American Gangster*. New York: William Morrow, 2005.

_____. *The Westies: Inside New York's Irish Mob*. New York: St. Martin's Griffin, 2006.

Erens, Patricia. *The Jew in American Cinema*. Bloomington: Indiana University Press, 1984.

Everett, William A., and Paul R. Laird. *The Cambridge Companion to the Musical*. Cambridge: Cambridge University Press, 2002.

Fleming, E.J. *Paul Bern: The Life and Famous Death of the MGM Director and Husband of Harlow*. Jefferson, NC: McFarland, 2009.

Frank, Rusty E. *Tap: The Greatest Tap Stars 1900–1955*. New York: Perseus/Da Capo, 1990.

Gabler, Neil. *Winchell: Gossip, Power, and the Culture of Celebrity*. New York: Vintage, 1995.

Gibson, Emily, and Barbara Firth. *The Original Million Dollar Mermaid: The Annette Kellerman Story*. Crow's Nest, N.S.W.: Allen and Unwin, 2000.

Goulekas, Karen F.: *Visual Effects in a Digital World: A Comprehensive Glossary of Over 7000 Visual Effects Terms*. San Francisco: Morgan Kauffman, 2001.

Granlund, Nils T., with Sid Feder and Ralph Hancock. *Blondes, Brunettes, and Bullets*. New York: David McKay, 1957.

Gussow, Mel. *Edward Albee: A Singular Journey*. New York: Applause Books, 2000.

Haine, Edgar A. *Disaster in the Air*. New York: Cornwall, 2000.

Harnisch, Larry. *Los Angeles Times*. Blogs: *The Daily Mirror*.

Heinze, Andrew R. *Adapting to Abundance*. New York: Columbia University Press, 1990.

Joshi, S.T. *A Dreamer and a Visionary: H.P. Lovecraft in His Time*. Liverpool: Liverpool University Press, 2001.

Kastrup, Allen. *The Swedish Heritage in America*. Swedish Council of America, 1975.

Katcher, Leo. *The Big Bankroll: The Life and Times of Arnold Rothstein*. New York: Harper, 1959.

Knowles, Mark. *Tap Roots: The Early History of Tap Dancing*. Jefferson, NC: McFarland, 2002.

Kulonen, Ulla-Maija, Irja Seurujarvi-Kari and Risto Pulkkinen (editors). *The Saami: A Cultural Encyclopedia*. UK: Cambridge University Press, *Polar Record* 42, Number 4, 2006.

Lawes, Lewis. *Twenty Thousand Years in Sing Sing*. New York: R. Long & R.R. Smith, 1932.

Leider, Emily Wortis. *Becoming Mae West*. Cambridge, MA: Da Capo Press, 2000.

Louvish, Simon. *Cecil B. DeMille: A Life in Art*. New York: Thomas Dunne Books, 2007.

McWilliams, Peter. *Ain't Nobody's Business If You Do*. Los Angeles: Prelude, 1998.

Nichols, Jeffrey D. "The Fall of Skliris, Czar of the Greeks." *History Blazer Magazine*, December, 1996.

Nowell-Smith, Geoffrey. *The Oxford History of World Cinema*. Oxford University Press, 1999.

Ostergren, Robert C. *A Community Transplanted*. Madison: University of Wisconsin Press, 1988.

Peretti, Burton W. *Nightclub City: Politics and Amusements in Manhattan*. Philadelphia: University of Pennsylvania Press, 2007.

Richman, Harry, with Richard Gehman. *A Hell of a Life*. New York: Duel Sloan and Pearce, 1966.

Rose, Frank. *The Agency: William Morris and the Hidden History of Show Business*. New York: HarperBusiness, 1995.

Schwarz, Daniel R. *Broadway Boogie Woogie: Damon Runyon and the Making of New York City*. New York: Palgrave Macmillan, 2003.

Scott, Allen J. *On Hollywood: The Place, the Industry*. Princeton, NJ: Princeton University Press, 2004.

Scranton, Philip. *Endless Novelty: Specialty Production and American Industrialization*. Princeton, NJ: Princeton University Press, 1998.

Shaw, Arnold. *The Jazz Age: Popular Music in the 1920s*. New York: Oxford University Press, 1987.

Simpson, Richard V. *Herreshoff Yachts: Seven Generations of Industrialists, Investors, and Ingenuity in Bristol*. Charleston, SC: History Press, 2007.

Taggert, Edward A. *Bootlegger*. iUniverse, New York: Writer's Showcase, 2003.

Trachtenberg, Leo. "Texas Guinan: Queen of the Night." New York: *City Journal*, Manhattan Institute, 1998.

Turkus, Burton B., and Sid Feder. *Murder, Inc.: The Story of the Syndicate*. New York: Da Capo Press, 1992.

Van Meter, Jonathan. *The Last Good Time: Skinny D'Amato, the Notorious 500 Club & the Rise and Fall of Atlantic City*. New York: Crown, 2003.

Weil, François, and Jody Gladding (translators). *A History of New York*. New York: Columbia University Press, 2004.

Weller, Sheila. *Dancing at Ciro's*. New York: St. Martin's, 2004.

Wertheim, Arthur Frank. *Vaudeville Wars: How the Keith-Albee and Orpheum Circuits Controlled the Big Time and Its Performers*. New York: Palgrave Macmillan, 2006.

Williams, Dawn. *Me and My Father's Shadow; A Daughter's Quest and Biography of Ted Lewis, the Jazz King*. Seal Beach, CA: Sunrise House, 2005.

Willis, Clint. *Wise Guys: Stories of Mobsters from New Jersey to Las Vegas.* New York: Thunder's Mouth/Avalon, 2003.

Wing, Ruth. *Blue Book of the Screen.* Hollywood, CA: Blue Book of the Screen, 1923.

Witham, Barry. *Theater in the United States 1750–1915.* Cambridge, MA: Cambridge University Press, 1996.

Index